DECLINE AND FALL?

DECLINE AND FALL?

Britain's Crisis in the Sixties

PAUL EINZIG

MACMILLAN
London · Melbourne · Toronto
ST MARTIN'S PRESS
New York
1969

© Paul Einzig 1969

Published by
MACMILLAN AND CO LTD
Little Essex Street London W C 2
and also at Bombay Calcutta and Madras
Macmillan South Africa (Publishers) Pty Ltd Johannesburg
The Macmillan Company of Australia Pty Ltd Melbourne
The Macmillan Company of Canada Ltd Toronto
St Martin's Press Inc New York
Gill and Macmillan Ltd Dublin

Library of Congress catalog card no. 69-17405

Printed in Great Britain by
R. & R. CLARK, LTD., EDINBURGH

CONTENTS

17487

Be not made a beggar by banqueting upon borrowing, when thou hast nothing in thy purse.

Ecclesiasticus 18:33

If any would not work, neither should he eat.

2 Thessalonians 3:10

PREFACE

To forestall any accusations that the hard things I have to say in this book about the British trade unionist worker are inspired by unfriendly feelings towards him, I hasten to say with the utmost emphasis in the very first sentence of the book that I am fully as keen on an increase of his standard of living as any Left-wing Socialist or any militant trade union leader. The main difference between my attitude and theirs is that I want the worker to earn and deserve his higher standard of living by contributing his due share towards the achievement of higher productivity in Britain. Most Left-wing Socialists and militant trade unionists are just not interested in that aspect of the problem. Their sole concern is to enforce an increase in the worker's money wages and they could hardly care less whether or not the size of the nation's real income — its total output of goods and services — is increased. Indeed their attitude and the worker's response to it actually tend to slow down that increase. The main object of this book is to show how utterly anti-social that attitude is.

I disclaim any political bias in this book. Although it is inevitably critical of the Labour Government in office and of the rank and file of its supporters, it has some very hard things to say also about their political opponents. As the reader will discover in due course, I blame both major parties for Britain's crisis. I fully expect this book to arouse as much resentment among Tories as among Socialists.

Another thing I want to make plain from the very outset is that this is *not* a book on foreign exchange or on the balance of payments crisis. Its subject is very much broader and infinitely more vital — Britain's crisis, of which the chronic adverse balance of payments and the frequently recurring crises of sterling are just outward symptoms. But as I am known mainly as a writer on foreign exchange — even though I have also written several books on much broader economic and political subjects — I deem it essential to emphasise that this book is addressed not to the specialist but to the general reader. Its subject must be of interest to everybody who has Britain's welfare at heart. Unless I succeed in convincing my readers that Britain's recurrent crises are not 'just sterling crises' my book will have failed to attain its object.

Nobody likes being told home truths such as this book contains. It would be an infinitely more popular task for me to reassure readers of this book about how wonderfully Britain is still doing, and to present them with a long list of 'what is right with Britain' instead of performing the uncongenial task of telling them 'what is wrong with Britain'. Thank goodness, there are still a great many spheres in which Britain is doing well, even though there are fewer such spheres than before. But would it be the best way to try to serve her interests if I were to state the obvious — that everything is not wrong with her ? I am convinced that her interests are better served by trying to make the public realise that far too many things are wrong and need righting.

To enumerate and discuss all things that are still right with Britain would admittedly fill a volume. But to enumerate and discuss all that has gone wrong with her would fill several volumes. I have tried to confine this book mainly to those aspects of Britain's decline which, in my opinion, have not received sufficient attention.

The view will probably be held in many quarters that even if all my criticisms were right I would be wrong in voicing them in public. Such things, they may feel, are better left unsaid. I strongly disagree with that attitude. In the eternal conflict between the 'don't publish it' school and the 'don't do it' school I have always found myself on the side of the latter, firmly convinced as I have always been that the right thing for governments is to abstain from doing things which, if published, create a bad impression, rather than let them continue to do them under a convenient cloak of secrecy.

Let me conclude my preliminary remarks on a purely personal note by saying with the utmost emphasis and with the utmost sincerity that, in spite of all my outspoken criticisms of the adverse changes in the British character since the War, I am firmly convinced that the British, with all their greatly aggravated faults and their greatly diminished virtues, are even now unquestionably the finest nation in the world. Never for a moment have I regretted having made my home in their midst and, in spite of the deterioration of the British character which I feel impelled to denounce in this book in no uncertain terms, I would not think of living anywhere else.

For one thing, I am convinced that Britain is one of the very few countries in which anyone can afford to risk antagonising the mighty — as I have done on innumerable occasions over a period of nearly half a century — without exposing himself to being persecuted, and even to being framed, as is the widespread practice in so many countries. I feel I can rely on British fairness for my outspoken diagnosis to be taken in the right spirit — even though the Jocelyn Hambro incident does make me wonder if, in criticising the Prime Minister, I might conceivably expose myself to some vendetta of a similarly un-British kind.

Gloomy as the picture which this book presents of Britain's prospects may be, it means to convey a faint glimmer of hope by the question mark affixed to its title *Decline and Fall ?* I have not abandoned all hope that the decline, which is only too obvious to everybody who does not deliberately turn a blind eye towards it, might not necessarily end in a fall. As this book is about to go to press the Government has just announced a set of tough measures which might conceivably go some way towards discouraging the nation from living beyond its means on borrowed money. I only wish I could believe that they might prove to be sufficient to halt Britain's decline.

Unfortunately the violent nation-wide outburst of indignation with which the belated imposition of sacrifices was received provides yet another flagrant instance to indicate the debasement of the British character. There were no such outcries

A 2

when much more severe sacrifices were imposed on the nation in 1931 and in 1940. The fact that the public is screaming before it is really hit by the measures augurs badly for the chances of their continued maintenance by the Government when they come to produce their full effect. As on all previous occasions the Government is certain to yield to pressure and relax them prematurely. The decline will then be resumed.

Even if, contrary to my pessimistic expectations, there should be an improvement of an apparently lasting character — for instance if the balance of payments should show a surplus in 1969 — it would be unwarranted optimism to assume that Britain has now turned the corner. Unless and until there is a basic change in the prevailing spirit, any such improvement is bound to be as temporary as the previous improvements had proved to be.

In spite of the disappointing response of the nation to long-overdue measures adopted in order to arrest its decline I still feel that all is not necessarily lost. This is because of my firm conviction that sooner or later the great qualities deeply ingrained in the British national character will come to assert themselves once more. Whether this will happen in my life-time is quite another question. I must thank my good fortune for having been able to witness Britain's national regeneration twice in my life, in 1931 and in 1940. And even if I be doomed to end my life without being able to witness Britain's national regeneration for a third time, I would infinitely prefer to be doomed here than be blessed anywhere else.

December 1968   P. E.

CHAPTER ONE

INTRODUCTORY

Is Britain really doomed to share the fate of the great empires of the past? Having exerted for many centuries a decisive influence on international politics, on the economic and social evolution of mankind, and on world history in general, is she on her way towards being reduced to a chapter in history textbooks, with only a minor and largely passive part to play in current world affairs? If so, her eclipse will puzzle students of history for many generations.

The decline and fall of the Egyptian, Babylonian, Assyrian, Persian, Roman, Byzantine, Spanish, Ottoman, Napoleonic, Habsburg and Hitlerite Empires had been the results of military defeats. In sharp contrast with all past experience, Britain is well on her way towards sharing the fate of these former world powers in spite of the fact that she emerged victorious from two World Wars, having played in both a decisive part in the achievement of victory. The traditional belief that, although Britain might lose battles, she is always bound to win the last battle has remained substantially valid right to our days. But, having won the second World War against heavy odds, she seems to have lost the peace — to all appearances, irretrievably.

Britain's decline would have been much more spectacular and dramatic if she had been defeated in the last War, but in final results it could hardly have been more fatal. Indeed it seems quite conceivable that, had she been defeated without being annihilated, she might have staged by now a recovery at least as impressive as the recoveries of each of the three defeated Axis Powers, Germany, Japan and Italy. For it was always in adversity that the British nation displayed its most admirable qualities, those qualities which had enabled it to achieve true greatness and maintain it for many centuries. And it is surely the deterioration of those qualities since the end of the last war that has doomed Britain to the decline it is our misfortune to witness.

We should hardly be human if we did not hope against hope that the present decline need not necessarily be final and that the history of former great empires need not necessarily repeat itself in Britain. After all, on two previous occasions within the lifetime of the older generation Britain experienced the symptoms of a major decline — during the late 'twenties and early 'thirties when Britain's crisis culminated in the suspension of the gold standard and the ensuing slump of sterling in 1931, and again during the immediate pre-war years and during the 'phoney war', when Britain's decline manifested itself in the inadequacy of her preparations to face the growing threat of Nazi aggression. On both occasions Britain staged a spectacular recovery at the eleventh hour and was able to resume her traditional role in world affairs after her temporary eclipse.

Is there no possibility that history might repeat itself on the present occasion? To find the answer we have to draw a comparison between the circumstances in which the three crises occurred. We have a remarkable account of the crisis of the 'twenties and early 'thirties in André Siegfried's *England's Crisis*, which laid bare systematically and relentlessly, but impartially, all that was wrong with Britain during the first half of the inter-war period as it was seen through the eyes of a friendly French observer. In their Preface, the translators of the book, H. H. Hemming and Doris Hemming, raised a pertinent question: 'Is England the victim of circumstances which are beyond her control, or is "the fault, dear Brutus... not in our stars, but in ourselves"?' The same question might well be asked again. But the answer would be quite different from what it was in 1931.

Even on that occasion the British nation had in many respects only itself to blame for its mounting difficulties. But it was justified in pleading in extenuation of its faults that circumstances had been strongly against it. The deflationary trend which was strangling Britain's economy, dependent as she had been on exports, had not been of Britain's own making; it had been world-wide. The same could be said about the speculative fever in Wall Street that superimposed financial difficulties over economic difficulties in the late 'twenties. American protectionism had not been Britain's fault, nor could she be blamed in any way for the highly vulnerable inter-national financial situation created by French insistence on the payment of reparations well in excess of Germany's capacity, and by the way the Bank of France, on the candid admission of one of its Governors, had misused its financial power over sterling for political ends.

It is true that Britain's own monetary policy, especially the return to the gold standard at the parity of 1914, had been an important contributory cause of the crisis. But at the time when this decision was taken it was possible to plead ignorance as a mitigating circumstance. Britain, in restoring the pre-war value of the pound, merely followed her traditions which ap-peared to be justified at the time on the basis of past experience.

As André Siegfried rightly observed, England usually looks abroad for the cause of her difficulties, which are always the fault of someone else. But today it would be quite impossible to argue convincingly that Britain's difficulties are the fault of other countries, or of the world trend, or even of her own ignorance of better policies. It is true, the argument that all Britain's troubles are due to the sacrifices this country had to make in the second World War while defending single-handed the world's freedom against heavy odds has still strong popular appeal at home if nowhere else. But the further we are removed in time from the war the less convincing that argument must sound even to ourselves.

Given modern methods of production and of financing pro-duction, two decades should be enough and more than enough for obliterating the physical, economic and financial damage caused by any non-nuclear war. Our defeated opponents have wiped out long ago the traces of devastation, invasion and prolonged enemy occupation. Britain suffered less physical devastations than either Germany or Italy or France or Soviet Russia, and yet these four countries have surpassed us in the speed of their physical reconstruction and in their further progress after all war damage was made good. Among the smaller countries Holland and Belgium had lost, through enemy occupation, devastations and confiscation of their investments in their former colonies, a much higher proportion of their national wealth and incomes than Britain. Yet they have managed to shrug off their losses and have achieved stability and prosperity in spite of them. The amazing way in which Israel has converted a desert into a prosperous country in spite of the exorbitant cost of her national defences sets yet another example of a national miracle. I could quote the examples of many other countries which have long overcome and forgotten their grave difficulties inherited from the war.

Britain alone among the former belligerent countries seems to feel still justified in trying to blame the war for her prolonged troubles, nearly a quarter of a century after the termination of hostilities. While in 1931 and in 1939 there may have been good reason for pretending that the fault was to some extent at any rate 'in our stars' and not in ourselves, in 1968 the question simply does not arise.

What is infinitely more important is that, regardless of the difference in the causes of Britain's present crisis, the reaction of the British people to them is different. In 1931, thanks to the shock caused by the suspension of the gold standard and by the sharp depreciation of sterling that followed it, the British nation pulled itself together and made a supreme effort to save the pound from its threatening collapse. The sacrifices imposed on it to that end were borne in the right spirit, fully in accordance with the finest British traditions. Instead of complaining about the unprecedented burden of the additional taxation imposed on them in order to save the pound, untold thousands of taxpayers queued up before tax collectors' offices to pay their December 31 instalments, many weeks before it was due, as soon as they received their first notices. That was only one small instance that characterised the British spirit in 1931.

In 1964–68 such a spirit was almost completely absent. During all the crises of the 'fifties and 'sixties most sections of the nation tried to contract out of the sacrifices and to pass on the burden to the other fellow. Indeed large sections of the public did their utmost to secure for themselves special benefits out of the circumstances accompanying the crises.

Unfortunately, even the spirit of national regeneration that saved the pound in the early 'thirties had proved to be short-lived. In spite of the growing menace of Nazi aggression, the British people soon relaxed its public-spirited effort. Before long the invigorating atmosphere that prevailed after the suspension of the gold standard gave way to the same state of apathy and selfishness which prevailed until the nation was aroused by the shock caused by the depreciation of sterling. The attempt in the late 'thirties to prevent rearmament from causing inflation by Chamberlain's proposal to introduce a National Defence Contribution encountered the utmost resistance, and the Government was forced to abandon the scheme. Although this, together with the gross inadequacy of the belated effort to rearm, was due to lack of inspiring leadership, the nation as a whole could not escape the blame. After all, there is something in the rule that every nation has the Government it deserves. It was not sheer coincidence that in 1940 when the British nation had its finest hour it had Churchill for its leader. Nation and leader truly deserved each other at that supreme moment.

But that rule does not always necessarily apply. During the phoney war responsibility for the slowness of Britain's rearmament rested solely with the Government. Sharp contrast arose between the attitude of the nation, which wanted by then to intensify its economic war effort and was willing and even eager to bear increased sacrifices, and that of the Government, which had not recovered from its discouraging experience with the National Defence Contribution. It did not dare to impose in 1939–40 sacrifices which the people would have been prepared to accept.

Once the menace and the imminence of the danger of invasion came to be realised in 1940 by Government and people alike, the same spirit which manifested itself so splendidly in 1931 became once more evident, only to an infinitely higher degree. When the author recollects the exhilarating experience of those days, or when he reads books or sees films on the Battle of Britain period, he finds it somewhat difficult to believe that the people he encounters or reads about today can possibly belong to the same race as the people who gave such a magnificent account of themselves in 1940.

Admittedly even amidst the deadly perils of 1940 there were instances of greed and short-sighted selfishness, of indolence and indifference. But the nation as a whole was truly inspired by what has come to be known as 'the spirit of Dunkirk'. That term will stand for self-denial in the public interest in face of mortal peril so long as English is spoken. If it had not been for that spirit Britain could not have survived as an independent nation. Had the men engaged in aircraft production slowed down for the sake of earning more overtime pay, or had they embarked on wildcat strikes at the slightest excuse, or had they been resisting measures aimed at increasing output or saving manpower, the R.A.F. could not possibly have been provided with the additional Spitfires that enabled them to win the Battle of Britain with a narrow margin.

Fortunately for Britain, those who did try to exploit the emergency of 1940 for their own benefit, or who tried at any rate to contract out of the sacrifices involved, constituted a small minority. Some workers did insist on 'danger money', but R.A.F. pilots were fighting on in spite of the obvious inadequacy of their pay. They did not go slow or work to rule during the Battle of Britain, when the fate of their country was in their hands, for the sake of hastening the settlement of an application for higher pay. Their discontent with the long-delayed rise when it was finally granted merely manifested itself in a wisecrack circulating in R.A.F. Officers' Messes, that 'never in the history of human relations have so many waited so long for so little'.

Unfortunately today the behaviour that was the exception in 1940 has become the rule, while the attitude that was the rule in 1940 has now become the rare exception. Almost all sections of the community are now much more interested in securing for themselves immunity from the sacrifices demanded by the situation. The spirit that prevails today may rightly be termed the inverted Dunkirk spirit. Everybody, or almost everybody, is trying to get as much as possible out of the community and to give the community as little as possible in return.

It is of course quite understandable that the peril which is now threatening Britain as a result of this attitude is not realised to anything like the extent to which the much more obvious and much more immediate peril of the Nazi invasion was realised in 1940. Most people now seem to be genuinely unaware of the effect of their attitude on Britain's national greatness. In any case the author suspects they are much more interested in being able to buy a better TV set, or the car they want, than in national greatness. But they are not even interested in the effect of their attitude on productivity, although it is bound to affect their own welfare as well as national prosperity in the long run, or national solvency and financial stability in the short run.

To understand such effects would require only an elementary knowledge of economics. The author is sure that even many of those who possess that knowledge prefer to pretend to ignore what is at stake. They persuade themselves without much difficulty that their attitude does not contribute towards increasing the country's difficulties. But there are people who are actually cynical enough to admit in their candid moments that they could not care less about the interests of their country so long as they can secure for themselves, their families or their trade unions the special advantages they want.

There could be no two opinions about the way in which every man, woman and child would have been affected by enemy invasion and occupation in 1940. But the way in which our present peril is likely to affect individuals is much more controversial, as indeed everything related to economic problems is bound to be. Everything related to economics is open to argument and, human nature being what it is, people are inclined to accept the line of argument which happens to suit their immediate interest — to be more precise, which happens to *appear* to them to suit their immediate interest. Or they simply try to ignore the inconvenient arguments out of existence.

The explanation of the difference between the British attitude in 1940 and in the 1960s is self-evident. The difference between the British attitude in the financial crisis of 1931 and in the financial crises of 1964–68 is not so simple to account for. In 1931 the country was not threatened by invasion any more than in the 1960s. But it was threatened by financial instability and the progressive aggravation of its chronic economic difficulties. They were different from its present difficulties, in that they were caused by deflation and not by inflation. But taking a long view they were no graver than the present difficulties. Yet the nation responded then splendidly to appeals to help the country in its effort to solve its problem. In the 1960s, on the other hand, the sum total of its response to appeals made in largely similar circumstances amounted to very little more than the decision of five Surbiton typists to work extra time without extra pay.

On both occasions sterling was under chronic pressure that developed into acute pressure from time to time. Why was it that while in 1931 the British nation rallied round the defence of its national currency, thirty-odd years later its behaviour showed an almost complete indifference towards the fate of sterling? There are several reasons, the most important of which are the following:

(1) Mass unemployment, record numbers of bankruptcies, falling Stock Exchange prices, slumping commodity prices in the early 'thirties made everybody painfully aware that we were in the middle of a grave crisis. But in the 'sixties everything appeared to be all right on the surface and there were but few outward indications of

our deep-seated troubles. Even after the series of acute sterling crises during 1964–68, a relatively slight increase in unemployment which has been fluctuating around the half million mark in 1967–68 has been the only symptom complained of by most people. After all, almost everybody is employed at ever-increasing wages or salaries. Profits are holding up reasonably well and are increasing in many instances, and there has been no appreciable increase in bankruptcies. Temporary setbacks apart, the Stock Exchange has been registering new record levels. It is very difficult to convince most people that all these apparent symptoms of prosperity are really symptoms of inflation in its early stages, and that in spite of them — perhaps because of them — they are heading towards a grave crisis, the prevention of which calls for supreme efforts and self-denial.

(2) In 1931 the British public realised that Britain had to fend for herself. Although the United States and France did grant Britain credits to a total of £130 million, this was almost exactly the amount of our gold reserve which was earmarked to secure the credits, so that they did not add to the resources available for the defence of sterling. Co-operation between Central Banks was in its infancy and it suffered a sharp setback as a result of the international economic and financial crises which induced most Governments and Central Banks to adopt an isolationist attitude. The British public had to realise in 1931 that it depended entirely on its own efforts if it wanted to save sterling. By sharp contrast, the British public in the 'sixties, having been thoroughly pampered and spoilt ever since the end of the war by the ease with which the United States and other countries were always willing to come to the rescue of sterling, came to take it for granted that foreign aid would always be forthcoming whenever needed. 'Something will turn up.' So why should they worry unduly about another and yet another sterling crisis? They all

came to an end sooner or later without causing a major disaster, thanks to foreign assistance granted at the eleventh hour.

(3) At the time of the 1931 crisis the experience of the extreme depreciation of the German mark having occurred only eight years earlier was still fresh in everybody's mind. By the 'sixties the memory of that experience became very dim. Very little was known here about the more recent extreme inflationary experiences of China, Greece and Hungary after the second World War, and in any case, unlike Germany, none of these countries is comparable with Britain. Above all, since 1931 the 'it can't happen here' school has gained ground considerably.

(4) The generation of 1931 had been brought up in the belief that monetary stability must be high on our list of priorities and that it was not only a matter of national prestige and integrity but it was also to our vital interest to make sacrifices for the sake of preventing a depreciation of sterling. But in the meantime the will to resist adverse pressure on the pound had been undermined by the influence of those in favour of taking the line of least resistance and of yielding to pressure by means of frequent devaluations or by adopting the system of freely floating exchange rates. The maintenance of the internal stability of sterling now occupies a very low place in the list of our priorities, and even the maintenance of its international stability has ceased to enjoy top priority. Even though Mr. Wilson had claimed before November 1967 that sterling's defence was a matter of top priority, he devalued nevertheless. Only very few people still think about it in terms of defending it 'with the last drop of our blood'.

(5) Over and above all, recent years have witnessed a progressive debasement of the British character. A mentality of sponging on the community and on other nations as a matter of course has come to prevail. Selfishness

and impatient greed demanding the advent of a millennium immediately have gained ground and 'growth-
hysteria' has become a national disease. At the same
time the desire to serve the public interest has declined
sharply. Hard-faced trade unionists quite frankly admit
that the only thing in which they are interested is to get
the maximum of exclusive advantage for their members,
and seldom worry about the effect of their selfishness on
the rest of the community.

This loss of the eminent qualities of the British character is
by no means absolutely irretrievable. On the contrary, it
seems highly probably that, should the situation of 1940 recur
today, the British nation's response would be similar to what
it was in 1940. It is even possible to hope — though quite
frankly with much less assurance — that should the public
ever become really frightened about the likelihood of an
extreme depreciation of sterling in the same way as it was
frightened in 1931, its response might be similar to what it was
in 1931. But if the debasement of the British character is
allowed to continue too long, the point of no return might be
passed at some stage.

CHAPTER TWO

HOW *PAX BRITANNICA* HAD BEEN ACHIEVED

BEFORE examining the causes of Britain's decline from the zenith of her power and influence, attained in the 19th century and maintained more or less continuously until the second World War, let us examine briefly the reasons why she had succeeded in achieving and maintaining such a position. It is not easy for the new generation to believe that only thirty years ago Britain was *the* leading world power. Today the United States and the Soviet Union compete for that position, with China appearing on the horizon as a potential contestant for supremacy. France made a bid for the lead among the powers of the second rank and might well have achieved it if it had not been for the disturbing events of May–June 1968 and their consequences. Even West Germany's influence is now overshadowing that of Britain, at any rate in the economic and financial sphere, while in the Far East Japan has achieved a position challenging comparison with that of Britain.

Yet less than a generation ago Britain's supremacy appeared to be incontestable. It is true, she carried disarmament too far between the Wars, but neither this nor sterling's vulnerability in the 'twenties and 'thirties appeared to have affected her immense international prestige. The growing military and economic power of the United States since the first World War tended to become an increasingly important potential influence in the international situation. But since the United States reverted to isolationism after the Paris Peace Conference, the weight of her considerable military strength played no active role in the maintenance of the precarious European balance of power that had come to be threatened by the Nazi menace. As for Soviet Russia, right until the successful stand she made to Hitler's invading armies before Moscow in the winter of 1941, she was generally looked upon as a clumsy and inefficient giant fully preoccupied with her domestic difficulties.

During the 'thirties Britain was generally assumed to be the Great Power whose influence was apt to play a decisive role. This view is known to have been shared by Hitler and by Stalin. The former's envious admiration for Britain had been well known and his ambition to become the ruler of the European continent had rested on the assumption, encouraged by the Peace Ballot, the Oxford Union resolution, and by Ribbentrop's misleading reports, that Britain would abstain from standing in his way.

As for Stalin, when in March 1935 Mr. Eden saw him in the Kremlin, the all-powerful dictator, ruling over the largest country in the world with a population three times that of the U.K., pointed to a vast map displayed in his study and exclaimed: 'Is it not remarkable that such a small island should be in a position to determine the prospects of world peace?' The meeting took place under the shadow of the growing Nazi threat, and Stalin's remark was meant to convey that Britain and Britain alone had the power to check that threat by making it clear that she would make a determined stand against Nazi aggression. With France weakened by a succession of political and financial crises and scandals, and with the United States suffering from an apparently incurable economic depression — apart altogether from her unwillingness ever to play again an active part in European politics — no other nation carried sufficient weight to stand a chance of being able to call a halt to Hitler.

Of course when Stalin was talking about 'a small island' he overlooked the fact — although it was glaring at him from the map he was facing — that at that time the British Commonwealth and Empire had a very real meaning and was the source of immense power for Britain. Having been misled by his own

propaganda, he had assumed that the 'oppressed and exploited' peoples of the British family of nations had been a
source of weakness and not of strength. Yet as the experience
of the first World War proved, and that of the second World
War was soon to prove again, the Commonwealth and Empire
was in those days no mere geographical notion. The old
Dominions and many of the overseas countries under British
control had been a source of great strength, not only as suppliers
of economic war potential but also as sources of manpower of
the highest fighting quality.

How had England, and later the United Kingdom, succeeded
in acquiring such a vast Empire? Not in the way in which
other nations under the leadership of some outstanding, ruthlessly ambitious tyrant sought to achieve it. British history
showed no periods comparable to those of Louis XIV and
Napoleon in French history or of Charlemagne, Charles V and
Hitler in German history, or of Peter the Great and Stalin in
Russian history. It recorded no spectacular British attempts
at world conquest by wars of aggression leading to military
victories or by systematic subversions in foreign countries. The
achievement of world power by Britain had been a very
gradual and on the whole unspectacular process, spread over a
very long period and interrupted by occasional setbacks. It
never depended on the success of the world-conquering design
of some outstanding leader. Overseas possessions had been
picked up piecemeal, usually as incidental results of wars
fought over the maintenance of the balance of power in
Europe.

The reason why England won the last battle in almost every
war was to be found largely in her economic strength that had
enabled her to persevere through adverse periods until the
fortunes of war had turned in her favour. Admittedly her
geographical position had helped her greatly, because it had
safeguarded her to a large extent from the worst consequences
of any temporary military reverses. It had enabled her to fight
her wars on foreign soil, sparing her own homeland the devastations inflicted by wars on the continent on both victors and

vanquished. But this circumstance, important as it had been, would not explain by itself why a small and sparsely populated country — as Britain was until well into the nineteenth century, possessing no great wealth in natural resources — had been able to stand up to countries incomparably richer in wealth and manpower.

The comparative ease of defending the British Isles against invasion and the possession of a naval power making it possible to conquer overseas territories may provide part of the explanation. But it was the country's economic strength, enabling Britain to pursue long and costly wars and to subsidise powerful allies, that must have been the main reason why Britain had become a world power. And since England had not possessed immense mineral or other natural resources, such economic strength could only be achieved thanks to the qualities inherent in the British national character.

Until comparatively recently the British nation was indeed a hard-working and thrifty race. And ever since the days of the Danegeld in the tenth century it was willing to share its hard-earned income with the central authority that governed it. Under its Parliamentary system its taxation — which had been traditionally higher than that of other countries — had been a largely self-imposed sacrifice enabling kings and governments gradually to expand Britain's overseas domains and to maintain a balance of power on the European continent.

Britain's wars in the 16th and 17th centuries had been basically almost entirely defensive, forced upon her by the imperialist designs of Spain or France. It was not until the 18th century that she came to pursue the wars of expansion that yielded for her valuable overseas territories in North America and in other continents. Her wealth secured from overseas trade and shipping had undoubtedly helped. But until a comparatively late stage in her history she was not supreme even in these spheres; she was a poor second to Holland and was from time to time inferior also to other countries. She never possessed the gold and silver resources of the Spanish overseas empire, nor until the second half of the

18th century the industrial skill of the French and German peoples. Not until the immigration of Huguenots did industrial skill begin to develop in Britain to a noteworthy extent. But once it made a start it came to advance in a remarkable way. British technological inventions laid the foundations of the industrial revolution that secured for Britain her uncontested industrial, financial and political supremacy for a century and a half.

Britain's most valuable national asset had always been the character of her people. The Germans are admittedly more thorough, the Americans more efficient, the French and the Italians more brilliant. British people are not so hard-working as Germans or Italians, nor so thrifty as the French, the Dutch or the Swiss. On the other hand, they are eminently law-abiding, fundamentally honest, dependable and truthful. Above all, they are, or were until recently, as public-spirited as any nation and more so than most nations. Their traditional patriotism — the term is used advisedly, in spite of its disparaging definition by Dr. Johnson — always manifested itself in unspectacular deeds instead of flamboyant words.

The British people's proverbial willingness to render unto Caesar what is Caesar's by paying their high taxes was in sharp contrast with the attitude of the French and of most other continental nations towards taxation. The otherwise glorious history of Holland records many instances of leading Dutch manufacturers and merchants trading for the sake of profit with the enemy invading their country. The extent to which exchange control has been evaded in the U.K. since its adoption in 1939 has been quite negligible compared with the experience of France and other countries.

Over and above all, Britain had become the leading world power thanks to the steadfastness of purpose which had been an outstanding quality of the British character. Whenever under acute menace, the British nation subordinated all other considerations to its overriding determination to overcome the crisis. Undaunted by temporary setbacks, Britain held out firmly against heavy odds until she won the final victory over her formidable opponents or wore them down until they grew

tired of the contest. Their overwhelming power had not inti-
midated her into surrenders. Because she proverbially 'did
not know when she was beaten' she went on fighting in adverse
circumstances amidst which other nations would have given
up, and usually ended by winning the last battle.

Although it is easy to find many faults with British rule in
the colonies, in recent times Britain had been superior to other
colonial rulers in her treatment of the conquered peoples. The
relative degree of fairness and humanitarianism with which she
had fulfilled her role had never been recognised by the subject
races so long as British rule continued, but now that they are
independent it is often nostalgically recalled.

The author himself heard Mme. Pandit say on a semi-public
occasion how fortunate it was for India when fighting for
her independence that she had the British for her opponent.
British exploitation of the colonies is a myth. Throughout the
19th century and right until the second World War, the amount
of British money pouring into the colonies in the form of new
investment or current expenditure generally exceeded the
amounts received from the colonies in the form of profits and
dividends. Even after 1945, when the granting of independence
to the colonies was obviously a mere question of time, the U.K.
continued to subsidise them heavily under the Colonial Development and Welfare Acts instead of letting them spend their own
accumulating sterling balances.

In public administration and in business dealings British
people had acquired a world-wide reputation for integrity.
'The Englishman's word is his bond' is a proverb well known
all over the five continents. The degree of corruption in
British public service was, and probably still is, lower than
anywhere in the world. Indeed, the much-abused public
schools and Oxbridge had created between them a ruling class
which, with all its limitations and deficiencies, was incorrup-
tible, eminently public-spirited and fair-minded. In international relations a Briton's word was generally regarded as
absolutely dependable, even though foreign diplomats resented
the British method of telling the truth in the hope that their

antagonists would not believe it. Frequent reference to 'Perfidious Albion' usually expressed impotent envy rather than genuine belief.

The fact that, when Sir Stafford Cripps devalued sterling in 1949 in spite of his repeated denials of his intention to do so, there was a world-wide uproar of indignation, was itself the highest possible tribute, showing the degree to which the word of a British statesman had been trusted as a matter of course. Whenever some foreign Government dishonoured its oft-repeated pledge not to devalue it hardly caused any surprise or indignation. But it had been taken for granted that a British Government would honour its pledge.

Admittedly the proverbial truthfulness of British people was very often merely technical. British politicians, diplomats and businessmen, in their discussions with their opposite numbers at home or abroad, had always been in the habit of going out of their way to ensure that what they said was technically true, even if at times the technical accuracy of their statements concealed inaccuracies of substance. But surely it indicated a higher degree of ethics and of civilised behaviour that they deemed it worth while to go to so much trouble for the sake of avoiding having to tell a barefaced lie. Even those who regarded this attitude towards truth as hypocritical readily accepted with curious inconsistency the Englishman's reputation for telling the truth and for keeping his word. There must have been many instances in which the British character placed British statesmen, diplomats and businessmen at a disadvantage in dealing with more tortuous-minded and less straightforward peoples. Nevertheless the British character was on balance a valuable national asset.

In 1945 it looked for a while as if the whole of Europe had been well on its way towards succumbing to Communist aggression or subversion. The United States alone had enough power to safeguard the survival of any country against the overwhelming might of the Soviet Union. Indeed the prospects of survival of democracy and freedom of all countries of Western Europe appeared to depend on the degree of financial and military support which the United States was willing to give them. But America's resources, formidable as they were, were not unlimited and her Government had to limit her commitments. A leading American statesman is known to have observed off the record on one occasion that, since the means of the United States are not sufficient to defend the whole of Europe, the one thing in Europe that was considered to be worth salvaging from an American point of view was the British character.

The British character was the main asset that had helped Britain through the second World War until Germany's strength came to be impaired by the Russian winter and until the United States came to mobilise her immense strength. It was the main asset that safeguarded the British nation from succumbing to Communist or Fascist extremism during the dark days of economic depression in the 'thirties. It was British willpower that saved Britain from the worst currency chaos experienced by all her European Allies and her former enemies after the first World War, and that had enabled her to retain and regain her financial power and prestige in spite of the heavy losses suffered through that war and its aftermath.

Had the British character remained what it had been much of the time between the Wars, there could be no doubt that Britain would soon have overcome the losses she had suffered during the second World War. The British nation would have put first things first and would have concentrated on recovering Britain's standing as an equal of the United States and of Soviet Russia, instead of abdicating its historical role and accepting a secondary part for the sake of the immediate advantages of raising the standard of living without having to work harder to achieve that end. Indeed there would have been no need for Britain to sacrifice the desired increase of her standard of living at the same time as regaining her economic strength and retaining her traditional international standing. By working harder, or even by abstaining from relaxing their efforts, the British workers could have ensured for themselves a well-deserved higher standard of living. This could have been done without having to sacrifice national greatness for the sake of being able to eat bigger and better meals, by simply earning and therefore deserving the increase.

Mankind must have benefited considerably from Britain's greatness during the long period of the *Pax Britannica*. Britain's superior naval strength had been used most of the time for maintaining peace and for ensuring safe trading for the benefit of all. British trade, industry and finance had contributed extensively towards the development of the five continents. To say that this had been also beneficial to Britain is merely to say that the British had been human. But while other nations that had achieved widespread influence outside their borders had inspired mostly fear, the British had also inspired respect, mingled, as it was bound to be, with envy and jealousy. Britain's unpopularity as a world power had been merely the measure of her superiority.

In the financial sphere the pound sterling was a symbol of integrity, so much so that the British authorities had been able to maintain sterling stable in terms of gold with the aid of a relatively small gold reserve. The international gold standard before 1914 was really a sterling standard based on implicit confidence in sterling.

Every nation, big or small, believes that it possesses certain qualities that justify its claim of superiority over all other nations. But until 1914 and to some extent even until the second World War, practically all nations had a grudging admiration for Britain's economic, financial and naval power, and for the integrity of the British character. Even those who would not think of acknowledging their admiration for Britain in public regarded the British as a race apart. There was an all but universal consciousness of Britain's superiority. Many people may have hated her because of that. But they could not help feeling that British greatness was an influence making for world stability, even if it meant the stability based on the *status quo*. If we compare *Pax Britannica* with the conditions of uncertainty in which the world has been living ever since Britain has lost her leading role, there can be no doubt that nostalgia for the happy days when Britannia ruled the waves and London ruled the international monetary system is not confined to Britain alone.

The author would not like to conclude this chapter without making it clear that, notwithstanding the tribute he paid to Britain as she had been in the days prior to her present decline, he is fully aware that the world of *Pax Britannica* was very far from being an ideal world. Conditions in Britain itself left a great deal to be desired. Although in the 19th century Britain was able to combine a high degree of progress with a high degree of monetary stability, this result could only be achieved at the cost of immense human suffering. Nobody with any humane feeling today — or for that matter with any political common sense — would like to put the clock back even if it were possible to do so. Today the masses would simply not stand for the degree of injustice and privation to which their forerunners had submitted as a matter of course a hundred years ago, and even until much more recently.

In retrospect the great achievements of the industrial revolution that had brought Britain to the pinnacle of her power may appear gratifying, just as it is a gratifying heritage for France to possess Versailles regardless of the costs of its creation in terms of human suffering in the 17th century. Today ambition to achieve greatness has to be reconciled with the spirit of the time, with the need for achieving our economic and political ends without a ruthless disregard for social considerations. The two aims, economic progress and a high standard of living for all, are not incompatible, provided that the workers are prepared to earn and deserve their progress towards prosperity instead of expecting it as a free gift from the community, a bounty which need not be earned and deserved. Thanks to technological innovations it would now be possible to combine economic expansion and national greatness with a standard of living that respect for the human dignity of industrial workers demands, if only they discovered the advantages of reconciling their interests with those of the community, instead of trying to secure gains for themselves at the expense of the rest of the community.

CHAPTER THREE

DECLINE SINCE 1945

THE history of Britain's decline since the end of the second World War is a sad tale that must surely be unexampled in the annals of victorious nations. Of course a nation which has achieved victory after a superhuman exertion is always tempted to enjoy the fruits of its victory rather than continue to make efforts and sacrifices for the sake of ensuring that it retains the superiority of its power achieved at such high cost. But the decline of power resulting from such relaxation was in the past usually a slow process and it did not become obvious until another war came to disclose the weakness of the former victor. This was the case of Britain and of France in 1940. Until then the victorious nations of the first World War lived on their past reputation and, thanks to the prestige derived from it, they retained much of the influence achieved through their victory in 1918.

It is surely unusual that a victorious nation should lose its power, influence and prestige during a period of peace in the complete absence of a military reverse. Yet this is what happened to Britain. Since 1945 she only took part in a few minor wars which could not have reserved her leading position and in which Britain gave in any case a good account of herself. Nevertheless it would be idle to deny that today Britain is incomparably weaker than she had been before the last War.

From a military point of view the extent to which Britain's governments have reduced the strength of her fighting services since 1945 for the sake of being able to speed up the increase of the standard of living and to increase public expenditure has gravely impaired her national security. The Royal Navy, which had been supreme for centuries, is now a mere shadow of its old self.   Regiments with splendid traditions have been disbanded.   Even the Territorial Army has been sacrificed to the Government's reluctance to cut civil expenditure or, to be exact, to moderate its increase.   Muddle in military aircraft planning has cast gloom over the prospects of the R.A.F.   As for the decision to disband even Civil Defence, it amounts to informing Britain's potential enemies that she has no intention of defending herself against adversaries capable of destroying her towns by nuclear weapons.

In addition to relinquishing the Colonial Empire, Britain has also deliberately forfeited her claim to the support of the loyal old Dominions in a future war.   The decision, endorsed by all political parties during the 'sixties, to try to join the European Common Market at the cost of sacrificing special relationships with the Commonwealth made Australia, New Zealand and Canada realise that they could no longer rely on Britain for safeguarding their prosperity.   And the decision taken by the Labour Government in 1967 to withdraw in a few years from Britain's military bases east of Suez has made Australia and New Zealand realise that they could no longer count on Britain even for their security and for their national survival.   After their heavy sacrifices to help Britain in two European wars in which they had little or no direct interest, they were forced to realise that Britain would not be in a position to reciprocate if and when it should be their turn to need urgent military assistance.

So the English-speaking Dominions are drifting into the American sphere of influence.   It would not be surprising if this trend were followed to its logical conclusion — separation from the Commonwealth and adhesion to the United States. But even if they were to remain in the Commonwealth in outward form, Britain could hardly expect to be able to depend on their military assistance in a European war to anything like the extent comparable to the generous help she received from them in the Wars of 1914 and 1939.

Admittedly the granting of independence to the colonies and protectorates was in accordance with world trends.   The days

B

when it was possible to rule over nations in face of their determination to gain independence are over — except for the two
new imperialist-colonialist Powers, Soviet Russia and Communist China, both of which have proved that colonisation
is still possible for nations which are ruthless enough to rule
conquered nations with totalitarian brutality.   It may be a
matter of opinion whether the granting of independence to
many British colonies was not grossly premature, and whether
it would not have been wiser and more in accordance with the
interests of the populations of the colonies themselves to prepare
them for independence more adequately before plunging them
into independence.   But admittedly an attempt to defer the
inevitable change might have necessitated heavy expenditure
in terms of money and of human lives.   For this reason it is
tempting to argue that to a very large degree Britain was fated
to decline because the loss of her Colonial Empire was the
inevitable result of the greatly increased desire of colonial
peoples to gain independence at once.

   Anyone arguing on such lines is well advised to study the
recent histories of France, Holland and Belgium.   These
countries, too, relinquished most of their colonial territories
after the War, yet their relative standing in the world has not
diminished as a result of having ceased to be colonial powers.
In the case of France it became, in fact, greatly enhanced, for
some ten years at any rate, thanks to the determination aroused
in them by General de Gaulle to blot out the memories of the
humiliating defeat of 1940 and of the subsequent German
occupation.   Even though the events of May and June 1968
deprived France of much of the prestige gained, the fact that
it had been possible for her to achieve such prestige at all is
well worth remembering.

   Holland and Belgium have managed to overcome by sheer
hard work the heavy losses they had suffered in terms of
national wealth and income resulting from the confiscation of
their immense investments in their former colonies.   They are
now more prosperous than ever before, and their influence in
European affairs is no negligible quantity.

It is only Britain who, having lost practically the whole of her Empire, has made no visible effort to regain her old prestige and power. Yet this could have been achieved through sheer hard work, by which Britain could have reduced her external debts to manageable proportions. She could have produced an export surplus, placing her once more in a position to assist friendly countries in need of economic and financial assistance. Admittedly, during recent years Britain has been exporting considerable amounts of capital, but she has done so at the cost of increasing her external short-term debts and therefore making sterling more vulnerable. Had she helped other countries out of strength instead of helping them out of weakness, she might have retained her political and economic prestige and influence.

Anyone who doubts that a strong balance of payments is a source of strength not only from an economic point of view but also from a political point of view should remember the experience of West Germany since the War. She has become a highly respected power, thanks to her persistent balance of payment surpluses, and her voice now carries considerable weight in the council of nations. She has achieved prestige not through rearmament but through a supreme effort to regain her economic strength. Today Germany is industrially and financially stronger than Britain. Her financial strength rests on solid reserves, and not on nominal reserves which are more than outweighed by external short-term liabilities as in the case of the United States and of Britain.

Whenever excessive domestic growth begins to produce its adverse effect on the German balance of payments the authorities take drastic corrective action and the balance of payments surplus soon reappears. The size of German export surpluses and their persistence show what a hard-working nation is capable of achieving. The seventeenth-century English pamphleteer's words concerning the Dutch may be applied perfectly to present-day Germany:—

> Were they with force not able to invade?
> No matter, they'll conquer the world by trade.

Switzerland, Holland and Sweden — to mention only these three countries — command universal respect and by no means inconsiderable influence in world affairs, even though their populations are only a fraction of that of Britain. Through sheer hard work they have maintained and increased their financial strength in spite of the rapid progress of their economic growth, so that they are now in a position to assist other countries instead of depending on assistance from others for their stability.

All the three major defeated countries have recovered their economic power and have even raised it well above the pre-War level. They command, therefore, political power and prestige. As for Soviet Russia — a country which had suffered more devastation and many more casualties than any other with the possible exception of Germany — she has reconstructed her destroyed towns and villages and has built up a formidable industrial capacity at the same time as maintaining her immense military strength.

Why is it that Britain alone has lost the peace after having won the War? Such gains and achievements as Britain has been able to show since 1945 are incomparably less impressive than those of most other countries. It is true, most of her blitzed districts have at long last been reconstructed. Some British industries have been modernised, but in this respect she is, generally speaking, behind Germany, France, Italy, the Soviet Union and Japan, not to speak of the United States. Her industrial productive capacity has increased, but not to an extent comparable with that of most of her rivals.

Although there has been a spectacular increase in British national income in terms of money, this has been largely the result of the depreciation of the inflated monetary unit. Calculated in terms of constant prices, the increase is not nearly impressive enough. Undoubtedly, we are better off than before the war. And of course, as Keynes would observe, we now earn a great deal more than we had at the time of the Black Death. The increase in the gross national product is in accordance with the secular trend, which may be interrupted by wars and other disasters but which is always resumed as a matter of course as soon as the cause of the setback ceases to operate. But unless and until the increase of our figures should compare favourably with those of other advanced countries, it is not impressive.

It is often argued that even if Britain's economic achievement is comparatively poor she has good reason for being proud of her achievements in the sphere of social services. Britain can indeed claim credit for having initiated the Welfare State with the adoption of the Beveridge Plan at a time when more prosperous nations that could afford it better had made no such progress in the social sphere. But in the meantime the social services of a number of other advanced industrial countries have caught up with, and surpassed, those of Britain. These countries have been in a much better position to be increasingly generous in assisting the lower income groups during the last two decades, because their working classes have contributed more wholeheartedly towards the national effort required for earning the costs of the increased benefits. Indeed, today Britain is less favourably placed to afford the smaller benefits than are several Western European countries to pay the higher benefits. Moreover, unlike Britain, these countries did not increase their social service benefits on borrowed money. More will be said on this subject in Chapter 10.

Another item on the credit side of Britain's balance sheet of achievements since the War has been the reconstruction of her portfolio of foreign investments depleted during the War. But that achievement again is heavily offset by items on the debit side of the balance sheet — the increase in Britain's long-term and short-term foreign liabilities and the increase in foreign investments in British industries. Some 25 per cent of British key industries is now owned or controlled by American interests.

On the debit side of the balance sheet there is the sharp decline of Britain's relative share in world trade in general and of her share in the trade of the Commonwealth in particular. There is the decline in Britain's relative share in the world output of goods by some of her key industries such as steel and shipbuilding. The proportion of ships sailing under the British flag has contracted considerably. Sterling is no longer the principal currency in international trade and its role in international finance has also diminished owing to the decline of world confidence in it. For the same reason London's formerly unassailable role as the world's banking centre has also suffered a decline, at any rate in a relative sense.

Since Britain is obviously unable to repay her external short-term debts it is essential for her to ensure that the confidence of foreign holders of sterling in the stability of sterling is upheld, so that they should have no cause to insist on repayment. But the perennial balance of payments deficit is hardly confidence-inspiring, nor is sterling's record since the war, having been devalued on two occasions. A succession of currency debasements had been the characteristic feature of the period of decline of the Roman Empire. It had been largely the result of the perennial balance of payments deficit that drained relentlessly her supply of precious metals, used up largely to pay for imported grain required by the Roman Welfare State. History seems to be repeating itself to an alarming degree.

What has been the main cause of Britain's decline? There has been no basic change in the trend of world trade similar to the one that caused the decline of Venice and other Medieval Italian cities. There has been nothing comparable to the exhaustion of Spain's precious metal resources in the New World. And, as already pointed out earlier, there has been no military defeat, no lost wars, to account for the decline.

The answer is, the author regrets to say, the deterioration of some of those qualities of the British character which had been responsible for the achievement of British greatness. But for this, Britain might have been able to hold her own in spite of all adverse circumstances.

Britain has ceased to be a leading world power, partly because the relative importance of the United States and of the Soviet Union has increased. With her much smaller population Britain would have found it difficult to keep pace with the expansion of the two dynamic giants. Difficult, certainly, but not impossible. By strengthening her relations with the old Dominions and, as far as practicable, with other countries of the Commonwealth, she might have remained a power that would bear comparison with the United States and the Soviet Union. But Britain has deliberately neglected her special relationship with the Commonwealth. And she has now adopted a policy calculated to destroy what is left of that special relationship.

The Little Englander policy that has always been dear to the hearts of the Left has been allowed to prevail, this time with the wholehearted endorsement of the Conservative Party. One country after another has ended its allegiance to the Crown. As pointed out earlier, this has been inevitable. But the pace of the disintegration is open to argument. Almost the only British territory for which the Labour Government has been putting up a tolerably stiff fight is Gibraltar — and that solely because the claimant happens to be Franco's Spain. If the Spanish Republic had not been overthrown before the war, Gibraltar would have been handed over on a silver salver to a fellow-Socialist regime long before now.

But apart altogether from the virtual disappearance of the Commonwealth and Empire — the former is still kept in precarious existence even though it has ceased to have any inner meaning, apart from what remains of Britain's special relationship with the English-speaking old Dominions — Britain would have declined in any case to the rank of a second-class power because of the deterioration of the British character. The Empire was built up and maintained by the devotion of the British people to the cause of their country. That devotion seems to have declined to vanishing point. Everybody, or at any rate the overwhelming majority, is now for himself and for himself alone. The indifference of so many workers and employers towards the vital interests of their country, their refusal to notice the crisis simply because they themselves have been doing well, makes all the difference to Britain's position and prospects. While before and during the War British people were probably the most public-spirited people in the world, today they probably rank among the least public-spirited.

One of the manifestations of this change in the attitude of the British people has been the increase in the degree of tax-avoidance and tax evasion. Britons have become much more reluctant to render unto Caesar what is Caesar's. Admittedly this is largely Caesar's own fault. The governments that have succeeded each other have been competing with each other in the degree of their extravagance, and Parliament has become increasingly reluctant to spend its time on checking the official spending spree. No wonder taxpayers have become increasingly reluctant to surrender an increasingly large proportion of their incomes to governments which are so keen on wasting their money.

Many thousands of accountants and solicitors are busy advising their clients how to avoid their taxes lawfully. But many millions of the lower income groups, too, have found ways, even without receiving professional advice, for evading their taxes unlawfully. No taxes are paid by those who earn good incomes through regular pilfering. Garage mechanics, repair and maintenance workers, etc., execute work for their firm's customers after hours at half cost and pay no tax on this illicit income. Old-age pensioners undertake jobs on the understanding that their employers keep quiet about it, otherwise their earnings are deducted from their inadequate pensions. Nothing is ever said about all this, yet the sum total of all such loss of revenue must surely exceed that of the total losses through evasion by the rich.

Britain is barely able to hold her own even as a second-class Power, owing to the unwillingness of her people to make the effort and self-sacrifice needed in order to become once more self-supporting. British people really seem to imagine that they can retain their self-respect, even if they cannot retain the respect of other peoples for a nation which prefers to borrow rather than work hard for the sake of paying its way. Before the war it was some Balkan States and the lesser Latin American Republics that had been looked upon with contempt because

of their inability ever to meet their debts — except by borrowing even more. Has Britain sunk so low as to assume a similar
role? The rate of interest that the British Government has to
pay on its loans is about equal to the rates paid by professional
defaulters before the war.

Until 1964 Britain managed somehow to hold her own. In
the course of her ups and downs, her liabilities incurred during
lean years were settled during the fat years. Since 1964, however, she has had, internationally speaking, no fat years,
although her leanness has varied in degree. She has become a
perennial borrower, quite incapable of getting out of the red.
A country cannot command respect if its government has to
depend on the willingness of other countries to help it out with
loans again and again. It cannot have influence if it is obviously not in a position to help others financially — except out
of borrowed money, thereby aggravating its own difficulties.

The extent to which a country's ability to play the part of an
international financial centre enables it to wield power and
influence can be illustrated by many historical examples.
During the Middle Ages and for some time after the Renais-
sance, Florence, Venice and Genoa had been powerful far
beyond the extent of their military resources, because of their
role as financial centres. In the 18th century the international
financial role of Amsterdam enabled Holland to participate in
the wars against Louis XIV on an equal footing with England
and with the German Empire. Britain's own supremacy
during the 18th and 19th centuries was due as much to London's
increasingly important international financial role as to the
superiority of her industries and to the strength of her Navy.

But the Labour Government seems to have decided to ignore
the teachings of history. It has become the official policy to
abandon London's role as an international financial centre.
In any case, the distrust in sterling has gone a long way
towards weakening London's international role, although,
thanks to the skill, experience and integrity of the London
banking community, it has succeeded in maintaining a high
degree of activity and even in attracting an increasing number

of foreign banks and in assuming new international banking functions.

By keeping down the measures applied in order to defend sterling to an indispensable minimum, and by relaxing them as soon as the acute attacks are passed, the Government has failed to inspire the degree of confidence in sterling that is necessary for maintaining its role as an international currency. Indeed it is now the officially declared policy to abandon that role and to terminate sterling's role as an international currency, a role which has been maintained up to now to a remarkable degree. Yet that role represents an immense influence in world affairs. General de Gaulle would have given anything to be able to acquire it, and a reunited Germany would be certain to make a bid to secure the financial lead for Frankfurt or Berlin. Meanwhile New York will have to play that role, in spite of the disadvantages of its geographical position.

The way in which Britain is deliberately abdicating her historical role even beyond the extent to which she is forced to do so by circumstances is really amazing. Her industries have ceased to enjoy a quasi-monopolistic position in the world's markets. In spite of this, she could and should have retained a high proportion of her power and influence by strengthening London's role as a world banking centre instead of deliberately weakening it. So far from trying to mitigate Britain's decline, the Government is aggravating it by weakening her even in the sphere where she could more than hold her own.

The effects of Britain's decline is not realised by Government supporters who resent the Government's inability or unwillingness to influence the foreign policies and military policies of the United States and other countries in accordance with pure Socialist principles. They refuse to see that the decline of Britain's military and financial power has necessarily reduced her influence on the policies of foreign governments. If they really believe in their Pacifist principles then surely they must realise that Britain's declining influence has been a change for the worse from the point of view of world peace. But while they want Britain to enforce their pacifist policies at the conference table they have done their best to deprive her of the means by which she could make herself felt.

Their attitude is characterised by the same lack of realism that inspired them, or their forerunners, in the 'thirties, when they insisted in the notorious Peace Ballot that Britain should disarm, and in the Oxford Union's resolution that British people should not fight for King and Country. They wanted Britain to disarm stark naked, but they demanded that she should defend other countries against aggression. The logical outcome of their policy was the Munich surrender. Their present successful insistence on disarmament and on policies that weaken Britain's financial power as well as her political and military power has ensured that she is not in a position to enforce their views in the Vietnam War or in any other international political sphere.

CHAPTER FOUR

JEKYLL-AND-HYDE GOVERNMENT

IT is doubtless tempting to put all the blame for Britain's decline on the Labour Government, but to do so would be neither correct nor fair. Although the crisis has come to the surface and has become greatly aggravated since Mr. Wilson assumed office in 1964, the Socialist contention that he had inherited a mess is not without justification. Admittedly on the face of it the nation appeared to be on the whole happy under most of the thirteen years of Tory rule. Beneath the comparatively smooth surface there were, however, influences making for a grave crisis. Indeed the Labour Party took over a difficult situation, so difficult that under Socialist rule only a Government of supermen could have put it right. And Mr. Wilson and his team were far from being supermen.

The Labour Government's inherited difficulties were not confined to the increased trade deficit the Conservative Government incurred by adopting reflationary measures to make quite sure that there would be no recession on the eve of the coming general election. That itself was bad enough, even if the Tory claim that it could have been put right by a Conservative Government in the same way as the crises of 1951, 1957 and 1961 had been dealt with is quite possibly justified.

But we must bear in mind that, although Tory Chancellors of the Exchequer had been able to get the country out of the recessions they had brought about in order to relieve the over-load on the economy, on each subsequent occasion the exercise proved to be more and more difficult. Mr. Heathcoat Amory had a more difficult task than Mr. Butler; Mr. Selwyn Lloyd and Mr. Maudling had a much more difficult task than Mr. Heathcoat Amory. In order to relieve the overload, Mr. Selwyn Lloyd had to administer such a dose of deflation that his successor had quite a job in reflating the economy. Confronted in 1963 with the prospects of persistent recession in the summer and the early autumn, Mr. Maudling administered an overdose of reflation especially in his Budget, causing an almost peace-time record trade deficit. The Conservative regime had incurred grave responsibility by deliberately abstaining from tackling in good time the balance of payments crisis that was mounting towards the end of its term of office. The fact that Mr. Maudling was merely following Mr. Gaitskell's example when in 1951 he did absolutely nothing on the eve of the election — he even admitted in Parliament that during his electioneering tour he was not even kept informed about the daily outflow of gold — to deal with the run on sterling, is no acceptable excuse. Tories are expected to be more responsible than Socialists in matters of finance and their bad example provided the Labour Government with an excuse for behaving even more irresponsibly.

But Tory responsibility for the crisis of 1964 was not confined to its pre-election reflation. Throughout the whole period of the thirteen years of Tory rule the public was allowed and indeed encouraged to develop an attitude of mind which made the solution of the difficulties developing beneath the smooth surface all but impossible. It is of course arguable that the Conservative Government, if re-elected, would have commanded sufficient confidence to apply the necessary deflationary measures in its own time, as there would have been no run on the pound. Even so, it is hardly an acceptable principle that a Conservative Government should perpetuate itself by deliberately creating a mess before each election, on the assumption that the existence of a mess makes its re-election imperative because of the inability of the Socialists to clear it up. Such a system would bring about a one-party State in practice.

Unfortunately for Britain, during recent times even the two-party system has not worked satisfactorily owing to the unscrupulous competition of the two parties for popularity. There is a perturbing degree of similarity between the circumstances of Britain's present decline and that of Poland two centuries ago. In both instances the impartial historian can trace the root of the decline to the ruthless rivalry between two opposing political factions fighting for supremacy. In both instances adherents of both parties were firmly convinced that they and they alone would be able to save the country and that their opponents would ruin it. Politicians on both sides found it therefore easy to convince themselves that their use of unscrupulous methods adopted to keep their opponents out of office at all costs was not a selfish bid for power but a patriotic attempt to save the country from ruin.

In 18th-century Poland the Czartoryski faction and the Potocki faction had both resorted to unpatriotic devices in order to defeat their political rivals. No matter how damaging their policies had been to Poland they had convinced themselves that such policies had been justified on the grounds that anything preventing the opposing faction from achieving power would be to the interest of Poland in the long run, even if it produced 'temporary' disadvantages and perils for the nation. The judgment of history condemns them for having caused Poland's decline that culminated in her final fall, for the sake of pursuing their selfish and unscrupulous ambitions.

I wonder if the judgment of history on the British Conservative and Labour Parties during the 'sixties will be very much different if and when Britain should come to pay the full price for their selfish rivalry? Will their motive — their desire to save Britain from their opponents' misrule — be accepted as a mitigating circumstance any more than it is accepted by history when judging the similar behaviour of the rival parties in 18th-century Poland? After all it is not the intention of the parties — good as they themselves think it may be — that matters but the ultimate destination to which the road paved with such good intentions is fated to lead.

Admittedly, neither of the two principal British parties can be accused today of emulating the ultimate crime of two Polish parties in the 18th century that had led to the downfall of their country — that for the sake of strengthening their position against each other they invited the two external enemies of their country, Russia and Prussia, to intervene. Apart from the British Communist Party, which would gladly convert Britain into a satellite of Soviet Russia as the only conceivable means for them to achieve power, and the pre-war British Fascists, many of whom would have welcomed Hitler with open arms, no party would be capable of such treason. But both major British parties have been guilty of aiding and encouraging the enemy within — the trade unions' greed and short-sighted selfishness, which has been the main cause of Britain's decline. Both parties were too eager to secure at all costs the largest possible proportion of trade union votes. It was this attitude of Conservatives and Socialists, whether in or out of office, that has generated in the minds of workers the assumption that they have only rights and no duties towards the community, and that it is their birthright to demand and receive the one-sided concessions made to them by both parties without having to earn or deserve them.

It never seems to have occurred to any post-war government to make it a condition for the costly concessions following each other in close succession that trade unions should be required to reciprocate the favours received by abolishing or mitigating their restrictive practices. Nor did they insist sufficiently that the workers should give the *quid pro quo* for the costly concessions by doing a fair day's work for their increased pay and for their other benefits. The Tories were, if anything, even guiltier in this respect than the Socialists, for by playing the part of Santa Claus while in office they made it impossible for their Socialist successors to be less magnanimous with their concessions or to insist on *quid pro quo*.

Competitive 'bribing' for the sake of attracting the supporters and potential supporters of the rival faction had been a familiar feature of 18th-century political life in Poland, and also of British political life since the War. One of the most effective means to that end is lavish spending of public money.

We shall see in the next chapter how Mr. Maudling provided a formula for increasing public expenditure by reversing the traditional rule to cut our coat according to our cloth.

Mr. Wilson and Mr. Callaghan have been the subject of a great deal of richly deserved criticism for the inadequacy of their measures in defence of sterling during 1964–67. But, to give them their due, we must admit that they might have behaved even worse — in fact a great deal worse. Their critics are apt to forget that they might have devalued immediately on assuming office, blaming their predecessors — not without justification — for having left behind a mess that they could not have cleared up in any other way. (If it is true that it was Lord Balogh who dissuaded Mr. Wilson from devaluing in 1964 the Conservative Party ought to have an equestrian statue of him erected in front of the Central Office.) The Labour Government could have adopted water-tight exchange control, blocking even foreign balances. They could have reversed the trend towards freer trade by adopting quotas and bilateral trading methods. Instead, they defended sterling with only a slight tightening of exchange control and continued their predecessors' free trade policy apart from one temporary lapse in the form of an import surcharge. They abstained from commandeering privately held foreign investments, even though they did realise officially held foreign investments.

Nor is the list of points in mitigation of their offences confined to purely negative matters. The Labour Government did adopt many unpopular measures for the sake of restoring the balance of the economy. They did apply credit squeezes and even resorted to wage restraint culminating in the wage freeze enacted in 1966 and in the adoption of the Prices and Incomes Act in 1968. All these acts of Dr. Jekyll do deserve recognition, and the Government's critics were less than generous by their refusal to admit it.

Having said all this, it must be added that Mr. Hyde had acted most irresponsibly in many respects, so that the favourable effects of Dr. Jekyll's policies have been much more than wiped out. While Dr. Jekyll was trying to act in the public interest, Mr. Hyde's acts were guided by purely sectional party and class interests. Mr. Wilson, having antagonised the Left wing of his Party by his public-spirited acts, felt impelled to appease the disaffected elements by granting them concessions which the country could not afford in the middle of a crisis, by abstaining from the adoption of sufficiently firm measures called for by the situation and by mitigating those measures much too soon. The measures adopted by Dr. Jekyll to damp down excessive consumer demand were not sufficiently effective. Except for a brief period from July 1966, they were always 'too late and too little'. And they were always removed too soon. In all fairness we must add, however, that what is remarkable is not that a Labour Government should be so reluctant in adopting and retaining such un-Socialist and even anti-Socialist measures but that it had adopted them at all.

The Dr. Jekyll side of the Government did make some efforts to check wage inflation by the adoption of an incomes policy. The fact that a serious attempt was made to restrain and even freeze wages is an important point in favour of Mr. Wilson. Even more than the policy of credit squeeze resulting in an increase in unemployment, it tended to make the Government unpopular among the workers, all the more so as the Conservative Opposition exploited unscrupulously the inevitable unpopularity of these measures. The behaviour of Tory politicians in resisting wage restraint which their Governments never had the courage or political honesty to apply is reminiscent of the behaviour of the Czartoryski and Potocki factions at their worst in 17th-century Poland. In face of this attitude of the Opposition it is surprising that the Labour Government perseveres to any extent with such a politically suicidal course. The blame for the inadequacy of its efforts in this respect rests largely with the Conservatives who were not prepared to abstain from exploiting the situation, let alone agree to pursue a bi-partisan policy in that sphere for the sake of restoring a balanced economy.

But Dr. Jekyll's well-meaning if inadequate efforts in the right direction must not blind us towards Mr. Hyde's disastrous moves in the wrong direction. The list of Mr. Hyde's misdeeds is indeed very long. It begins with one of the first Cabinet decisions taken after assuming office — to grant Ministers and Members of Parliament a substantial increase of their salaries. To do this in the middle of an acute crisis was about the most irresponsible act of selfishness committed in Britain in modern times.

It must be conceded that, having regard to their heavy responsibilities and the long hours and hard work that the performance of their duties entails, politicians within the Government and outside it had been grossly underpaid. They are far from being overpaid even now, by comparison with salaries paid to Ministers and Members of Parliament in other leading countries, or with remunerations of executives in the business world, or even with the increased scales of pay to senior Government officials. In examining the case for their higher salaries and pensions, it is utterly irrelevant to argue, as some people do, that a great many of them would not be able to earn outside politics anything like their present increased salaries. An increase of their pay had long been overdue, and there is even a valid case for a further increase — at the appropriate moment.

But to choose the moment of an acute crisis for remedying the admittedly genuine long-standing grievance of Ministers and Members of Parliament, and to proceed with the matter in such an indecent haste after the advent of the Labour Government, was, to quote Talleyrand's immortal words, more than a crime — it was a grave mistake. It recalls the behaviour of victorious dictators in certain backward countries, whose first act on assuming power is to distribute largesse among their henchmen as a reward for helping them to overthrow the previous regime. The only difference is that while such dictators have their defeated opponents shot, imprisoned or exiled, the Labour Government of 1964 gave them a share in the spoils in the form of raising their salaries too, together with those of Government supporters.

It was one of the most striking manifestations of the deterioration of the British character that the Conservative Opposition, instead of denouncing the unfortunate timing of the increase, accepted it with alacrity with only one single dissenting voice. They must surely have realised the demoralising effect of setting such an example when the fate of the country's economy depended on the willingness of the public to practise self-restraint. Yet they eagerly accepted the increase and did not even divide the House against it. Sir Cyril Osborne was the only Tory Member who spoke against it at the time.

It is the favourite argument of Government supporters and Opposition apologists trying to excuse the inexcusable that, after all, Government and Parliament merely followed the recommendations of an all-Party Committee. Quite so. But there is no passage in the Report of that Committee which recommends the granting of the increase in the middle of an acute crisis.

When early in 1965 Mr. Wilson went so far as to invoke the 'spirit of Dunkirk' in exhorting the British public to practise the self-restraint which he himself was unwilling to practise, the author felt impelled to protest in *The Times*, pointing out that had Mr. Churchill, on assuming office in 1940, made it one of his most urgent tasks to raise his own salary and that of his colleagues, the term 'spirit of Dunkirk' would not have found its way into the vocabulary of the English language. Had Mr. Wilson and his colleagues really imagined that, having granted themselves generous pay increases and pensions, they would be able to impress the public with the imperative necessity for renouncing excessive wage increases? If only they had confined themselves to passing legislation providing for the long-overdue increase of their remuneration but defer-ring its actual application until after the crisis they would have commanded respect and moral authority, enabling them to exhort the country successfully to follow their lead. But evidently Mr. Hyde was too impatient to obtain his rise. As a result, he forfeited his right to preach patience and self-restraint to others.

Another act of Mr. Hyde was the increase of pensions and

other social service benefits. Justified and long overdue as such increases had undoubtedly been, they were ill-timed in the middle of a crisis. The 'gnomes' interpreted them as indicating that the Government was keener on buying popularity by pursuing Socialist policies than on restoring a balanced economy.

While Dr. Jekyll did go some way towards curtailing excessive consumer demand, Mr. Hyde ensured that the deflationary measures did not go far enough to be effective and that they were relaxed as soon as sterling appeared to be free of acute pressure for a few weeks. It was the Government's declared intention to apply deflation without tears, ignoring or pretending to ignore the fact that deflation can only help to the extent to which it hurts. Those who reminded the Government of this elementary fact of life were denounced in 1964 by a certain Minister as 'sado-masochists', implying that they wanted to derive perverted pleasure from inflicting pain on others and on themselves by adopting deflationary measures that would really hurt.

Mr. Hyde preferred to postpone the taking of the bitter medicine in sufficiently big doses, in the hope that someone else might solve our problem for us — that something might happen in some part of the world, obviating the necessity for us to take the medicine. The result of this policy was that the crisis has now been dragging on for four solid years. A sharp dose of deflation, swiftly administered, might have cured Britain in a matter of months as it did on past occasions and as it did in other countries. The very gradual ineffective administration of inadequate doses, accompanied as they were by inflationary measures, merely prolonged our agony. It did not even save sterling from eventual devaluation, and it prevented that act from bringing relief.

Dr. Jekyll's wage freeze in 1966 was effective solely because it was accompanied by a short-lived but effective deflationary drive. Otherwise the trade unions would have remained in a too strong bargaining position and would not have stood for the wage freeze. But Mr. Hyde removed both squeeze and freeze before the danger to sterling passed. When the wage freeze and the 'severe' restraint that followed it came to an end in July 1967, a very large number of wage demands was put forward and pressed rigorously. In many instances wage increases were demanded with retrospective effect so that they wiped out completely the achievements of the wage freeze.

In spite of this, the Government proceeded with the relaxation of the squeeze by reducing the restrictions on hire-purchase credits in August. Apart from the material effect of that move on domestic demand, its psychological effect abroad was disastrous. It was interpreted as an indication that the Government, frightened by the evidence of its unpopularity as indicated by by-election results, was no longer prepared to defend sterling at the cost of incurring more unpopularity. Mr. Hyde gained definitely the upper hand. He triumphed in November when the Government decided to abandon the defence of sterling and to devalue, without even taking adequate measures to ensure the success of the devaluation.

Dr. Jekyll's influence prevailed whenever the Government decided to stand up to the trade unions. But Mr. Hyde ensured that the Government was unable to stand up to the trade unions effectively, by rescinding unconditionally the House of Lords ruling on the Rooke *v.* Barnard case. Had that decision been allowed to stand trade union leaders would have been exposed to legal action for damages whenever they misused their power and thereby victimised individuals. For that reason trade union leaders might have been willing to co-operate with the Government in return for legisation to relieve them of the threat of such action. Instead the subservient Mr. Hyde hastened to concede them their immunity as a free gift without any *quid pro quo*. Had Dr. Jekyll made the repeal of the Rooke *v.* Barnard ruling conditional on removing at least some restrictive practices the resulting increase in productivity might have obviated the necessity for tougher measures of squeeze and freeze. It is not surprising that the Government, having given away such a valuable bargaining weapon, found trade unions non-cooperative.

Dr. Jekyll was fully aware that overfull employment was the

main cause of the country's economic difficulties. But Mr. Hyde pursued policies accentuating the prevailing scarcities of labour. Indeed during 1965 and early in 1966 Ministers and other Government spokesmen actually boasted of the Government's achievement in succeeding in increasing the degree of overfull employment.

Over and above all, Mr. Hyde succeeded beyond measure in inducing the Government to spend more and more in the public sector. In doing so he cancelled out all the beneficial effects of Dr. Jekyll's efforts to curtail spending in the private sector of the economy. More will be said about this in the next chapter.

The belated efforts of Mr. Jenkins to adopt relatively tough measures in November 1968 instead of continuing to rely on the delayed effects of the devaluation to correct the balance of payments deserve recognition. It was the legitimate task of the Opposition to criticise the Government for its unwarranted delay in adopting these measures, also to criticise the choice of the measures. But the violent attacks on the Government for deflating was another manifestation of the deterioration of the British character. This effort to cash in on the unpopularity of Dr. Jekyll's effort played straight into Mr. Hyde's hands.

CHAPTER FIVE

IRRESPONSIBLE SPENDING SPREE

In few spheres has national demoralisation during recent years been so glaringly obvious as in the sphere of public spending. It has been proceeding regardless of sterling crises. In the TV news bulletin on April 27, 1968, the Prime Minister was shown engaged in laying the foundation stone for a £350,000 swimming pool in his constituency. Of course it must have been a very popular act to make a public gesture implying endorsement of the decision of local authorities to provide his constituents with an additional swimming pool. Like almost every increase in public expenditure, it satisfies certain sectional interests, while the other side of the picture — the increase in total expenditure — is hardly noticed by anyone. After all, the additional burden this item represents is an infinitesimal fraction of the total of public spending. It is only slightly over $1\frac{1}{2}$d. per head of the population, taking the country as a whole. It is so easy and so tempting to slide into incurring similar items of expenditure by the thousand, for each one of them adds merely a few pence, or a few shillings at the most, to individual burdens. But their grand total is a formidable figure and it amounts to inflation.

The fact that Mr. Wilson, while preaching self-restraint to everybody, actually went out of his way on this occasion to publicise his endorsement of an item of luxury spending in his constituency in the middle of a campaign preaching restraint could not have passed unnoticed. It must have reminded the 'gnomes' of the striking difference between the Prime Minister's words and his actions. Given the fact that sterling had just recovered from an acute crisis and was hovering on the brink of another, the ill-timed initiation of such expenditure, small as the amount involved was to be, must have gone some way towards increasing distrust in sterling abroad. Such kind of public spending was ruthlessly checked in 1931, but in 1968 the British nation was simply incapable of self-restraint for the sake of saving the pound.

Over centuries Britain had built up for herself an enviable world-wide reputation for sound finance. Until the first World War she was generally looked upon as the model of responsible budgeting, towards which foreign Governments, Parliaments and nations had been accustomed to look for an inspiring example. This reputation was maintained during the first World War which was financed to a much higher degree by increased taxation instead of by borrowing or by inflation than in any other European belligerent country. Between the Wars, too, Britain set an example by the conversion of the gigantic 5% War Loan. She provided guidance for Governments struggling with their post-war deficits.

In this respect, as in so many respects, Britain can no longer trade on her past reputation. For in recent years she has acquired an unenviable reputation for irresponsible public spending. The self-restraint that characterised British public expenditure in the past has long been discarded. Governments succeeding each other since the second World War, and local authorities guided and inspired by them, have been simply incapable of resisting the temptation or the public pressure to spend well beyond their means. They have simply felt they must provide this or that costly improvement, even though they must have been fully aware that the nation obviously could not afford it unless and until it succeeded in increasing its productivity and in restoring a balanced economy.

The trouble is that every Minister and Member of Parliament, indeed every individual and organisation that is able to influence spending policy, has his own piece of pet extravagance, for the sake of which they are all for departing from their basic policy of curtailing public expenditure. In theory they are all for curtailing public spending, but each of them would like to make just one exception in favour of one pet project. The sum total of the 'exceptions' proposed from various influential quarters must necessarily be gross overspending. The ease with which the Government can increase taxation and borrowing makes it very tempting to make many 'exceptions' and to indulge in a non-stop irresponsible spending spree as a result.

Although it would be difficult to find acceptable excuses for the Government's inability to restrain growing pressure for increased spending in time of crisis, this does not of course mean that Tory propaganda is right in claiming that public overspending alone has been responsible for the inflationary increase of consumer spending and therefore for the balance of payments deficit and the sterling crises. This line of propaganda was suddenly adopted in May 1968 for the purpose of providing an excuse for the otherwise inexcusable attack on the Government's policy of wage restraint. The Conservative Opposition, having decided that it stood to gain by exploiting for party-political purposes the inevitable unpopularity of the Government's well-meaning efforts to check unearned wage increases, felt the need for inventing some form of theoretical foundation for its irresponsible policy so as to lend it the appearance of respectability. Otherwise it would have been unmistakably obvious that the Opposition was advocating or at any rate excusing wage increases solely for the sake of attracting trade unionist votes.

In an attempt to avoid acquiring a bad reputation for their flagrant lack of patriotism, Conservatives had to pretend that they did not believe wage increases were inflationary. So they enunciated a new creed — that the only thing that causes inflation is overspending by the Government, but for which it would not matter if trade unions were allowed and even encouraged to press for higher and higher wages. Tories who professed to believe this nonsense conveniently forgot that while in office they too were in favour of restraining wage increases — even if they never had the courage to try to adopt and enforce a policy to that end. They also forgot that they too were indulging in a non-stop increase of public expenditure, and even laid down the principle that the amount of revenue must be adjusted to whatever level of expenditure they chose to agree upon.

The attitude of the two opposing political factions that caused the ruin of 18th-century Poland had nothing on the attitude of those politicians in present-day Britain who actually encourage the wage-plunder, regardless of the obvious effect of unearned wage increases on exports through causing an increase in costs and in domestic demand for imported goods and for goods that could otherwise be exported.

The obvious truth is that inflation in Britain has been the combined effect of overspending in both public and private sectors. The Labour Government's policy of trying to restrain private spending while letting loose an orgy of public spending was of course hopelessly mistaken. The Opposition was equally wrong, however, in advocating a similarly one-sided policy in the opposite sense, to restrain spending in the public sector while actually encouraging the increase of spending power in the private sector.

But the fact that the Opposition is now pursuing an irresponsible and mischievous policy which is certain to make it more difficult for the Government to restrain overspending in the private sector does not in any way mitigate the blame attached to the Government's equally irresponsible and mischievous policy of overspending in the public sector.

Excess of expenditure over revenue is no longer called Budgetary deficit — it is now disguised under the name of 'Exchequer borrowing'; and in giving it that name the Government seems to have succeeded in misleading not only simpletons but even some experts whose names are household words into believing that Britain has a revenue surplus. Whatever it is called, it increases the public debt and, to a large extent, it forms the basis for credit expansion.

The British attitude towards the public debt has undergone a remarkable change through the centuries. Until the end of the 17th century it was looked upon as the reigning sovereign's personal debt which he was supposed to repay before his death. Although this was seldom actually done — Henry VII was one of the few exceptions and has secured for himself a favourable place in history largely because, instead of leaving debts behind, he actually left behind a well-filled Treasury to his successor — the principle was there. During the 18th century the impersonal character of the public debt as the liability of the immortal state came to be admitted. Nevertheless it was still assumed that sooner or later all Government debts had to be repaid. Various ingenious sinking fund schemes were proposed and some of them were adopted and operated for a time. Had they been carried through the public debt might have been wiped out — only to reappear in times of war.

But the public debt contracted during the Napoleonic Wars remained substantially unchanged—temporary ups and downs apart — till 1914, even though the principle that it ought to be reduced and wiped out remained upheld in theory. The sharp increase in the public debt during the first World War made no basic difference to this praiseworthy but unrealistic attitude. It was still vaguely hoped that conversions and a series of revenue surpluses might at any rate reduce its burden to manageable proportions. After the second World War, how-ever, any idea of ever repaying or even drastically reducing the public debt was given up. It came to be accepted as a matter of course that the State, being eternal, is entitled to have permanent debts and to increase their total year after year.

This change of attitude did not come immediately after the War. Although Dr. Dalton's name has come to be regarded as a byword for unsound finance owing to the consequences of his policy of cheap money and to his unfortunate remark about 'spending with a song in his heart', he did lay down the rule that, taking one year with another, the Budget must be balanced. His idea was to pursue a Keynesian counter-cyclical fiscal policy, deliberately unbalancing the Budget during recessions and producing a revenue surplus during booms. Dalton's successor, Sir Stafford Cripps, has gone down in history as the apostle of austerity — even though his record was

spoilt by the devaluation of 1949 — while Gaitskell was pre-
prepared to incur unpopularity by imposing National Health
Services charges for the sake of reducing the Budgetary deficit.
The fact that his highly unpopular measure did not prevent
his election as Leader of the Labour Party is an indication of
the high level at which British character still stood before its
more recent deterioration.

During the Conservative regime of 1951–64 efforts were
undoubtedly made to uphold sound financial principles. Taxation was repeatedly reduced, and Mr. Selwyn Lloyd even had
the political courage to give long-overdue relief to upper-
middle-class income groups by raising the surtax exemption
limit from its unrealistic pre-war figure. But the basic fact of
the situation had been the unwarranted degree of the increase
in public expenditure. Mr. Thorneycroft resigned because the
Cabinet refused to endorse his proposal to cut Estimates by
some £50 million. By curious coincidence the most important
passage in his resignation speech was worded almost identically
with the resignation speech of Lord Randolph Churchill some
seventy years earlier. The main difference was that, while the
latter resigned over a difference of half a million pounds, the
amount of overspending which impelled Mr. Thorneycroft to
give up the Chancellorship was exactly a hundred times larger.
So progress has undoubtedly been made.

In the late 'fifties a new principle was laid down that increase
in public expenditure is justified so long as its extent did not
exceed that of the national income. This is a highly dangerous
doctrine, all the more so for being so plausible. In addition to
justifying a perennial Budgetary deficit, it has created a self-
aggravating built-in 'inflator' because an increase in public
spending inevitably increases the total of the national money
income. This means that under the new doctrine increased
public spending automatically provides its own justification.
Owing to the 'multiplier-effect' of any increase in public
expenditure — that is, the money once spent is re-spent again
and again — it tends to increase national income by much
more than its own amount.

An even more disastrous doctrine, which was adopted towards the close of the Tory regime, was the rule laid down by Mr. Maudling in his Budget statement of April 14, 1964 — that 'by far away the largest factor in determining the amount of revenue is agreed level of expenditure'. This rule, referred to briefly earlier on, amounted distinctly to the abandonment of the policy of reducing taxation pursued hitherto by Conservative Governments. In view of the non-stop increase in spending and the growing pressure for its further increase, it could mean only higher and higher taxes to adjust revenue to higher and ever-higher expenditure. It is true that an increase in the national income means a higher yield even in the absence of additions to taxation. But when an increase in expenditure precedes the increase in the national income, the automatic increase in the yield of taxation necessarily lags behind it and the time lag provides ample occasion for inflation.

The Maudling principle was bad enough. But the Plowden principle was even worse. The Plowden Report (1962) condemns the policy of 'stop-go-stop' pursued until then by all Governments since the War, by which threatening inflationary booms were halted at an early stage instead of being allowed to proceed until they got out of control. Thanks to this counter-cyclical policy, Britain and many other countries were spared for two decades the disastrous consequences of non-stop inflationary booms and the major slumps and prolonged depressions that would have followed them as night follows day. The Plowden Committee in its wisdom condemned that system, mainly because it interfered with planned public expenditure.

What the Plowden formula implies is that, since the expenditure of the public sector of the economy must be treated as sacrosanct and must not be reduced in any conceivable circumstances, all the spending cuts required for the sake of reducing the overload on the economy should be made exclusively in the private sector of the economy. As the public sector must not be squeezed the private sector must bear the full burden of the restrictive measures. It did not seem to matter to the

Plowden Committee if businessmen whose plans are upset by credit squeezes, hire-purchase restrictions, Selective Employment Tax, etc., feel frustrated, nor even if workers made redundant by this one-sided policy feel frustrated, so long as a handful of senior officials are spared that feeling. Yet it has become to a large extent the basis of Government policy under Tories and Socialists alike.

The extent to which 'Plowdenism' came to guide Government policy has been particularly striking during Mr. Wilson's term of office. Although token cuts were made from time to time in public spending — to be exact, the extent of its increase was from time to time somewhat reduced only to be increased again to new record figures through supplementary estimates — it was allowed, nevertheless, to grow in every Budget year after year at an alarming pace.

Anyone who has no information about Britain's financial plight and judges her situation by the amounts that her public authorities feel able and justified in spending must imagine that she must indeed be a happy carefree country. There seems to be no such thing as a crisis as far as the public sector is concerned, though it is of course possible to argue that, had it not been for our balance of payments difficulties and sterling crises, the public sector would have overspent to an even higher degree.

All the deflationary efforts the Government was prepared to make for the defence of sterling were directed by the Wilson Government to the private sector. The reason why the measures of squeeze applied here and the various degrees of wage freeze and price restraint had failed to save the pound from devaluation was that their effort was much more than cancelled out by the inflationary effect of ever-increasing public spending. All the sacrifices forced on the private sector were in vain. Even during the course of the much-advertised economy drive that was supposed to follow devaluation in January 1968 the sum total of the cuts in the Estimates for 1968–69 was a reduction of the extent of their projected increases by a mere £300 million. In accordance with the

Maudling doctrine quoted above, the rest was to be raised by additional taxation.

When one reads Press reports from Germany or from other countries indicating from time to time that public opinion there is still gravely concerned whenever there is a Budgetary deficit, it does bring home to us the stage which the British nation has reached on the slippery slope leading to financial ruin. Hardly anybody here feels strongly about any additional expenditure nowadays solely on the ground that it would increase the Budgetary deficit and the public debt. Seemingly the only thing that matters to the British public and to British Governments is to promote progress towards a higher standard of living. It does not matter to them if that means an increase in the Budgetary deficit. After all, they say, in return for fictitious book entries the country receives additional real goods or services. The only argument that might carry some weight with them is that overspending increases the balance of payments deficit.

It would be of course too much to expect the man in the street to realise that there is a connection between Budgetary deficit and balance of payments deficit. If Tory propaganda, by its deliberately one-sided exaggeration of the importance of that connection, should succeed in drawing attention to its existence and importance then it would render a public service from this point of view, even if this were done for the wrong reason.

It is true, during the late 'fifties and early 'sixties, a handful of Members of Parliament began to take an active interest in scrutinising Estimates. On several occasions they successfully insisted on debating Estimates instead of passing them undebated 'on the nod'. But the overwhelming majority of Members infinitely preferred to spend Parliament's limited time on repetitive speeches dealing with broad generalities rather than performing their traditional role as the taxpayer's watchdog. So after a while the Members who would have liked to do their duty gave up the unequal struggle.

Parliament recently relaxed its interest even in the detailed control of taxation. It meekly accepted the Government's

decision that the all-important Committee stage of the Finance
Bill should be taken by a Standing Committee of 50 Members
instead of being taken by a Committee of the whole House.
It is at the Committee stage that the provisions introducing new
taxes or changing existing ones are scrutinised closely clause by
clause, line by line. Until now every Member was given an
opportunity to contribute to the debate on any clause in which
his constituents were interested or on which he had some
special knowledge. Every Member had the right to move
amendments to any such clause and the debates had to continue until everybody had said everything they wanted to say.
But as from 1968 only 50 Members will have that privilege.
To add insult to injury, the Government applied the guillotine
to the Finance Bill of 1968, surely one of the longest and most
involved Finance Bills providing for a record increase in
taxation. So the technicalities of the taxation measures its
clauses contain — those boring details which may determine
the fate of you or me for decades — will be passed without
adequate scrutiny on the Committee stage.

That the Government was anxious to escape detailed
scrutiny is understandable. But that the Commons, with
seven centuries of traditions behind them in the control of
taxation, have accepted this limitation of their functions is yet
another deplorable instance of the decline of Parliament and
of the nation which has the Parliament it deserves.

Having regard to the Government's unwillingness to check,
or at least adequately moderate, the increase of its expenditure,
and to Parliament's unwillingness to use its constitutional
powers to force the Executive to do so, is it surprising that
exhortations by politicians trying to induce the private sector
to practise self-restraint fall on deaf ears? They are as futile
as moralising in *The Doctor's Dilemma*, Act III, the effect of
which, according to Shaw's character Dubedat at whom it
was aimed, was that it 'merely left a little carbonic acid gas
behind that spoilt the air'. That is about the sum total of
the effect of exhortation speeches, in or outside Parliament,
so long as Government and Parliament are not prepared to set

an example by practising the self-restraint they preach. They must go beyond moralising and show they are willing and able to resist pressure in favour of more public spending during periods when this is quite obviously against the public interest. But, as we saw in the last chapter, they are not even prepared to make a gesture by deferring at least part of the ill-timed increase of their salaries until the crisis is overcome. When early in 1968 Mr. Wilson was pressed in the House to do something in that sense he side-stepped the issue by saying that the time for such a decision had not arrived yet.

Of course it must be readily admitted that a high proportion of the increase in expenditure is for useful and necessary purposes. The country certainly needs more houses and hospitals and schools and roads, and better public services in general. The satisfaction of some of these requirements is even more important from the point of view of raising the standard of living than the availability of more spending power for consumers' use in the private sector. But it is wrong that our understandable and legitimate desires for such improvements should be satisfied at a time when the country's financial situation is critical. It is a matter of elementary prudence and common sense that during periods of crisis all expenditure that is not absolutely indispensable and urgent should be cut down or deferred. This was done in the 'twenties when the Geddes Axe was wielded ruthlessly but effectively. It was done again in 1931, perhaps a little too ruthlessly but very effectively. It was done in respect of spending on civilian requirements during both World Wars. Why could it not be done again?

To urge restraint in public spending is not preaching austerity for its own sake. It would not mean abandoning much-needed improvements. It would be a case of *reculer pour mieux sauter* — to cut our spending, public and private alike, until the resulting restoration of a balanced and solvent economy enables us to go ahead once more. The British public, which has willingly submitted to drastic cuts on past occasions, is not trying on the present occasion to impress its elected representatives with its willingness to accept sacrifices. It is because in the

C

meantime Britons have become so thoroughly pampered and spoilt that they want to have everything at once, regardless of what the country can afford at present. Neither the public nor its rulers seem to be capable of self-denial or self-restraint.

Nothing could indicate the debasement of the British character more clearly than the fact that overspending through running into debts has come to be taken as a matter of course. Even the fact that domestic overspending does not merely lead to an increase of the domestic public debt but, indirectly, to the country's increase of its external short-term debts does not seem to cause any public concern, although it gives major headaches in official quarters. It would be difficult to make the public realise that to live beyond our means as a country and to become indebted to the rest of the world in consequence is something that is understandable for a developing country but for a developed country it is something to be ashamed of.

During the 'twenties foreign Finance Ministers who had been guilty of that self-same offence and who came to London to beg for assistance were treated to outspoken lectures by senior Treasury officials. Such humiliating experience had done them and their countries more good than the loans they had succeeded in negotiating over here. If only the U.S. and other Governments which repeatedly helped Britain since the end of the second World War and especially since 1964 had been sufficiently tough with our negotiators to make them realise that, by repeatedly resorting to requests for assistance, they and their country have lost caste, the Government might have made a more determined effort to avoid having to go through such a humiliating experience again and again.

To some extent Britain lives on her past prestige and for that reason those who assisted her financially treated her negotiators with more respect than they had deserved on the basis of their country's more recent performance. In July 1968 the Central Banks who agreed at Basle on the principle of a $2,000 million loan did not even insist on a 'letter of intent' declaring the Government's intention of good behaviour. If only they had insisted on strict financial control as the price of their assistance, it might have made the British public realise how far their country has declined. This realisation and the effects of such control might have saved Britain from her worst enemy — the selfishness and greed of her people.

In the complete absence of public pressure in favour of checking the spending spree, the Government's occasional gestures to indicate its desire to reduce the Budgetary deficit were confined overwhelmingly to the revenue side of the Budget. Following on the devaluation of 1967, a planned increase in expenditure was cut only by 30 per cent and the remaining 70 per cent was covered by additional taxation. Expenditure cuts were not as much as mentioned when Mr. Jenkins announced his new batch of measures in November 1968 to avert a second devaluation.

CHAPTER SIX

GUNS OR LUXURIES?

IT was one of Hitler's most familiar pre-war slogans, coined for the sake of justifying the austerity inflicted on the German people in order to be able to rearm, that Germany must have to choose between guns and butter. He had evidently hoped to acquire for Germany, with the aid of her guns, the butter produced by other nations. The unspoken slogan of present-day Left-wing Socialists who are in favour of total disarmament is that Britain must have to choose between guns and more luxuries.

It is not as if they had any reason to suspect that present-day Britain, under a Labour Government, or indeed under any conceivable Government, might use her guns for 'Imperialist-Colonialist' conquests at a time when she is about to give up her last few remaining colonial possessions one after another. But military weakness is one of the basic aims of British Left-wing Socialists. Moreover, any further reduction of expenditure on defence provides additional scope for overspending by the Civil Departments. Above all, the effect of such cuts on the balance of payments is hoped to enable the Government to relax its resistance to unearned wage increases.

Confronted with the necessity of reducing public expenditure, the Labour Government chose to take the line of least resistance. Instead of economising more than the absolute minimum in spheres where economies would encounter resistance, it resorted to drastic cuts in defence costs. At the same time as reducing expenditure, it was able to curry favour with its Left-wing supporters by weakening Britain's defence forces. Of any cuts in spending, cuts in defence expenditure were liable to encounter the least resistance and to earn the highest degree of approval from the Government's supporters.

National defence has always occupied a low place even in the list of priorities of moderate Socialists. Before the War the Labour Party was firmly opposed to conscription right up to the outbreak of the War, even after the occupation of Prague by Hitler made war a virtual certainty. With typical inconsistency, this attitude had not prevented them from agitating in favour of armed intervention to resist aggression against Manchuria, China, Ethiopia, Spain, Czechoslovakia, etc. They expected Britain to play the part of the knight-errant always ready to come to the rescue of any country, the political regime of which they found sympathetic, if attacked by a country whose political regime they disliked. But they firmly refused to provide the knight with the armour and weapons without which he would have stood no chance against aggressors armed to the teeth. This curious lack of logic found full expression in the 'peace ballot', the result of which must have given much comfort and encouragement to potential aggressors and must have been largely responsible for Hitler's decision to risk a World War.

Admittedly, after the War Mr. Attlee, learning a lesson from pre-war mistakes through his first-hand experience in the war-time Coalition Government, maintained a reasonable armed strength. He even went so far as to produce an atom bomb in great secrecy. Knowing that a very substantial section of the Labour Party would oppose it, no provisions were made for its considerable cost in the Estimates, and no Supplementary Estimates were introduced, for fear that the majority of Socialists might vote against it. The atomic piles were financed through the Civil Contingencies Fund under the subhead of 'public buildings in Great Britain'. Nobody outside the Attlee Government has ever been able to discover the way in which the millions required for the rest of the expenditure had been raised.

Lord Attlee has been criticised even by Tories, at any rate for the way in which he had circumvented Parliamentary control, even though they must have been aware that it was the only way in which it was politically possible to produce an atom bomb under a Labour Government. Yet he deserves credit for ensuring that so long as he was Prime Minister Britain retained her power to defend herself and her prestige in world policies. As a result he was able to deal with Washington on an equal footing and thanks to his influence, backed by British armed strength in the Far East, the continued presence of which in Korea was essential to the U.S., he was able to prevent a major war with China which might easily have developed into the third World War.

President Truman would certainly not have listened to Attlee's advice to avoid a full-scale war with China if Britain had not provided a high proportion of the fighting forces engaged in Korea. No doubt Mr. Wilson would have been able to influence President Johnson in respect of Vietnam to the same extent as his Socialist predecessors had been able to influence President Truman in respect of China if Britain's armed strength had been maintained at the level at which it stood at the time of the war in Korea.

But national defence was weakened considerably during the thirteen years of Conservative rule. The Tories must bear the responsibility among other things for the termination of National Service. The cost of defence had to be allowed to increase, largely because of the rising costs of defence equipment, but the fighting strength of the three Services was drastically reduced both in absolute terms and in relation to the military strength of other countries.

Moreover, much of the limited amount allotted for defence was spent wastefully. The Army of the Rhine, for instance, had almost as many civilian employees as soldiers. This was an utterly unrealistic arrangement. Undoubtedly, it was comfortable for officers and men to let various auxiliary functions be performed by German civilians, men and women, but this only meant that, since in a shooting war these tens of thousands of employees could not remain attached to the Army as camp followers, the Army would have to reorganise itself completely at short notice and in difficult circumstances by allocating to Service personnel the tasks formerly performed by civilians. So if real fighting should ever begin, the actual fighting strength of most formations of the British forces would have to be reduced from its unrealistic level maintained for statistical purposes by the employment of civilians to do jobs which would have to be done by soldiers in a shooting war. This make-believe cost the taxpayer and the balance of payments tens of millions of pounds every year.

From the moment the Wilson Government assumed office in 1964 it was subjected to strong and increasing pressure, not only on the part of the Left wing but even from more moderate elements in the Labour Party, to make drastic cuts in defence expenditure in preference to making economies in other spending. Cut after cut was made, and by 1967 a stage was reached when the remaining military strength was no longer sufficient to meet minimum requirements based on existing commitments overseas. It was then decided to relinquish gradually practically all commitments east of Suez and to make further cuts in service expenditure.

Beyond doubt it must be tempting for Governments, whether Conservative or Labour, to economise on national defence so as to achieve popularity by being able with comparative impunity to spend more on other objectives and to pursue expansionary economic policies in general. Cuts in other directions always encounter strong resistance from vested interests and are unpopular, while cuts in defence costs are only resented by the dwindling number of patriots who still give national security and national greatness a high priority in their scheme of things. As their views are out of fashion the Government of the day can afford to ignore them, while cuts in other directions are liable to lose votes for it.

Admittedly, as we pointed out in Chapter 3, it is in accordance with British traditions to disarm extensively between wars. Thanks to Britain's insular position it had not been considered necessary for her to maintain large standing professional armies, or to have conscription in time of peace.

By maintaining her sea power Britain was able to feel that her security against invasion was adequate. When involved in a war overseas that gave her sufficient time for rearming in order to intervene decisively when she was ready. The traditional policy of disarming between wars was based partly on the traditional belief that, even if Britain should suffer reverses during the early phases of the war because of her inadequate initial preparedness for it, she was always bound to win the last battle and would therefore emerge victorious from the war.

This policy, in addition to her immunity from invasion, was largely responsible for Britain's growing prosperity because, while most continental countries had to spend a high proportion of their resources on permanent military preparedness, Britain was able to make productive use of those resources between wars. This was possible until the development of air power came to expose Britain to sudden devastating attacks, the possibility of which came to call for a high degree of permanent preparedness. For this reason alone the traditional policy of disarmament between wars has now become hopelessly out of date.

Britain was able to win the last battle in most major wars of the 18th century, in the Napoleonic Wars and in the first World War, because her insular position, her sea power and her financial resources had given her time to raise, train and equip armies over a period of years, and because in the meantime she could afford, thanks to her financial strength, to subsidise continental allies. Owing to the increased importance of air power, she was only able to escape defeat in the second World War by a very narrow margin in 1940. That experience alone, together with the decline of Britain's financial capacity to subsidise allies, should make the British nation realise that it has not concluded a contract with providence to ensure that on all future occasions it would necessarily win the last battle. It is therefore no longer safe for Britain to relapse into a state of unpreparedness between wars.

Moreover, weapons have become much more complicated and their production now requires much more time than in the old days. In the changed situation anything up to ten years have to pass between the appearance of a new weapon on the drawing board and its readiness for actual operational use. Those in favour of extreme disarmament want to reduce Britain to a state of helplessness by depriving her of deterrents. The countries which have the new weapons ready in large quantities would then be placed in a position to defeat and even annihilate her long before she would have the chance to make good her deficiency in such weapons.

Britain's unpreparedness in 1939, which was largely due to successful Socialist propaganda against rearmament during the 'thirties, must surely have been one of the causes of the second World War. It cost many lost battles during the early years of the War. Had it not been for Hitler's error of judgment in attacking Soviet Russia before invading Britain, and had it not been for Japan's error of judgment in bringing the United States into the War, it might have cost the very existence of Britain as an independent nation.

When Left-wing politicians and writers talk about 'guilty men' they mean the politicians responsible for the Munich surrender. But there would have been no Munich surrender had Socialists not succeeded in influencing British public opinion against rearmament. They are the real 'guilty men', having prevented the National Government by pressure of public opinion from preparing adequately for the showdown with Hitler, even though it was obvious that such a showdown was a mere question of time. Owing to the high level of unemployment in Britain during the 'thirties it would have been easy to rearm sufficiently to deter Hitler from risking a war over Czechoslovakia.

But most of the Bourbons of the Labour Party have learnt nothing and have forgotten nothing from their pre-war experience in misguided pacifism. They are quite prepared and even eager to make the same mistake all over again. They have reverted to their pre-war policy aiming at extreme disarmament which, as already pointed out, does not prevent them from pressing the Government to make Socialist policies

C 2

and principles prevail in British foreign policy. They never cease urging Mr. Wilson to influence the United States in foreign policy and military policy in that direction. Being utterly devoid of elementary common sense, they are unaware of the glaringly obvious fact that a nation has to be strong in order to make its voice heard in the council of nations. It would be quite useless for a British Labour Government to try to influence the foreign policies and military policies of other countries in the interest of peace so long as she is not strong either in a military sense or in a financial sense to ensure that her views command respect. It is utterly perplexing how our Socialists can imagine that the Labour Government could dictate American policy in Vietnam and elsewhere so long as Britain, so far from being able to help the United States in a military or financial sense, depends on her for her national security and for her financial stability.

This brings us to the impact of our declining financial strength on national defence. We saw above that in past wars Britain was able to gain time for making good her initial unpreparedness largely because from the very outset she was in a position to assist her allies with loans and subsidies. But during the 'sixties there has been, simultaneously with the decline of Britain's military strength, also a sharp decline in her financial strength. Nor has this been altogether sheer coincidence. It was Britain's weakening in the international financial sphere that impelled her Government to cut military expenditure in general and military expenditure abroad in particular beyond the limit to which disarmament was compatible with freedom from fear. And conversely, her weakening in the international financial sphere was due to some degree to the decline of Britain's striking power and of her power to stand up for her rights.

Financial weakness jeopardises the country's national security in the following ways:

(1) The Government is reluctant to aggravate pressure on sterling by increasing defence costs and is strongly tempted to reduce them below danger level.

(2) Britain's potential enemies, being well aware of this, pursue their policies on the assumption that Britain would give way every time rather than cause a further weakening of sterling by holding on to the territories threatened by them. Even formerly friendly countries, such as Spain and the Argentine, feel they can now afford to press their claims for slices out of the disintegrating Empire.

(3) At home the United Kingdom itself is seriously threatened with becoming a disunited kingdom as a result of separatist movements in Scotland and in Wales, and even in the Isle of Man. There are also other causes, and possibly Britain's financial weakness and the resulting military weakness may only play a marginal role in encouraging the separatist movements. But it should not be disregarded.

(4) Deflationary measures adopted in order to defend monetary stability tend to reduce Britain's industrial strength or at any rate handicap its increase, thereby reducing or keeping down her industrial war potential.

(5) Cuts in defence spending reduce the capacity of the British arms industry both directly and indirectly through discouraging arms exports. This latter effect is produced through an increase in the cost per unit in the absence of large and steady orders by the British Government. Moreover, many foreign Governments, no longer content with buying shop-soiled Spitfires, refuse to place orders for new models of British arms unless they have been tested through their current operational use by the British Forces.

(6) Financial weakness reduces Britain's prestige, so that even the same amount of military strength would carry less political power and influence.

(7) Reduction of gold and foreign exchange resources and increase of external short-term liabilities are detrimental to Britain's capacity to subsidise allies or to keep essential military bases in friendly countries.

(8) For the same reason, Britain will not be able to afford to assist uncommitted nations financially and will be unable to save them from Imperialist-Colonialist-Communist invasion or subversion.

(9) Britain's dependence on foreign assistance makes her national security and even her national survival dependent on the willingness of foreign Governments, Parliaments and public opinions to continue to assist her at critical moments.

This latter point emerges forcefully from Britain's experience in 1939–41 when the time-lag between the 'cash-and-carry' system and the 'lend-lease' system — a time-lag which was prolonged by the 'scraping the barrel' rule under which Britain was not to benefit by 'lend-lease' until her last dollar resources were expended — greatly reduced Britain's capacity to finance her war requirements in face of the danger of invasion. An even more prolonged time-lag might have played a decisive part in determining the outcome of the War if Hitler had decided to change his time-table and invade Britain before invading Soviet Russia. The gross inadequacy of Britain's own financial resources might have prevented her from importing at the most critical moment the arms and other goods that had been vital for her defence.

The reduction of Britain's naval and air strength has now proceeded well beyond danger point. It is no longer sufficient to deter the Soviet Union from attacking her on the assumption that she would receive no immediate assistance or no timely assistance from the United States — for instance, in an election year when involvement in another European war might be deemed unpopular. What makes matters even worse is that, as we observed in Chapter 3, this time Britain could not even depend on the military support of those members of the Commonwealth which had supported her enthusiastically in two World Wars. Although, owing to General de Gaulle's veto of her admission into the Common Market, her Government has not been able as yet to jettison Australia, New Zealand and other loyal Commonwealth countries, the declared intention of doing so as soon as possible has materially weakened Britain's potential strength in a war.

Even if General de Gaulle's veto should be removed, military assistance from Western Europe would depend on assistance from the United States. Should America choose, for the reason mentioned above, to keep aloof, Britain's assistance would of course be welcomed by her European NATO allies if they themselves were attacked, but it is doubtful whether we could depend on reciprocity. If Soviet Russia should single out Britain for attack without invading Germany, the Low Countries, the Scandinavian countries, France or Italy, these countries might not be prepared to risk exposing themselves to Soviet invasion by coming to Britain's aid without being certain of full-scale American support.

Britain's decision to abandon such military bases as Aden and Singapore, mainly for financial reasons, has made our friends east of Suez realise that it would be difficult, if not impossible, for her to come to their rescue in good time and to a sufficient extent. According to expert opinion, a refusal by Arab States to allow our military transport planes to cross their air space would greatly handicap such an operation. Moreover, even if the development of air transport on a large scale were to make it possible to transfer entire divisions to the invaded countries in a matter of days or weeks — we are of course very far from that, and the required divisions might not be available immediately after the disbanding of military units decided upon in 1968 — the withdrawal of British garrisons might prove to be of decisive importance.

Imperialist-Colonialist-Communist Russia and China believe in the rule that 'nature abhors a vacuum' and to their minds any country in which there is no American or British garrison could be regarded as a vacuum to be filled by them as a matter of course. To replace the potential military value of friends to be jettisoned by our Common Market and East of Suez policies by an increase in our own armed strength would impose a heavy burden on Britain which she could not afford.

Rearmament would take even longer to get into its stride

on the next occasion than it did in the two World Wars when
the delay cost many a lost battle. The increased delay must be
expected not only because modern weapons take longer to
produce but also because Britain has reduced her industrial
capacity for arms production to a higher degree than ever
before. Between the Wars that capacity was well maintained
thanks to Britain's flourishing export trade in arms. But for
this, our aircraft production would have been much slower in
getting into its stride during the late 'thirties and early 'forties.
As the Battle of Britain was won only by a very narrow
margin it seems reasonable to assume that, had the military
aircraft industry been dismantled to a high degree between the
Wars, the Battle of Britain would have been lost and Hitler
would have conquered Britain. The small number of R.A.F.
fighters that remained airworthy when the losses of the Luft-
waffe reached the limit beyond which Hitler was not prepared
to allow it to be weakened further saved Britain and the world
from Nazi domination. And the reason why the British aircraft industry was able to produce those fighters was that its
capacity was kept reasonably high in spite of inter-war disarmament, thanks to the freedom to export warplanes.

Under Left-wing pressure the Labour Government has prevented the aircraft industry from accepting orders from South
Africa and from other countries whose political regimes or
policies Left-wing Socialists disapprove of or whose Governments have incurred the disapproval of the United Nations.
At the same time its exporting capacity has been fatally reduced
by the discontinuation of important Government projects
which would have produced planes eminently suitable for
export. So on the occasion of the next major war British
rearmament will be much slower in getting into its stride than
it did after 1914 and 1939, because this time it will be necessary
first to re-expand the arms industry.

It is argued, of course, that anyhow there would be no time
for rearmament in the next war, because the use of nuclear
weapons would decide its outcome in a matter of weeks, if not
days. But we are by no means certain whether the next war

would be fought with conventional weapons or with nuclear weapons and we cannot afford to base our policies entirely on the assumption that nuclear weapons would necessarily be used. In a prolonged war fought with conventional weapons — a possibility which we could only ignore at our peril — Britain would be placed at a considerable disadvantage because of the reduction of her arms industries as a result of Socialist dogmatism.

Socialists like to present the arguments around disarmament as a conflict between 'freedom from want' and 'freedom from fear'. But this argument constitutes yet another out-of-date picture. Since the War freedom from want has been achieved in Britain to a very large extent, thanks to the Welfare State and full employment. The choice is no longer between guns and butter as it was to a large degree before the War, but between guns and luxuries. Today cuts in national defence expenditure are demanded not in order to raise above subsistence level the standard of living of half-starved millions, but largely in order to be able to avoid pursuing a deflationary policy which would tend to prevent luxury-spending. Freedom from fear is jeopardised not for the sake of achieving freedom from want but for the sake of being able to concede more to the trade unions without having to insist on *quid pro quo*.

The defence cuts have already greatly weakened Britain's influence which she would and could have used in the interests of peace. We said earlier that had she been armed properly in the late 'thirties there might have been no second World War. By disarming excessively Britain is now increasing the likelihood of a third World War which she might be able to prevent if only she retained adequate military and financial power and the prestige that goes with it.

All this of course is in the realm of conjecture. Nearer to concrete realities are the economic consequences of disarmament in the form of relinquishing Britain's East-of-Suez military commitments. This helps the Government to abstain from more unpopular cuts in expenditure and at the same time to appease its Left-wing supporters. Economic arguments in favour of the policy are entirely untenable. The proposed withdrawals will expose British capital and enterprise in the Persian Gulf and further east to nationalisation on more or less confiscatory terms. This would mean a capital loss of the order of £1,000 million, while the loss of current foreign exchange earnings from these investments would much more than wipe out the savings of foreign exchange that are hoped to be achieved through the closing down of military bases. Loss of British control over Middle East oil means that instead of importing oil payable in sterling Britain would have to import oil payable in dollars.

Britain is certain to lose a great many friends and staunch supporters in the East as a result of the mere announcement of her intention to withdraw from East of Suez by 1971. Her show of strength on the occasion of the 'confrontation' with Soekarno's Indonesia must have greatly encouraged anti-Communist elements in that country. In all probability it saved Indonesia from coming under Communist domination, which would have produced disastrous effects on the whole of South-East Asia. Scuttling of Britain's East-of-Suez interests by the Labour Government is liable to lead pro-British elements throughout non-Communist Asia to the conclusion that they have been backing the losing side. Many of them will be strongly tempted to change sides while the going is good. This is liable to tip the balance in favour of Left-wing Governments. In any case, as the adoption of Communist regimes would yield high immediate benefits to the countries concerned in the form of seizing British property, there would be strong temptations to drift Leftward. In the Persian Gulf the withdrawal of British garrisons is certain to be followed by the overthrow of pro-British regimes and they will be replaced by pro-Soviet regimes. This would weaken the chances of the survival of the existing regime in Iran, too, and the substantial British capital invested in that country would also be thrown in jeopardy.

Offers made by some Persian Gulf Protectorates to cover the full costs of the British forces maintained on their territories were contemptuously rejected by the Government, even though their acceptance would have removed the ostensible financial reason for the withdrawal of British bases. No doubt the Government wished to curry favour with the Left wing of the Party by making this gesture to show that it could not be induced by mere financial considerations to maintain garrisons east of Suez for the sake of safeguarding the financial interests of Big Business and of rich investors in oil companies at the cost of bolstering up 'reactionary' regimes.

Many Left-wing Socialists seem to be so utterly ignorant of elementary economics as to be genuinely unaware of the fact — with which every undergraduate may reasonably be expected to be familiar — that the earnings on British investments abroad benefit not only the companies directly concerned who earn them and their shareholders who receive them in the form of dividends, but every man, woman and child in Britain. Earnings on foreign investments constitute a most important invisible export item without which the Government would have to resort to infinitely more drastic squeezes and freezes in order to ensure that reduced imports are covered by increased visible exports. I suspect many of those in the Government who rejected the offer of the Arabian oil Protectorates are fully familiar with this, but they pretend to be obtuse because to them propaganda appears to be more important than prosperity. They would gladly jettison invisible exports of £100 million or more for the sake of impressing their Left-wing supporters with their gesture of hostility to 'big business'.

Some Ministers at any rate must surely remember that in 1939–41 it was the dollar credits raised on the security of privately held dollar investments that paid for our essential imports. They must surely realise — unless they are utterly devoid of any vestige of statesmanship — that in future wars foreign investments would become once more an indispensable reserve on which Britain's survival might well depend. But British Socialism is the religion of envy and spite. Socialist hatred of investing classes and of business is apt to darken their vision.

This attitude was illustrated by Lord Dalton's refusal in

1945–46 to support British holders of Japanese pre-war bonds
in their endeavours to enlist official support in their negotiations
for an acceptable settlement of their unpaid claims. 'Serves
them right for investing in Japan' was the answer of a Chancellor of the Exchequer who, as a former lecturer in finance at
the London School of Economics, had no excuse for ignoring
elementary economics. Yet he did not appear to mind if the
country as a whole lost the millions lent to Japan before the war
so long as he and his fellow-Socialists had the satisfaction of
inflicting losses on the hated investors by deliberately abstaining
from safeguarding their legitimate interests. Needless to say,
a settlement was reached eventually, but through no thanks
to Lord Dalton.

In many instances the underlying motives of the pressure to
reduce defence spending cannot even be explained on the
ground of Socialist illiteracy in economics or of Socialist envy
and spite. Such pressure is liable to have much more sinister
motives. Fellow-travellers and crypto-Communists are naturally anxious that Britain should depend for her vital military
and civilian oil requirements on imports from outside the
sterling area, so that, owing to her reduced foreign exchange
reserves, her fighting services and industries should be exposed
to the risk of being paralysed in case of a war. They are also
anxious that Britain should relinquish her nuclear striking
power and reduce to a minimum her conventional weapons,
and even her civil defences, in order that she should be at the
mercy of Communist blackmail.

The same people who would like to see Britain completely
disarmed are of course equally anxious that we should terminate our special relationship with the United States. One
of their objects in trying to induce the Government to dis-
sociate itself openly from the United States over the Vietnam
War is to antagonise American opinion. Britain would then
cease to be in a position to assume that the United States
would come to her rescue in the case of Communist aggression.
Should these fellow-travellers and crypto-Communists attain
their end, circumstances would be liable to arise in which

Britain would come to be faced with the choice between destruction and unconditional surrender. They hope that in such a situation her choice would be determined by the popular decadent slogan: 'Better red than dead'.

On the basis of the above argument, the inescapable conclusion is that those in favour of extreme disarmament are either knaves or fools. They are knaves if their object is to place this country in a position where it has no choice but unconditional surrender to Communist domination to avoid total destruction. They are fools if they are not aware that such a result would follow logically, naturally and inevitably from the adoption of the policy they advocate in good faith.

Drastic cuts in the cost of national defence would not even buy Britain economic stability. The resources saved in the Estimates for 1968–69 through defence cuts are certain to be spent on something else — judging by the increase of our total Estimate — instead of being used for strengthening our financial stability. In order to ensure that defence cuts — or for that matter any cuts of public or private spending — should strengthen Britain's finances it would be necessary for British official opinion, political opinion and public opinion to undergo a far-reaching change. We should discard the belief, inherited from the stable days of the 19th century, that we are able to maintain the stability of sterling on a very small reserve. In changed conditions much stronger reserves are required. Unless we realise this, and unless we are prepared to aim at reinforcing our reserves even at the cost of hard work and sacrifices, cuts in defence spending would simply mean that any resulting improvement in the balance of payments would induce the Government to yield to pressure in favour of policies leading to a further increase in public or private spending in other directions. Guns would be discarded, not for the sake of solving the crisis, but solely for the sake of providing Labour supporters with more luxuries without requiring them to work for them and earn them.

CHAPTER SEVEN

THE 'ENGLISH DISEASE'

THE term 'English disease' was coined in West Germany during the early 'sixties when the cessation of the heavy influx of refugees from East Germany was beginning to cause acute scarcities of labour. This was beginning to affect the hitherto exemplary behaviour of German workers in a sense similar to the way in which British workers had been affected by overfull employment, even though not nearly to the same extent. It was then stated on frequent occasions in the West German Press that the West German workers had caught the 'English disease'.

The real medical meaning of the term *Englische Krankheit* is of course rickets, though why rickets is regarded in Germany, and in other countries where the medical term is used in the same sense, as a specifically English sickness is rather obscure. But it is easily understandable why the unhelpful labour attitudes arising from shortages of manpower have come to be regarded everywhere as a characteristically English pheno-menon. Wherever on the Continent workers are criticised for unwillingness to give an honest day's work for their pay, for restrictive practices, for absenteeism, for wildcat strikes, or for bloody-mindedness in general, the term 'English disease' is meant to imply that they have come to follow the bad example of their British fellow-workers. (On the Continent reference to 'English' usually means 'British', but on the present occasion at any rate Irish, Scottish and Welsh workers in the U.K. have no cause to be offended because of the omission to include them specifically under the collective term 'British'.)

It is difficult to imagine any more damning indictment of

the behaviour of British workers than the fact that it has become a byword for indolence, insolence and inefficiency on the Continent. Moreover, the suggestion that continental workers who behave without due regard for the public interest have 'caught' the 'English disease' is clearly meant to imply that the British example is infectious and that, had it not been for the demoralising effect of that example, continental workers would not have adopted their objectionable attitude.

Were Pitt alive today, he might be inclined to adapt his historical Guildhall pronouncement of 1805 to present-day conditions by declaring that 'England has ruined herself by her lack of exertions and will ruin Europe by her example'. It seems highly probable that the disastrous behaviour of French workers in May 1968 was to some extent at any rate the result of their realisation of the extent to which their British opposite numbers had been able to get away with things during the past ten years. Owing to the difference between the Anglo-Saxon and Gallic temperament, their brief but violent outburst greatly surpassed any manifestation of the 'English disease', so much so that some concern was beginning to be felt in Britain about the possibility of British workers catching the 'French disease'.

Frequency of references abroad to the 'English disease' shows that condemnation of the British trade unionist workers' behaviour is not confined to British quarters which might be suspected of being prejudiced against them. Foreign commentators on their behaviour cannot be suspected of similar bias. After all, foreign industrial countries owe their prosperity largely to the decline in Britain's competitive capacity as a result of the behaviour of British workers.

Every man, woman and child in industrial countries stands to benefit directly or indirectly by the inadequacy of British exports caused by high British costs and by long and uncertain delivery dates. Germans and other continentals who have got into the habit of talking about the 'English disease' have indeed no cause to condemn the behaviour of the British worker, so that their condemnation implied in the use of the term is quite impartial. Their only grievance against the British worker is that workers in their own country have now come to follow his example to some slight degree.

Continental newspapers frequently publish stories on the behaviour of British workers, providing their readers with fictitious exaggerations, some of them based on instances that had actually occurred. Such stories may sound incredible to continental readers unaccustomed to the standards of behaviour of British workers. To us they sound too near the truth to be really funny. It is a case of *se non è vero è ben trovato*. For instance the story was going round on the continent some years ago that most of the hundreds of redundant aircraft workers who left Britain in the early 'sixties to find jobs in Holland, Germany and Switzerland gradually drifted back to Britain because, to their astonishment and dismay, they found that on the continent they were expected to work for their pay and they did not care for that unusual experience.

It is, of course, sheer coincidence that one of the symptoms of rickets, as of the 'English disease' in the non-medical sense of the term, is a swollen head, and that its main remedy is large doses of vitamins. What is unfortunate from a British point of view is that, while foreign observers of Britain readily diagnose and condemn the 'English disease', in Britain itself nine people out of ten are unaware that anything is fundamentally wrong. Although the British Press frequently quotes continental references to the 'English disease', this does not seem to bring home to British workers the full extent to which the inadequacy of their negative contribution to the nation's economic effort is condemned or ridiculed by impartial observers abroad. It does not seem to occur to them that the frequent disparaging references abroad to their behaviour are nothing short of a national disgrace for which the British working classes, and even the British nation itself, have every reason to be thoroughly ashamed. No amount of effort by the Donovan Report to find other scapegoats can cancel out the unanimous verdict of disinterested world opinions.

England's defeat at a test match or some other international sports event, or the inadequate number of prizes won by British athletes at Olympic Games, worries people in this country incomparably more than the unenviable notoriety gained by the British working man abroad. Indeed some British writers go out of their way to try to explain away the 'English disease' by suggesting that the term simply means the chronic balance of payments deficit and the frequently recurrent sterling crises! The fact that German workers were often accused of having caught the 'English disease' even at times when the German balance of payments had a large surplus and the German Mark was at a premium effectively disposes of that tendentious mis-interpretation of the meaning of the term. The distortion of the meaning of 'English disease' cannot get round the fact that in West Germany — to quote only one example — the 'English disease' has not been sufficiently severe most of the time to affect the balance of payments or the exchange, even though it did cause from time to time a certain amount of inconvenience to employers and to the community in general.

The main cause of the 'English disease' is that far too many British workers don't feel they owe it to their self-respect to give full value for their pay. While in Germany work is a quasi-religious cult, in Britain today idleness is a quasi-religious cult. Is it a wonder that Germany is progressing from strength to strength while Britain is stagnating and declining?

The above generalisation, as indeed other generalisations throughout this book, is admittedly less than fair to millions of British workers who do realise that they have duties as well as rights and who act accordingly. It is hard on them that they should be bracketed with those workers who fully deserve to be indicted at home and abroad for their anti-social behaviour. It is not the fault of the conscientious workers that they are unable to swim against the tide without incurring the active hostility of their fellow-workers. The least that is liable to happen if they should try to work harder than others is that, after due warning to emulate the slow pace of their fellow-workers, they are 'sent to Coventry'. But they might in given circumstances be expelled from their unions and might even meet with accidents. I have failed to discover in the Donovan

Report any condemnation of this aspect of the workers' behaviour and any adequate appreciation of its effect on output, even though it is liable to be of the utmost importance.

Are British workers really unaware of what their fellow-workers and others in countries all over the five continents think of them? Perhaps they just could not care less, or are so full of self-admiration — expressed at times in correspondence columns of newspapers — that they simply refuse to believe that others do not share the high opinion they have formed of themselves. Unless they come to realise that the 'English disease' has made them the objects of contempt and ridicule abroad, and that it has doomed their country to non-stop decline, there can be no hope for a national regeneration which alone could cure Britain of the 'English disease'.

The reason why most people in Britain are unaware of the 'English disease' is that they themselves are doing reasonably well. Indeed it is true to say that most of them have never felt so prosperous. The impression of well-being is of course a phenomenon that always accompanies the early phases of inflation. Most people have now more money to spend than ever before, even allowing for the higher prices they have to pay for everything. Their money incomes and, in a great many instances, also their real incomes increase year after year. The Government and the local authorities are overspending to improve their housing, education, health services, etc. Although from time to time the authorities admit the need for economies and occasionally they actually make some token reductions, they continue to spend recklessly large and increasing amounts of money which they do not possess and are unable or unwilling to collect in the form of additional taxation or rates. They prefer to take the line of least resistance by resorting to borrowing to cover their deficits, paying usurious interest rates at the ratepayer's expense. They seem to be no more ashamed of the disreputable practice of perennial borrowing than workers are of the 'English disease'.

It is often argued that surely the 'English disease' cannot be as bad as all that. After all, Britain's production is undoubtedly increasing, even if its increase compares unfavourably with that of most other industrial countries. A source from which comfort is derived is that satisfactory British successes are recorded from time to time in a number of spheres. British inventive genius is still second to none, in spite of all the disincentive effect produced by egalitarian trends affecting earnings and taxation penalising success, that is the main cause of the brain drain. But it is precisely because British inventive genius is so outstanding that Britain's actual industrial achievements in the form of higher output must be regarded as so utterly unsatisfactory. If only the British workers worked as hard as their foreign opposite numbers Britain would undoubtedly hold the lead in increased productivity and in industrial expansion, at any rate in Europe. Were it not for the multitude of British inventions since the war the 'English disease' might have reduced the standard of living in Britain to well below pre-war level.

In many other spheres where British achievements don't depend on the attitude of the British workers, Britain is second to none among nations. For instance, every now and again a Briton wins a Nobel Prize or some other international award. Thank goodness Britain is holding her own in various cultural spheres even if she has lost her lead in the spheres of sport and athletics.

In the sphere of industry and trade, too, British firms very often score over their foreign rivals by securing some important contract for capital goods in face of fierce foreign competition. But the fact that such successes always make front page headlines nowadays instead of being taken for granted as in the old days shows the extent to which the British public is starved of success stories in the sphere of industry and trade and to which it is in need of reassuring itself on every possible occasion that in that vital sphere Britain still holds her own.

So long as most people in this country feel complacent about their conditions it is a hopeless task to try to convince them that the reason for Britain's decline is precisely because they are better off than they deserve to be on the strength of their own productive efforts. If only they were content with a slower pace of progress towards a higher standard of living, or alternatively if only they were prepared to work harder in order to earn and deserve the accelerated improvement instead of expecting to obtain it as a free gift, the 'English disease' would soon become an evil memory.

The most obvious outward manifestation of the 'English disease' has been the chronic weakness of sterling, that thermometer indicating the ups and downs of the nation's economic health. The man in the street need not be a specialist in foreign exchange, or even familiar with economics in general, to realise that something must be fundamentally wrong with our economy when sterling drifts from one crisis into another. What proportion of the public realises the close connection between these crises and the workers' behaviour? It is of course a much more rewarding line to blame the 'gnomes' of Zürich or the wicked foreigners in general who withdraw their sterling deposits when our behaviour makes them lose confidence in sterling, or merchants who want to safeguard themselves against being bankrupted through losses caused by a devaluation, by covering their exchange risks. But the chronic balance of payments deficit speaks for itself, and the persistent increase of Britain's external short-term liabilities since 1964 cannot be argued out of existence.

To what extent are British industrial workers themselves to blame for the 'English disease'? The change in their attitude since the War is attributable in part at least to the change in the balance of power in their favour. Unfortunately, it is only too tempting to take full advantage of such a change. But full employment is not confined to Britain, nor is the Welfare State, the existence of which has further strengthened the workers' bargaining position, an exclusively British institution. It is noteworthy that, even though industrial workers in other countries with full employment and a Welfare State did catch the 'English disease' from time to time, they never caught it to anything like the extent to which it prevails in its country of origin. Is it because British workers are basically work-shy?

Whatever unfavourable qualities may be inherent in them, they must surely have some very basic good qualities to account for the fact that in the past, until comparatively recently, Britain was at the spearhead of industrial progress and of human progress in many other spheres. It is arguable that Britain's industrial superiority in the past was due to the fact that she had been first in the field of modern industrialisation. Now that this advantage has ceased, any unfavourable basic qualities the British industrial worker may possess have come to the fore and have produced their full effect.

One cannot believe that this is anything like the full explanation. Even if the British worker, unlike the German worker, does not like work for its own sake, normally he used to give a very good account of himself in former times. His attitude has deteriorated because he has been pampered and spoilt by Governments, politicians, trade unions and employers since the War. He would have had to possess a particularly strong character to survive such an overdose of pampering without being spoilt. We shall see in Chapters 9 and 10 how his belief that full employment and the Welfare State are his birthright for which he owes absolutely nothing to the community has deprived him of the full benefit which these two institutions are potentially capable of conferring on him. It has also effectively deprived his country of the full benefits of technological progress.

Unfortunately British workers behave either as if they did not know that, as a result of the 'English disease', Britain is well on the road to ruin or as if they did not care what would happen to Britain so long as they themselves can continue to get more and more pay for less and less work. They really seem to believe that they can contract out of the fate of their country, and that their country may decline and fall without dragging them down with it. Even the Donovan Report admits that there have been occasions on which trade unions 'see little connection between the efficiency of industry and the living standard of their members'. This reluctant admission was the understatement of the year.

Shipbuilding workers, whose bargaining power had greatly increased through their association with engineering workers in the same federation, were getting increase after increase during recessions in spite of the decline of their industry, due largely to their restrictive practices. An executive of one of the shipyards remarked that his workers would expect to get a substantial rise the day before the last of the British shipyards would close for lack of orders.

If the workers fail to realise the identity of their interests with those of their firms and with those of their industries, there seems to be little hope for making them realise the identity of their interests with those of their country. Nor has the Donovan Report, with its effort to put the main blame on managements, made the task of bringing them to a realisation of their true interests any easier. It has reinforced the workers' hope that all they have to do is to wait for an increase in the efficiency of managements to raise their standard of living, and that they themselves need not exert themselves to assist towards the achievement of that end. Yet surely it is a matter of elementary common sense that the standard of living of the working classes cannot be increased or even maintained in the long run if, owing to the inadequacy of the workers' exertions, their country is doomed to decline. It is Britain's tragedy that her workers refuse to see this basic truth.

How long will British workers be able to continue to live in a fool's paradise? They shrugged off the devaluation as something that did not concern them, and they continued to behave in such a way as to make the defence of sterling even at its lower level difficult if not impossible. The 'English disease' continued as before. Evidently devaluation was no cure for it, as indeed it could not be. It is not patent medicines that the patient requires, but a resurgence of his vitality and of his will to cure himself — that is, the same cure as for rickets, a good dose of vitamins and a deflation of his swollen head. Popular use of the term 'English disease' abroad should make him realise that, even though he may consider himself the salt of the earth, that view is not shared by anyone else.

CHAPTER EIGHT

THE 'SICK MAN OF EUROPE'

ONE of the results of the 'English disease' is that Britain has
come to be looked upon as 'the sick man of Europe'. Of
course, just as there is always bound to be an 'oldest man' in
every village, there has always been a 'sick man of Europe' —
whichever country happens to be the most obviously on the
decline. But this is the first time that Britain has come to
inherit that undignified title which had in the past usually
indicated contempt rather than compassion.

The role of 'the sick man of Europe' was played by the
Roman Empire during its period of decline, between the third
and fifth centuries A.D. Its decline was largely due to large-
scale parasitism under the Welfare State, expressed by the
popular slogan of *panem et circenses*. Thereafter its successor,
the Byzantine Empire, took over that role, together with the
causes responsible for it. Interruptions apart, it continued to
play that role until the capture of Constantinople by the Turks
in 1453. Spain was the next declining European empire,
gradually losing her role as a world power during the 17th
century and continuing to decline in the following century.
Her decline, let it be noted, is all but generally attributed to
the easy acquisition of wealth by her population, thanks to the
exploitation of the New World, as a result of which Spaniards
had 'never had it so good', and a high proportion of them had
got out of the habit of living on the proceeds of hard and honest
work. On a much smaller scale, Poland assumed the role of
'the sick man of Europe' in the late 18th century until she
disappeared from the map. More will be said about the
circumstances of her decline and fall in Chapter 9.

The term 'the sick man of Europe' was first actually applied to the declining Ottoman Empire during the 19th century, especially after the battle of Navarino. Having reached its zenith towards the end of the 17th century when Turkish guns were battering the walls of Vienna, it underwent an almost uninterrupted decline throughout the 18th and 19th centuries and the early part of our century. Its governments were hopelessly inefficient and mostly corrupt, its administration and legal system were antiquated and rigid, its people utterly demoralised. By the middle of the 19th century its total disintegration came to be looked upon as a mere question of time. The possibility of its collapse was for many decades a source of constant anxiety for Europe, because rival claims on its territories had been the potential cause of war. After a series of military defeats Turkey staged a recovery, however, in the early 'twenties, under Kemal Atatürk, who, having led them to victory against Greece, forced through a programme of drastic reforms. Under his inspiration the Turks recovered their national pride and, within reduced limits, the country has become a reasonably stable if minor member of the community of nations.

It has become fashionable to consider in retrospect the Austro-Hungarian Monarchy as having been another 'sick man of Europe' before 1914. Actually it had been a stable and efficiently run Empire and its problems of national minorities had been much less troublesome than the Irish problem had been to Britain. Had it not been for the outcome of the first World War it might have adapted itself to changed circumstances and might have become a miniature League of Nations.

On the other hand there was much justification for regarding France as 'the sick man of Europe' during the 'twenties and 'thirties, owing to the endless succession of political crises and the decline of political and financial standards of morality. Even the shock caused by the defeat of 1940 and the resulting enemy occupation had not been sufficient to arouse the French people and to bring about a national regeneration. Confused political and financial conditions continued for years after the liberation of France, until in 1958 General de Gaulle, by the force of his character and personality, succeeded in restoring her to her rightful place among the leading European nations and in achieving some years of political and economic stability and a high degree of financial and political power. It is as yet premature to form an opinion whether the relapse experienced in May and June 1968 will produce lasting adverse results and will reduce France to her former role of a 'sick man'. Possibly this would occur anyway after the disappearance of de Gaulle from the Élysée. But her example during her spell of stability gives some indication of what Britain, given right leadership and adequate response to such leadership, might have achieved and might still achieve.

Meanwhile it is Britain that has now come to be generally looked upon as 'the sick man of Europe'. Because of her inability to resist temptation to live beyond her means, and because her ability to intensify her productive efforts seems to have declined, she is unable to keep pace with the progress achieved by other advanced nations which are at a comparable stage of evolution. What is even worse, she has apparently lost her ability and even her will to maintain a well-balanced economy and a stable currency. Her financial instability has become in recent years a source of permanent anxiety for Europe and for the rest of the world, because it is rightly assumed that a collapse of sterling would trigger off a world-wide currency chaos comparable with the one that followed the suspension of the gold standard in 1931.

We saw in Chapter 2 that in the past Britain was looked upon all over the world as the outstanding example of financial strength, stability and integrity. The second World War had left Britain financially exhausted and during the decades that followed no serious attempt was made to restore her financial power. Her successive Governments were all much more interested in the more popular effort of stepping up the process of raising the standard of living of her people than in consolidating her achievements and placing them on sound

foundations by restoring her financial strength, thereby preparing the way for a further spell of progress.

The proceeds of the big American loan of 1946 were dissipated in a matter of weeks as a result of the ill-advised premature restoration of sterling's convertibility. Thereupon the
Attlee Government, instead of making a supreme effort to
ensure that Britain should work out her own salvation and
become self-supporting, adopted the comfortable course of
depending on assistance from the United States by accepting
Marshall Aid. American subsidies shielded Britain from the
worst consequences of her inadequate economic performance —
though not from recurrent sterling crises — while her Government was busily engaged in nationalisations and in the estab-
lishment of the Welfare State on borrowed money. These
preoccupations left little time for concentrating on an effort to
increase productivity. Its policy to place party and class
interests above national interests was bound to inspire distrust
in sterling and in 1949 it had to be devalued.

During the 'fifties and the early 'sixties the British economy
was holding its own precariously. It was largely at the mercy
of even relatively minor adverse trends, having no adequate
technical strength to resist them. From time to time it had to
cope with waves of distrust in sterling in the absence of efforts
to strengthen the basic position, except in times of acute crisis.
But it is to the credit of all Governments prior to 1964 that,
thanks to the systematic application of the much-abused
'stop–go' policy, no runaway inflation was allowed to develop,
and the pre-war cycles of booms and slumps were not allowed
to return. In spite of her huge external short-term liabilities
and her small reserves, under Conservative Governments
Britain was able for a long time to live on her past reputation
for sound finance and foreign holders of sterling gave her most of
the time the benefit of the doubt, in the sense that departures
from sound finance were looked upon as temporary. Confidence
was weakened from time to time, but the large majority of
foreign holders of sterling took it for granted that adequate
measures would be adopted in good time, so that there were no

mass withdrawals of foreign balances. It was easy to restore confidence by gestures conveying the impression that basically Britain was still inspired by sound principles.

The large trade deficit that was allowed to develop during the last year of Tory rule was the first major change which conveyed a vague feeling that Britain might assume the role of the sick man of Europe. Such a feeling was by no means general, however. Indeed the *Neue Zürcher Zeitung* was very optimistic during the spring of 1964 about sterling's prospects in the autumn, in spite of the near-certainty of a Labour victory in the coming general election. Its influence delayed the development of a run on the pound on the eve of the election, and for a short time even after the Socialist victory. For some weeks the foreign exchange market gave the Labour Government the benefit of the doubt. Only when it became evident that under the Labour Government the defence of sterling would not enjoy the same priority as it had under its predecessor did sterling come under a cloud from November 1964. Its frequent acute crises during 1964–68 and the Labour Government's inability or unwillingness to deal with them effectively were responsible for Britain's unmistakable assumption of the role of 'the sick man of Europe'. Her perennial borrowing from the International Monetary Fund and from foreign Central Banks, and the adoption of unsound tactics of supporting sterling by means of gigantic forward selling of dollars which the authorities had not possessed, together with dubious manipulations of the official gold reserve figures and foreign trade figures, lowered Britain's prestige and gave rise to fears of worse crises to come.

Britain's financial prestige suffered a further blow in 1968 when she applied to the I.M.F. and to foreign Central Banks to provide facilities enabling her to guarantee the sterling holdings of Sterling Area countries. In order to realise the full extent of the decline this step implied we have to recall that after the first World War the Versailles Treaty, which provided for reparation payments in terms of 'gold dollars', 'gold francs' and 'gold lire', fixed sterling payments in 'pounds

D

sterling' pure and simple. Such was the prestige of sterling during the 'twenties that, while in the United States innumerable contracts were in terms of 'gold dollars', there were hardly any contracts in Britain in terms of 'gold pounds'. Their number was so small that it was not deemed worth while to legislate about them after the depreciation of sterling following on the suspension of the gold standard in 1931. But in 1968 the British Government deemed it necessary to offer holders of sterling an exchange guarantee.

Hardly anybody in Britain realises the extent to which her new role as a perennial borrower is humiliating and degrading. That is why no sufficiently strong public pressure has developed to force the Government to bring the shameful practice to an end. The fact that the British public is completely oblivious of anything being fundamentally wrong about it is yet another indication of the debasement of the British character. Everybody, or almost everybody, was greatly relieved on each occasion when, instead of tackling the problem in the hard way, the authorities succeeded in obtaining yet another instalment of foreign financial assistance obviating the immediate necessity for tough measures. Thanks to such assistance sterling was 'saved' on some half-dozen occasions after 1964. Each time the last-minute salvage was welcomed as a triumph, and the Government proudly announced its great success in persuading foreign Governments and Central Banks to grant large credit facilities. The fact that such facilities were always granted under the implied threat of a devaluation of sterling was of course the closely guarded secret of the negotiators.

After each successful operation the authorities came to display an unwarranted degree of optimism, with the usual adverse effect on the attitude of the trade unions. The latter could hardly be blamed if, in response to the official optimism, they came to feel justified in resuming their full pressure for excessive wage increases, pressure which they mitigated somewhat for a short time during the acute crisis. All the time the Government carefully concealed the full extent of the country's fundamental difficulties resulting from its extravagant public spending and from the inadequacy of its efforts to check the unwarranted wage increases.   Consequently the wages spree was resumed after each crisis, so that in a matter of months there was another acute crisis.   Again and again British representatives had to approach foreign Governments and Central Bankers for new credits and/or a renewal of previously granted credits.

As a result, since the advent of the Labour Government, Britain has become by far the largest foreign borrower. Borrowing abroad on a large scale is justified if the country is at an early stage of its economic development, or if it had suffered a gigantic degree of physical destruction through war, earthquake or other similar disaster. A country which comes under neither category has no right to mop up the supplies of credit that should be left available for more deserving cases. Yet Britain borrowed and borrowed again, to the full limit of her ability to do so.

What *has* happened to British pride? The younger generation does not of course remember the happy days when Britain was on the giving end. It is therefore understandable if the British post-war generation does not realise the degree of decline indicated by the unpalatable fact that it is now once-proud Britain that is receiving the loans and the accompanying lectures on sound finance by lenders. But even the survivors of the pre-war generation who had known Britain before her decline seem to take it as a matter of course that her representatives should go to Basle again and again to beg for another and yet another extension of the outstanding credits, or if possible for their increase, or for a new credit if the previous one had been repaid. Yet it is mainly because of the frequent applications for financial assistance, and because of Britain's apparent inability to clear herself of her external short-term liabilities, that she is now looked upon as 'the sick man of Europe'. The other symptoms of the 'English disease' can be concealed or they can be argued out of existence. But there is no way of getting round the widely publicised fact that Britain has become a perennial borrower.

Of course the Government did not altogether escape criticism from British side because of its foreign credit operations. It was often criticised by its own supporters — but not for borrowing again and again. That had come to be looked upon as part of the British way of life. It was criticised from time to time for the strings that were believed to have been attached to the loans. The Government was attacked for allowing foreign Governments or bankers to influence its policies in return for financial assistance. Britain could not afford to be too proud to borrow from foreign bankers, but she was expected to be too proud to permit her creditors to attach conditions to their loans, or indeed even to advise her Government how to behave in order to be able to repay her credits.

It seems to have come to be taken for granted by Britain that the world is supposed to owe her a living, and a good living at that. This at any rate is the conclusion emerging from the attitude of Left-wing Socialists towards real or imaginary strings attached to foreign credits. The very idea that the world should expect Britain to pursue policies that would enable her to repay the credits, or at any rate to abstain from asking for more, appeared to be outrageous to the Left-wing critics of the Government. They insist that the Government must obtain loans unconditionally and that it must be allowed to retain its sacred freedom to pursue unsound policies to its heart's desire. These critics would not care if Britain remained permanently indebted as a result of the frequent repetition of these salvage actions. They would like Britain to play the unattractive part of the insolent beggar demanding help but rejecting conditions, or even good advice that would go with the help.

In the domestic sphere the principle of 'no strings attached' means that the beneficiaries of concessions from employers or from the Government must insist on making it clear from the very outset that they feel under no obligation whatever for the concession, either to their employers or to the community. In the international sphere it means that recipients of loans disclaim any obligations towards their creditors or indeed towards the international monetary system the stability of which

depends on the willingness of the borrower to make good use of
the loan granted for that purpose.   Britain is not too proud to
borrow again and again, but she must be too proud to borrow
on terms that would ever enable her to discontinue borrowing.

It is realised abroad to a far greater extent than in Britain
that her change of role from giver to receiver of assistance has
profound implications — that constant borrowing and repeated
renewal of loans is the outward symptom of material and moral
deterioration.   'The sick man of Europe' makes no adequate
effort to cure himself; he expects other nations to keep him in
permanent comfort and luxury during his permanent sickness.
So long as Britain continues to pursue the policies and practices
responsible for her sickness all the remedies she obtains from
abroad are bound to be wasted.   They do her absolutely no
good, but simply encourage her in her attitude of abstaining
from curing herself.

When before 1914 Turkey was 'the sick man of Europe' and
Imperial China was 'the sick man of Asia', financial assistance
by Britain and by other countries was granted to them on
conditions of imposing strict financial control on them.   When
in the 'twenties countries of central and south-eastern Europe
received financial aid from the League of Nations a Commissioner General was put in charge of their finances.   His powers
to veto unsound policies had helped the countries concerned
much more effectively than the international loans, the proceeds of which they would have wasted if it had not been for
the controlling hand of the Commissioner General.   It is a
thousand pities that the I.M.F. and foreign Central Banks that
have assisted Britain did not insist on imposing on her similar
controls as the price of assistance.   They would have been able
to save the British Government and the British people from
the consequences of their own irresponsible and reckless folly.
The imposition of such control would have been admittedly
extremely humiliating.   But the shock of having to submit to
such obvious humiliation might have produced a salutary effect,
while the much less obvious humiliation of having to beg for
assistance has been ignored.

Admittedly, each time the I.M.F. and the Central Banks grant or renew their credits, the Government lets them have a 'letter of intent' setting out the measures it means to adopt of its own free will, without being compelled to adopt them by any binding undertaking given as a condition of the loan. From time to time the I.M.F. send a committee to London to ascertain the extent to which the terms of the letter of intent are carried out. On the face of it this may appear to provide some safeguards to the creditors. In practice it is virtually meaningless. So long as the Government owes the I.M.F. and the Central Banks a substantial amount it holds all the trumps — because of the threat, expressed or implied, that unless the credits are renewed, or even unless more assistance is forthcoming, sterling would be devalued — for they would not be in a position to ensure repayment on maturity by refusing to renew the credits without risking a first-rate international crisis. Any such refusal would have a disastrous effect on sterling, and the creditors are just as anxious as the debtor that this should be avoided.

The Government must have felt safe in disregarding again and again the spirit, and occasionally even the letter, of its various undertakings, in the reasonably certain knowledge that the foreign creditors would continue to bolster up the pound in any case. Yet the possibility that a stage might be reached at which the creditors might risk a showdown has always been present. It would not be a hundred per cent safe for the Labour Government to assume that the risk does not exist. Until November 1967 it might have appeared reasonable for foreign Governments to assume that Mr. Wilson and Mr. Callaghan, having committed themselves to the defence of sterling in no uncertain terms, would resort to really tough measures in the absence of foreign assistance, rather than dishonour their pledge. It is possible that had help not been forthcoming in such generous doses during 1964–67 the Government would have reinforced sterling willy-nilly with the aid of more adequate domestic measures.

It might have been at any rate worth while for Mr. Henry Fowler, Secretary of the United States Treasury, on whose decision the extent of American aid to Britain mainly depended, to call Mr. Wilson's bluff during the years while the latter was still keen on defending sterling, by refusing assistance unless really effective steps were taken to restore the balance of the British economy. Instead of virtually underwriting sterling in the form of support which the United States could afford less and less amidst her own growing troubles, he ought to have taken a leaf out of the book of his near-namesake of a thousand years ago, Henry the Fowler, King of Germany, who, having paid tribute to the Hungarians for twelve years in order that they should abstain from raiding German territories, decided eventually to have a showdown and defeated them.

It would of course be futile to try to cure 'the sick man of Europe' by granting additional doses of financial aid. While such aid may be effective for resisting an acute speculative attack, a chronic weakness could not be cured by it. On the contrary, by allaying fears of a recurrence of the much-dreaded acute attacks, the 'sick man' is less inclined to go out of his way to achieve a basic improvement of his condition. The weakness of sterling is merely an outward symptom. Its artificial support merely amounts to bringing down the high temperature of the patient without dealing with its underlying cause. And it obviates the immediate necessity for the 'sick man' to try to heal himself.

Perhaps the worst aspect of Britain's role as 'the sick man of Europe' is that her decline is liable to drag the entire Western world down into the abyss. Another sterling devaluation, or the adoption of a freely fluctuating and depreciating sterling, is likely to lead to general currency chaos, competitive currency depreciation race, shrinkage of foreign trade similar to that experienced during the 'thirties. The ensuing slump in the demand for primary produce and in world commodity prices would give the Communists the chance to exploit the resulting misery of the populations of the primary producing countries. One country after another would become the victim of Communist subversion. 'The sick man of Europe' might easily infect the whole free world with his sickness.

CHAPTER NINE

OVERFULL EMPLOYMENT

During the dark days of depression between the Wars most people regarded the achievement of full employment as a Utopian dream. The horrors of large-scale unemployment came to be accepted as a permanent 'normal' state of affairs. It is true, some bold reformers — foremost amongst them was Keynes — claimed to have discovered the formula under which imaginative official policies could create a high degree of employment, if not full employment. But everybody else had simply assumed that the British working classes were doomed to perpetual large-scale unemployment. In the 'twenties and the 'thirties it would have taken a gross overdose of optimism for any prophet to risk a prediction that during the 'fifties and 'sixties permanent full employment and indeed overfull employment would prevail in Britain.

It had not occurred to those who before the War were agitating for the adoption of policies to create full employment, or to those who merely regarded it as an ideal but unattainable state of affairs, that a high degree of employment, too, was apt to give rise to a set of difficulties. They simply assumed that if only Britain could attain and maintain full employment she could live happily for ever after. Now we know better.

Although our problems arising from full and overfull employment are fundamentally different from the problems of the intolerable state of mass unemployment that kept many of us awake in the inter-war years, they are grave problems nevertheless and are the source of much trouble. The main difference between the two sets of problems is that while the problems of unemployment arise inevitably from unemployment, the problems arising from full employment are man-made and, given a little good sense and goodwill, could and should be avoided.

Scarcity of manpower for industrial requirements ensured full employment during the War. But even after demobilisation full employment was soon restored. What we all considered to be unattainable before the War became reality. During two decades Britain experienced almost uninterrupted full employment that developed into overfull employment from time to time. The younger generation of workers who had had no experience of large-scale unemployment is not in a position to appreciate what an immense blessing it is for them never to have to worry whether next week's pay packet would be forthcoming. There are nowadays almost always vacancies and workers can usually change their jobs whenever they feel like it. They can safely take it for granted that even if for some reason they should lose their jobs they could almost invariably step into some other job, provided that they are willing to change their occupation and/or their residence.

It is true during 1966–68 unemployment tended to increase from time to time, fluctuating round the half-million mark — a high figure for post-war conditions. Its persistence gave rise to arguments that Britain was no longer fully employed. But the fact that one had to wait months for repair work or for the delivery of materials required for such work speaks more convincingly than any figures. It was conclusive evidence that full employment still existed and the economy was overloaded.

There were admittedly spells of redundancies from time to time in certain industries during the 'fifties and 'sixties and there was relatively high unemployment in certain districts. But for anyone willing to move or to take up a new occupation unemployment presented no insurmountable problem. A senior Government official whose job is to deal with problems arising from redundancies told the author that, on each occasion, by the time his Department set out to take steps to find jobs for the victims of progress most of them had already found jobs with the greatest ease on their own initiative.

Which is as it should be. It is a shocking idea to suggest, as

D 2

some economists, bankers and politicians do, that it is necessary to create and maintain deliberately a permanent pool of
unemployed, for the sake of securing the required degree of
flexibility of the labour market in order to ensure the possibility
of redeployment and for the sake of securing a reasonable
balance of power between employers and trade unions. Everybody who can work and wants to work should have a chance
to work, so that the permanently unemployed should be confined to the unemployables.

Like the Welfare State, full employment is a blessing for the
attainment and maintenance of which it is well worth the
community's while to pay a price in the form of the inevitable
economic disadvantages associated with it. But it is utterly
wrong for the workers and their unions deliberately to increase
the price which the community has to pay for the creation and
maintenance of a state of affairs which is wholly to their
advantage. They should not misuse the balance of power
changed in their favour by full employment, on the complacent
assumption that the sky is the limit to the price which the
community is prepared to pay for the maintenance of full
employment.

Unfortunately, it is often inevitable that measures adopted
from time to time in order to relieve the overload on the
economy should give rise to unemployment. Likewise, redundancy is the price which has to be paid for progress, whether
in the form of technological innovation, improved organisation
of work or increase of efficiency through amalgamations of
firms. But to favour progress, even though it has such deplorable side effects, is not the same as setting out to increase unemployment deliberately and to lay down the rule that there
must be a certain minimum percentage of permanent unemployment as a matter of considered policy.

Under the influence of British experience in the misuse of
full employment during recent years, the school of thought
that favours such a cruel policy has been gaining ground. It
is a great pity that trade unions and their members cannot be
made to realise that their attitude of short-sighted greed and

selfishness leads not only to deflationary measures that create unemployment but even to a growing demand for the adoption of the evil policy of maintaining a permanent pool of unemployed so as to obviate the necessity for having to resort to deflation from time to time. Even the Labour Government was flirting with that idea for a while. This fact, if nothing else, should make the trade unions realise that the extent to which full employment can be achieved and maintained in the long run depends very largely on the extent to which it is or is not misused by those who primarily benefit by it.

Britain's decline has been largely due to the fact that politicians of both parties have succeeded in conveying to trade unions and to workers in general the impression that there is absolutely no limit to the extent of economic disadvantages which the community is prepared to accept as the price to pay for the social advantages of full employment. Beyond doubt, to a very large extent the social considerations against unemployment must be allowed to prevail over economic considerations. Even if it were advantageous economically that unemployment should rise above, say, one million, the social disadvantages of such a large-scale unemployment — unless quite temporary — must outweigh the economic advantages of increased productivity derived from the change in the balance of power in favour of employers. But to a very large extent the misuse of the balance of power in favour of workers as a result of full employment carries its own punishment — unemployment is liable to increase not because of any deliberate policy pursued to that end but because of inexorable economic tendencies generated by the misuse of full employment.

We shall see in the next chapter that in Britain the blessings of the Welfare State were kept down, and its disadvantages greatly increased, by the ill-advised way in which the policy was presented to the workers and by the wrong spirit in which the beneficiaries of the Welfare State responded to the benefits conferred on them. The same is unfortunately true also for the way in which the policy of full employment was presented and in which the workers responded to it. Like the Welfare

State, it has produced an unnecessary extent of demoralisation of the working classes, and this has been largely responsible for Britain's decline.

The change in the balance of power between employers and employees resulting from full employment has been grossly misused by organised labour for the purpose of holding the community to ransom. Scarcities of labour have been exploited by enforcing undeserved and unearned wage increases and by failing to give a fair day's work for the increased pay. To some extent, this is, alas, in accordance with the basic character of human nature, with the basic economic principle of supply and demand, and with the principle of 'free for all' on which the Western economic system is based. But owing to the creation of labour monopolies in the form of trade unions, the exploitation of the community was not merely a result of the natural working of *laisser-faire* but was very largely the result of the misuse of monopolistic powers.

Although trade union leaders are open to criticism for misusing their increased power, in fairness it must be admitted that their militant attitude merely represents the view of the large majority of the rank and file in favour of holding out for the maximum of benefits obtainable. There is always pressure, often stimulated by Communists and other troublemakers whose aim is to bring about strikes and to aggravate wage inflation, but more often it is due to the natural desire of all human beings to increase their incomes. Were trade unions to moderate their demands in the national interest beyond a certain point, their executive committees and officials would be voted out of office at the first opportunity. In the meantime there would be even more unofficial strikes which, according to the Donovan Report, already amount to 95 per cent of the total number of strikes. Of course this figure, which was to be quoted in practically every review of the Report, distorts the relative importance of official and unofficial strikes, because it does not allow for the difference in the number of those participating in official and unofficial strikes, nor for the difference in their duration. It forms part of the systematic whitewashing of

trade unions by the Report to play down the relative importance of official strikes.

Even so, the Donovan Report is right in claiming that as a
result of full employment the relative importance of national
bargaining between trade unions and employers' associations
covering entire industries and of bargaining at factory level
and shopfloor level in individual factories has changed considerably in favour of the latter. Whatever terms may be
acceptable to trade unions are very often unacceptable to shop
stewards and other representatives of working groups. Before
the ink is dry on national agreements signed by the workers'
official representatives, their unofficial negotiators set out to
enforce additional concessions.

In doing so, these negotiators may occasionally disregard the
wishes of their unions which are technically their superior
authority. But more often they are probably encouraged in
their unofficial action by their unions whose officials, without
wishing to dishonour agreements concluded for a definite
period, have no objection if the agreements are dishonoured
by the men and their local leaders. The author himself heard
on one occasion a nationally-known trade union leader, who
for some inscrutable reason has acquired a reputation for
statesmanlike moderation, say that if the men try to secure
improvements on the terms of nationally-negotiated agreements, 'more power to their elbow'.

The result of local wage demands — whether officially
encouraged or not — is a wage drift which accounts for a high
percentage of unearned wage increases. The extent of such
local wage increases, according to the Donovan Report, is now
much more substantial than before the War, when it was assumed that industry-wide agreements could cover almost all
requirements, leaving only minor issues to be settled by individual negotiations. Today the wage drift has become a major
and at times decisive factor in determining the extent of wage
inflation.

Shop stewards, who regard themselves not as local representatives of their trade unions but as representatives of the

workers against their trade unions as well as against their employers, are among the main instigators of the frequent troubles and are largely responsible for unofficial strikes and other forms of industrial action, and also for the resulting wage increases. It is characteristic of the heavily biased attitude of the Donovan Report that it goes out of its way to play down the anti-social attitude of shop stewards. 'It is often wide of the mark to describe shop stewards as trouble-makers. . . . For the most part the shop steward is viewed by others and views himself as an accepted, reasonable and even moderating influence, more as a lubricant than an irritant.' This may often be the case if they don't happen to be Communists, crypto-Communists, fellow-travellers, Trotskyites, Anarchists or Syndicalists. Some of them are astute enough to realise that such subversive elements among their fellow shop stewards have one thing in common with hard-faced economists and politicians who advocate the deliberate creation of a permanent pool of unemployed of 1,000,000 or more — their utter and complete indifference to the welfare of the British working classes. They create trouble solely in pursuit of their political ends.

Many people connected with industry in various capacities are satisfied that much more often than not shop stewards are the main cause of local trouble, whatever the Donovan Report may choose to say about it. But the main responsibility for Britain's difficulties caused by unearned wage increases, by the inadequacy of the workers' contribution to the productive effort, and by the various forms of industrial actions that disorganise the economy from time to time does not rest with trade unions or their members, nor even with shop stewards, whatever their political allegiance may be. It rests with politicians of both major parties who have succeeded in persuading the workers, or at any rate in allowing them to assume it in the absence of sufficiently emphatic words and actions pointing to the contrary, that full employment, like the Welfare State, is their absolute birthright for which they owe nothing whatsoever to the community. Needless to say, there had been no need actually to induce or encourage the workers to adopt that attitude, which suits them down to the ground in any case. But those politicians who share in the responsibility for policies and decisions conferring on the workers the benefits of full employment and the Welfare State ought to have made determined attempts to induce the beneficiaries to receive the benefits in the right spirit.

The conception that workers have only rights and no duties towards the community has become so deeply ingrained in their minds that any suggestion to the contrary must actually come to them as a surprise and a shock, not only to the workers themselves but to politicians and to members of the public in general.

Under the influence of Britain's experience during the inter-war period, it is not surprising that the creation and maintenance of full employment irrespective of its economic costs has come to be regarded as a fetish. Politicians who know that it is to their advantage to pursue a popular line — and there must be very few who don't — give it top priority among the aims of monetary and economic policies. There has been no effort to make beneficiaries of that policy realise that it is not their birthright but a concession on the part of the community that has to be earned and deserved. Admittedly, workers are often exhorted to work hard and exercise restraint in wage demands. But they have never been made to realise that the only way in which they could enjoy the full benefits of full employment in the long run would be by being willing to continue exerting themselves to the same extent as they or their forerunners had during the days of large-scale unemployment when they were driven to work by their constant fear of losing their jobs and being unable to find other jobs.

Workers are allowed and even encouraged to take it for granted that in the post-war world they are entitled to expect the Government in office to ensure for them the benefits of full employment, no matter how they behave. It has been tacitly understood that they are entitled to have it regardless of any decline in their productive efforts and regardless of the extent to which they abuse their stronger bargaining position.

Although they have been warned that such behaviour is apt to slow down progress towards a higher standard of living and might even endanger the continuity of full employment, any effect such warnings might have produced were cancelled out by the oft-repeated unconditional assurance that the Government aims at full employment at all costs. While before the devaluation of 1967 Mr. Wilson declared the maintenance of sterling as being at the top of the Government list of priorities, soon after devaluation he declared that full employment was heading the list.

On the basis of the experience of the decades since the war workers have come to assume that they can eat their cake and keep it. They have come to consider it a matter of course that, regardless of the extent to which they abuse their bargaining power, they can rely on the maintenance of full employment. Politicians of all parties compete with each other in their eagerness to reassure them that they would do their best to perpetuate this pleasant state of affairs. It is true, each Government that has held office since 1945 has had to resort to measures causing a temporary increase of unemployment. But the extent and duration of such spells of unemployment was not sufficient to induce workers to take official warnings seriously, even if it was sufficient to induce them to reinforce restrictive practices to safeguard themselves against the effect of unemployment, and to reduce the extent to which the measures are effective in curing the economic difficulties against which they are adopted.

In any case there has hardly ever been any *net* unemployment since the War. To explain this it is necessary to define the true meaning of full employment. Most people define it in terms of percentages — that is, full employment prevails if the proportion of unemployed is below a certain per cent of the total employables. Mr. Gaitskell, speaking with the authority of the chief economic expert of the Labour Party and a former Chancellor of the Exchequer, considered unemployment up to 5 per cent acceptable. But in recent years there was an outcry whenever unemployment rose to above 2 per cent.

In theory full employment is supposed to exist when the

number of unfilled vacancies equals the number of those seeking employment. In reality there must always be a number of unemployables and a number of workers are always in transit between jobs or are from time to time seasonally unemployed. Moreover, statistics of unfilled jobs always grossly understate the real number of vacancies. They only cover vacancies registered with Labour Exchanges; yet a number of employers never register their requirements, having been unable to obtain any workers through the Labour Exchange, or having obtained most unsatisfactory workers through them.

There have been at any time since the War at least a million unfilled vacancies in domestic services alone, but it would be hopeless to try to get cooks, chambermaids, gardeners, etc., through registering requirements at Labour Exchanges. Even chronic unemployed would consider it beneath their dignity to accept employment in which they are obliged to display a certain degree of courtesy towards their employers. Under the prevailing spirit it is deemed humiliating to do so. For a somewhat similar reason distributive trades have never enough labour to meet their greatly increased requirements resulting from the inflation of consumer demand. Some years ago the author had to stand in a long queue before being served in the shoe department of a well-known West End department store. When his turn came the grey-haired manager, serving single-handed, apologised for the delay and explained that it was impossible nowadays to get young men to serve in his department, because they deemed it beneath their dignity to assist customers with trying on shoes. The same able-bodied young men would not think it beneath their dignity to be kept by the community because they had refused such employment.

No doubt young men prefer employment in factories where they need not display any courtesy to customers or to employers' representatives and need not even deny themselves the satisfaction of calling the foremen names with impunity. They know they can depend on being backed by their fellow-workers against any attempt to penalise them for such behaviour. So while there may be scarcity of labour in factories there are unfilled vacancies in distributive trades and in domestic service. It is not real unemployment if men are out of work by choice, because they prefer to await vacancies in some particular occupation or in some particular district. During the winter of 1967–68 the number of unemployed included quite a few young men from industrial districts who, having taken jobs for a short time in South Coast seaside resorts, spent the rest of the winter in idleness on the dole.

It is correct to say that, ever since the War, even during periods when unemployment was temporarily well in excess of 2 per cent, there were in reality many more registered and unregistered vacancies than unemployed. Although many unemployed would not have been suitable to fill the vacancies available, many more jobs remained vacant simply because a great many unemployed preferred to remain unemployed rather than apply for jobs in which they could not display the same aggressive spirit and the same arrogance they display as factory workers, transport workers, etc. Allowing for this, it is true to contend that a state of overfull employment, or, at any rate, full employment, has prevailed in Britain almost all the time since the War.

Most of the time there were acute scarcities in various types of skilled labour, and from time to time also in unskilled labour. To a large degree such scarcities had been created or exaggerated artificially, as a result of restrictive practices, and of resistance to redeployment not only as between industries or as between factories of the same industry or even of the same firm, but even as between different departments in the same factory. There was, and still is, also much trade union resistance to the use of labour-saving equipment. Employers on their part contributed their share to the creation of labour scarcities by 'hoarding' labour rather than releasing the hands for which they had no use, for the benefit of rival firms that were short of manpower. Above all, the Selective Employment Tax has created permanent scarcities of labour in service industries while marginally encouraging manufacturing industries to hoard labour.

To some extent the inflationary effect of full employment is inevitable for the following reasons:

(1) The strengthening of the trade unions' bargaining position as a result of the change in the balance of power in their favour has led to bigger and more frequent demands for unearned wage increases and has weakened the ability and determination of employers to resist them. Consequently wages have increased to a higher degree in excess of productivity.

(2) Even if trade union leaders tried to moderate wage demands and other demands for concessions tending to cause an increase in costs, the rank and file would not stand for moderation and would accept the lead of militant shop stewards or of Left-wing infiltrators serving political ends by causing the maximum of trouble. Some firms are known to have signed contracts with Soviet purchasers as an insurance against Communist trouble-making. But they discovered that such contracts bought them no immunity from trouble-making by Trotskyites and other brands of Left-wingers.

(3) Increased wages caused a rise in prices not only through adding to costs but also through adding to demand for consumer goods and, once removed, to demand for capital equipment for increasing the output of consumer goods for satisfying the increased domestic demand.

(4) Employees of every kind work much less hard because there are no unemployed available to fill their jobs if they should be dismissed because of their unsatisfactory performance.

Such effects would have arisen even if full employment had not demoralised so many workers. Unfortunately, because full employment in Britain has made a great many workers power-drunk and bloody-minded, it has produced the following additional effects on their attitude to the detriment of productivity:

(5) The change in the balance of power has enabled trade unions to increase artificially the scarcity value of their

members by restrictive practices which have come to be applied more ruthlessly during periods of overfull employment than before the war during periods of large-scale unemployment.

(6) It has enabled workers to flout discipline, causing thereby decline in productivity and also longer and less certain delivery dates. In some instances it has caused a deterioration of the quality of manufactures in addition to the increase in their prices.

(7) It has encouraged trade unions to be trigger-happy about strikes, enabling them to enforce unearned wage demands by threatening employers with ruinously costly stoppages.

(8) It has enabled trade unions to resist automation and other forms of modernisation, unless it is adopted on terms that make the additional investment largely unprofitable to employers and to consumers alike.

As a result of this attitude the extent of the inflationary effect of full employment is unnecessarily large. According to the Brooking Institution's Report on Britain, this effect and its reaction on the balance of payments is higher in Britain than in most countries. It is because the workers are determined to retain their strong bargaining power that British consumers are deprived of the benefits of technological progress which could otherwise have increased the standard of living in Britain during recent years to at least the same extent as it has in other Western European countries.

In spite of this high economic and social cost of full employment, it is of course infinitely preferable to large-scale unemployment. If it were possible to decide between creeping inflation, such as we have witnessed in Britain in recent years, and deflation, such as we witnessed in Britain between the Wars, let us have inflation any day. But there are surely intermediate stages between the two extremes. The reason why so many people are becoming increasingly nostalgic for the return of the pre-war days when prices had been steady is that today's troubles are always felt more acutely than yesterday's troubles, even by those who had experience in both. But the younger generation had no experience of the evils of deflation, only in the smaller but none the less considerable evils of inflation. It would not be surprising, therefore, if a large and increasing section of British public opinion tended gradually to turn in favour of deflation involving a moderate but by no means inconsiderable increase in unemployment.

It is admittedly tempting for those unacquainted with the ruinous costs of deflation to arrive at the conclusion that it would be for the benefit of the community as a whole, because it would facilitate an increase of productivity. Paradoxical as it may sound, many people argue that more goods would be produced if only, say, 97 per cent of the working population were in employment than is the case when some 98 per cent are employed. Abuse of the privilege of full employment is likely to increase the number of those who share that harsh view. Their influence might affect the policy of a future Government, and possibly even that of the present Government — Mr, Callaghan, when Chancellor of the Exchequer, is alleged to have appeared at one time to be drifting unconsciously towards sharing that view—that, after all, a relatively moderate increase in unemployment and its maintenance at a certain level might be just the solution that is needed.

This depressing view is gaining in strength with each flagrant instance of misuse of power by trade unions or their members under the present state of virtually full employment. Already there is evidence of a growing feeling — not exclusively in 'reactionary' quarters — that, after all, the unemployed have only themselves to blame if large-scale unemployment were to return. It would be idle to deny that, owing to their behaviour during periods of full employment, workers have forfeited to a large degree the sympathies of the wider public at whose expense they had extorted far too many unearned wage increases.

This is a deplorable attitude to take. After all, it is far from certain or even probable that as a result of an increase in unemployment it would be those responsible for the decline

in productivity and for extortions of unearned wages who
would lose their jobs. More likely than not the conscientious
workers would be the first victims, if only because their dismissal would not be resisted by the militant workers to the same
extent as they would resist the dismissal of one of their numbers.
So an increase in unemployment as a 'punishment' of the
working classes for their failure to appreciate the blessings of
full employment would not even be rough justice — it would
be rough injustice.

However this may be, it would be to the vital interests
of industrial workers not to continue to antagonise public
opinion by misusing their power. At present they may think
they can well afford to ignore the unpopularity of their strikes.
'They are the masters now.' But they would be wiser to bear
in mind the risk attached to an increase in their unpopularity
and to the possibility of a return of conditions when they will
be once more in bad need of public sympathy. They should
balance that risk against the immediate advantages they stand
to gain by holding the community to ransom to the full extent
that is made possible by their present bargaining power.

Before the War the millions of unemployed in this country,
as in other industrial countries, had been the victims of monetary orthodoxy and of unenlightened pre-Keynesian economic
policies. Thanks largely to the all-but-universal acceptance of
a large part of Keynes's teachings, there should be no longer
any real danger for the workers that this country or the world
at large might relapse into unemployment because of a relapse
of their Governments into monetary orthodoxy and pre-
Keynesian economic short-sightedness. Their only danger is
that they themselves, by their own unreasonable and short-
sighted behaviour under full employment, might inflict on
themselves large-scale unemployment as the consequence of
their behaviour. They and they alone are now liable to create
mass unemployment by forcing Governments to adopt much
more drastic deflationary measures than those witnessed during
1964–68. Such measures, once adopted, might well become
self-aggravating. Resistance to them might well be weakened

by the effect produced by the misuse of full employment on public opinion, political opinion and official opinion. The future of Britain, and indeed even the fate of the free world, depends on the possibility of making British industrial workers realise this, before their behaviour forces the Government to risk the initiation of a deflationary spiral as an alternative to a runaway inflation. A slump in Britain could develop into a world-wide slump, with mass unemployment everywhere. It is hardly worth while for workers to risk such a disaster for the sake of the extra wages that they extort through the misuse of their excessive bargaining power.

CHAPTER TEN

THE WELFARE STATE

THE Welfare State is beyond doubt one of the noblest and finest ideals mankind has ever aimed at achieving. Its object is to ensure that every member of a community should be able to lead a decent human existence, that every man, woman and child should be safeguarded by the State against suffering want and against depending for their most essential requirements on the ups and downs of employment or on the caprices of private charity. Unfortunately the British experience with the Welfare State has provided a disheartening example of how even the noblest and finest ideas can be debased and discredited if applied and received in the wrong spirit.

After twenty years of experience in the working of the Welfare State, the term 'Welfare State' has come to be widely used in Britain as a term of abuse and of derision, mostly to account for flagrant instances of indolence and indiscipline. If workers arrive late or take days off, if their work is casual and negligent, if they go slow deliberately, if they inflict hardship on the public and on their fellow-workers by their wildcat strikes, if employers are unable to produce the goods on the delivery date of the contract, the Welfare State is blamed — unfortunately very often not without reason. Such criticisms should be directed not against the objective of the Welfare State but against its widespread misuse and against its effect on the workers' attitude.

Nothing could be more praiseworthy than the attempt to attain the real objective of the Welfare State, and in spite of her unfortunate experience with it Britain has every reason to be proud of having produced in the Beveridge Plan a basically correct formula for that attempt. With the elaboration and adoption of the Beveridge Plan Britain had undoubtedly given the world a lead, as she had in many other spheres during the centuries of her greatness.

It is true, some countries which had followed the British example of adopting the Welfare State actually surpassed their mentor in recent years. The benefits they now grant to those in need are now in many respects well in excess of the corresponding benefits granted in Britain. Certain classes of people who are covered abroad are excluded from the benefits under the British Welfare State. But credit for the initiation of the modern Welfare State does belong to Britain. We have every reason to be proud of this. Had it not been for the lead she gave soon after the War, world-wide progress towards the desired end would have been undoubtedly much slower. The fact that the United States with her incomparably higher standard of living is still far behind Britain in respect of the adoption of the Welfare State makes it appear probable that the prosperous countries of Western Europe would not have adopted their advanced systems if it had not been for the British lead.

It is all the more deplorable, indeed a major tragedy for Britain, that the inauguration and application of the Beveridge Plan's principles in an utterly wrong spirit and the resulting wrong response of the beneficiaries to its application should have worked out to the grave detriment of Britain's economic progress. Indeed it is no exaggeration to say that the public's misguided response to the application of the Welfare State, together with the misuse of full employment — another noble and fine objective gone wrong through its misapplication — have been among the main causes of Britain's decline. They are mainly responsible for the development of the 'English disease' and for assumption of the role of 'the sick man of Europe' by Britain.

The adverse results of the British experience lead one to ask whether those adverse effects are inherent in the institution of the Welfare State itself. Is it absolutely inevitable that the distribution of generous social service benefits should demoralise the recipients and should thereby handicap progress towards higher living standards for the whole community through an increase in productivity, in addition to handicapping specific increases that could be obtained by the lower income groups as a result of higher productivity? Surely it is not absolutely inevitable that demoralising effects of the Welfare State should jeopardise monetary and economic stability and should doom the country that had invented it to frequently recurrent financial crises and to non-stop inflation. It seems to me that the unfortunate result of the British experience is a special case, so that it would be wrong to infer from it conclusions concerning the Welfare State in general.

To find the answer it is necessary to recall the circumstances in which the Beveridge Plan was initiated. We must recall Lord Beveridge's words with which he presented his plan when it was first announced. 'To those who ask me, Can we afford to have it, my answer is, Can we afford *not* to have it?'

It was largely because of this fateful formula that Britain, having been victorious in the War, was doomed to lose the peace.

This may sound sheer rhetoric. But there can be no doubt that the mistaken psychology of the way in which the plan had been presented by its author — which had established the standard formula applied as a matter of course when each subsequent concession to the working classes was introduced — had an extremely demoralising effect. The unfortunately conceived formula implies that the benefits to be conferred are the recipient's birthright, to which he is entitled regardless of whether he will try to contribute towards the community's efforts to earn their costs. They are his, whether or not he will try to work harder to deserve it. They are his even if he should choose to work less hard than before, so that the community's total earnings would tend to decline simultaneously with the increase in the costs of his social benefits. Indeed they are his even if he should choose not to work at all. The Beveridge Plan and its subsequent amendments provide ample temptation and opportunity for avoiding work altogether. One is entitled to the benefits even if one should choose to lead a completely idle existence and to scrounge on the community.

The correct answer Lord Beveridge should have given should have sounded something like this: 'To those who ask me, Can we afford to have it? my answer is, We don't know yet. This is in the way of being an experiment. Whether we shall be able to afford it depends on you and *you* and YOU! If you help the community to earn the high costs of these benefits by working harder the benefits could be made permanent and they could even be increased in stages. But if you don't contribute your share towards earning their costs we might find that the benefits might have to be reduced or even repealed.'

It is argued sometimes that the presentation of the Beveridge Plan as a free and unconditional gift had been an act of statesmanlike wisdom. It had to be presented, the argument runs, as a reward for the splendid contribution made by the British people towards achieving victory. It is said that, had it not been for the way in which the reward was offered, without any strings attached to it, there might have been grave social unrest once the War was over. Those who argue on such lines must have a very low opinion of the character of the British working man during the War. Can anyone seriously believe that the people, having been promised benefits the extent of which exceeded their most optimistic hopes, might have broken into open revolution if attempts had been made to explain to them the elementary economic fact that the costs of the benefits would have to be earned somehow, the goods to meet the additional demand would have to be produced somehow, that they would not be conjured out of thin air?

But once they were told in almost so many words that the benefits would be a free gift for which, it was clearly implied if not actually stated, they owe absolutely no gratitude to the community, it had become difficult if not impossible to persuade them to show their appreciation by working, if not as hard as during the War, at any rate not less hard than before the war. By the way the plan was presented it conveyed the false impression that Britain would be bursting with prosperity once the War was over, and could well afford the costs of the Beveridge Plan, regardless of whether the workers contribute towards earning them.

Instead of presenting the Welfare State as manna from heaven it should have been presented as a major concession by a community impoverished by the War. It should have been made clear that the community could only afford such social progress if the working classes were to co-operate in its effort to regain and surpass its pre-war prosperity. Such an appeal might have inspired the workers to be at their best instead of encouraging and enabling them to be at their worst. There might have been a British miracle. Britain's productivity and standard of living might have risen and the differential in Britain's favour compared with the standard of living of most other advanced nations would have been maintained and even increased — unless the British people preferred to share their increased prosperity more generously with backward peoples. In either case Britain's prestige and power would have increased instead of declining, and she would have remained a first-class Power instead of becoming reduced to a second-class Power. It is most unfortunate that the Welfare State, which should have inspired the British working classes to make an effort comparable to that of German, Italian, Japanese, etc., working classes, should have induced them to relax their exertions, just at the moment when the community was at long last beginning to treat them more generously.

In spite of bitter disappointment over the disheartening results of the British experience with the Welfare State, it is not suggested here that its adoption was a mistake. There is indeed strong temptation to arrive at that conclusion and many people have yielded to the temptation. It is certainly not the object of this chapter or of this book to challenge the validity of the case overwhelmingly in favour of the Welfare State. For social, political and, above all, humanitarian arguments in its favour heavily outweigh the economic arguments against it. But it would serve no useful purpose to try to ignore the arguments against the Welfare State — in the form in which it has operated in Britain. On the debit side of the balance sheet there are weighty items — adverse effect on production, on prices, on the balance of payments, on sterling, and on Britain's standing in the world. There can be little doubt that Britain has sacrificed her national greatness in the form of superior financial, economic, political and military power largely for the sake of attempting to achieve national greatness through being the spearhead of progress in another sphere — in the sphere of providing its people with a degree of social security that had never before been attained.

It is arguable that the price paid for the adoption of the Welfare State has not been too high, since even its adoption in the wrong way has greatly reduced poverty and has raised the standard of living of lower income groups above subsistence level. Even conceding that argument as a matter of course, the operation of the Welfare State in Britain is open to censure because the price paid for its adoption, as for that of full employment, has been made quite unnecessarily high. The argument is that, had the Welfare State been introduced more intelligently, with more regard for human psychology and with less regard for increasing its popular political appeal, much greater results could have been achieved at incomparably lower costs.

This argument does not depend on unsupported opinion. Readers can find ample confirmation and evidence by studying the progress made by the Welfare State in several Western European industrial countries. Social services in most of these countries were much less advanced than in Britain at the time when the adoption of the Beveridge Plan was decided upon, but now they can boast of much more advanced social services than Britain. Those in this country who agitate in favour of stepping up the increase of our Welfare State benefits often quote facts and figures to show that other countries are now much more generous in allowing the lower income groups to share in their national prosperity. But the argument implied by the facts and figures they quote cuts both ways. It not only proves that Britain has lost her lead in the progress towards social security but also that the accelerated progress of other countries has not been prevented by any anti-social attitude of their workers. Unlike their British opposite numbers, they have not prevented the degree of increase in productivity that has been indispensable in order to justify the increased generosity of their respective Welfare States.

It is because in other countries the Welfare State has been adopted and received in the right spirit that they have been able to expand its scope without having to pay the price for it in the form of a national decline. None of these countries has witnessed in recent years such a demoralisation of their industrial workers as Britain. Although there have been occasional allusions in recent years to the appearance of symptoms of the 'English disease' amongst their workers, judging by their satisfactory balance of payments, by the increase of their productivity, and by the general dynamic spirit prevailing in the countries concerned, the extent to which the British example in the demoralising effect of the Welfare State has affected them must be very moderate.

The object of stressing the disadvantages resulting from the British Welfare State experience is not to present a case against the Welfare State as such. Those who benefit by the Welfare State or are in favour of it because they regard social considerations to be more important than economic considerations would not in any case be deterred from it by any warnings that it is liable to entail grave economic disadvantages to the community. But possibly they might heed the argument that, in the circumstances in which the Welfare State has been applied in Britain, it has entailed unnecessarily grave disadvantages which could and should have been avoided.

According to some definitions, the term Welfare State covers every method by which legislation and Government action assist in raising the standard of living of the lower income groups. From this point of view the policy of full employment, too, comes under the definition, and so do expansionary monetary and economic policies which, by changing the balance of power between employers and employees in favour of the latter, aim at strengthening their bargaining position, thereby enabling them to secure higher wages. For the purposes of the present chapter the definition of the Welfare State is confined to measures providing higher social service benefits in the broader sense of the term that covers education and housing as well as the National Health Service, unemployment and sickness benefits and various kinds of pensions.

To a large extent the Welfare State tends to produce inflationary effects, unless those effects are offset by an increase in the efforts by its beneficiaries to produce more. The following inflationary tendencies are inherent in the Welfare State:

(1) The Exchequer's contribution to the cost of the Welfare State increases public expenditure, which is inflationary, especially as the idea of genuinely balancing the budget seems to have now been abandoned.

(2) The contribution of employers to National Insurance tends to increase costs and prices.

(3) The contributions of employees in National Insurance leads to demands for increases in wages and therefore to higher costs and prices.

(4) Because the Welfare State provides assistance to beneficiaries 'from cradle to grave' it reduces their incentive to save. To the extent to which it actually reduces savings, or prevents their increase which would take place otherwise, it is inflationary.

(5) Because it brings about a redistribution of incomes it is inflationary on the Keynesian principle that an increase of lower incomes tends to increase demand for necessities to a higher degree than a corresponding reduction of higher incomes tends to reduce it.

(6) Because the Welfare State relieves parents of the cost of higher education of their children, of medical costs, of the cost of school meals, and of the maintenance of their aged relatives, a larger proportion of their incomes is available for spending on other goods and services.

Such inflationary effects are inevitable. But it is possible to argue that, unless the basic trend is already strongly inflationary and the Welfare State aggravates that trend, the social advantages of the progress of the Welfare State tend to compensate for the economic disadvantages of such inflationary effects. Unfortunately in Britain these disadvantages, instead of being mitigated by an effort of beneficiaries to show their gratitude to the community by working harder, have become gravely accentuated because of the wrong spirit in which the beneficiaries receive the costly benefits. Their attitude slackens their productive effort, and this unnecessarily adds to the inevitable inflationary effect of the Welfare State, by handicapping an increase in productivity which would otherwise have absorbed the extra costs.

The following are the *avoidable* inflationary effects of the Welfare State:

(1) The Welfare State tends to encourage absenteeism. It is tempting to take a few days off and draw sickness benefits. The high degree of absenteeism in Britain is one of the major causes why she is lagging behind other industrial nations in the expansion of her production. Even more working time is lost because of absenteeism than because of strikes.

(2) It is detrimental to employees' loyalty to employers. Social service benefits make workers less dependent on the goodwill of their firms created by long terms of service with them. Labour turnover has therefore increased; employees are more inclined to change their jobs for trifling reasons. This is detrimental to productivity.

(3) In certain circumstances beneficiaries are said to be able to get more money for not working than for working. Even if this is not the case, many beneficiaries feel that it is not worth their while to work if they consider that the differential between their wages when working and their benefits when not working is inadequate.

(4) The National Health Service is grossly misused, so that doctors have not enough time for genuine sufferers. They have to produce a vast number of unnecessary

prescriptions which increase public expenditure. It remains to be seen to what extent the recent re-introduction of prescription charges will stop this misuse to any considerable degree.

(5) Many people retire while still fit to work. They are discouraged from continuing work after retiring age is reached by the application of the earnings limit. This increases scarcity of labour, which is the reason why trade unions exert pressure to retain that rule. This is very short-sighted because in the due process of time trade union members will themselves be recipients of retirement benefits.

(6) The Welfare State has created a mentality in favour of depending on the community instead of making an effort to work out one's own salvation. It has discouraged zeal and initiative, because of the feeling that the community would now protect one from the worst consequences of one's indolence. Work has come to be looked upon as being purely optional instead of being a vital necessity in order to survive. In a Welfare State there is a feeling that one works only out of choice, and not out of necessity, if one wants to secure luxuries in addition to the necessities which are provided as a matter of course.

(7) This sponging mentality also manifests itself by a widespread feeling among workers in nationalised industries that theirs is not an industry which has to justify itself by being self-supporting but a social service that is entitled to expect to be subsidised by the State. Just like Government Departments, they feel they are not supposed to earn their keep but can depend on being kept by the taxpayer. They have no desire whatever to go out of their way to help national boards to become solvent. Employees of nationalised industries take it for granted that the large and ever-increasing deficit of their industry must be covered by the community in the same way as it covers the deficit on National

E

Insurance. They don't feel the need for contributing towards an effort to cover the deficit. For instance, railwaymen resisted for years the adoption of liner trains which, if they had been adopted before a high proportion of freights were diverted to the roads, might have made the railways solvent.

All these disadvantages are not inherent in the operation of the Welfare State. They have been added to those disadvantages which are inevitable, because the Beveridge Plan and its subsequent amendments had been applied in the wrong spirit — in the spirit that beneficiaries have only rights and no duties in relation to the community.

The application of the Welfare State in the wrong spirit tends to destroy family ties by relieving people to a large degree of their family responsibilities. Parents no longer consider it their foremost duty to make sacrifices for the sake of their children or for the sake of their aged parents. By being relieved of such duties they are enabled to buy more expensive TV sets or cars. Nothing could characterise more the new spirit than an indignant remark made by Mr. (now Lord) Robens in the course of a debate in the House of Commons on the inadequacy of retirement pensions, stating that the benefits are so utterly inadequate that many people actually have to subsidise their old parents. What an outrageous thought, to expect them to repay what their parents had spent on their upbringing!

It is in accordance with the spirit of the Welfare State in the way it operates in Britain to try to evade such responsibility. For many years after the initiation of the Welfare State there were daily SOS messages broadcast by the B.B.C. — indeed sometimes there were several of them before each news bulletin — calling on Mr. or Mrs. So-and-So, last heard of in some working-class district a number of years ago, to contact such and such a hospital where their father or mother was dangerously ill. Presumably in the majority of such cases the sons or daughters, having moved from their former residences, had severed all connections with their old parents, and had not even sent Christmas cards with their new addresses, just in case they might be asked for financial help which would be awkward to refuse. That wouldn't do at all, to meet such appeals. If they relieved their parents' misery they might not be able to afford the washing machine or the more expensive TV set on the possession of which they had set their hearts. Let the old folk live on their pension the best way they can. Such SOS messages have been much less frequent in recent years and it is to be hoped that the decline in their frequency means that in this respect at any rate the demoralising effect of the Welfare State on family ties has been wearing off during the last few years.

The adverse change in family spirit brought about by the Welfare State is strikingly illustrated by an eminent spokesman of the working-class point of view, the playwright Arnold Wesker, whose 'kitchen sink' plays disclose a close familiarity with working-class habits and mentality. In Act III of his play *Roots* there is perturbing evidence in support of this point. When the daughter of a working-class family who had come to lead a middle-class existence is jilted by her intellectual fiancé, she gets absolutely no sympathy from her family. Even her own mother is openly overjoyed by her daughter's humiliation and unhappiness, sneering at her for having tried to be superior to them.

No matter how disunited a middle-class or upper-class family would be, it would close its ranks as a matter of course in face of an affront to one of its members from outside the family. There can be little doubt that most workers' families adopted a similar attitude before the war. But the picture presented by Wesker, read in conjunction with the B.B.C. messages referred to above, reflects truly the destructive effect of the Welfare State on working classes' family ties.

This disadvantage arising from the adoption of the Welfare State is not an inevitable consequence of its adoption. It has been added to the disadvantages that are inherent in it, because it is applied in the wrong spirit. It is to be deplored. The Welfare State is a great institution if applied in the right spirit. There is, for instance, everything to be said for better schools and hospitals — provided that those who primarily benefit from them are made to realise that they must share in the community's effort to achieve such progress, even if it means that for the time being they have to defer that holiday on the Costa Brava. So long as they are allowed to assume that it is the one-sided duty of the community to provide them with better schools and hospital facilities without expecting them to contribute anything whatsoever towards the sacrifices involved, they can hardly be blamed if it does not even occur to them to volunteer to reciprocate the gifts of Santa Claus.

The only effective way to deal with this attitude would be to suspend all improvements of schools and hospitals until beneficiaries come to realise that there could be no further improvements unless they develop a spirit of co-operation by contributing within their means towards the sacrifices made for their benefit. The same applies to the sacrifices involved in other social service benefits. So long as workers take it for granted that such services are bound to be improved even in the complete absence of their co-operation they will see no reason for doing their duty to assist the community in its task of earning the cost of the improvements. Even if the principle that they must assist should be laid down it would not necessarily mean that all or most workers would be willing to restrain their demand for unearned wage increases if it meant that they would have to defer the purchase of their new TV set so that the community could afford the cost of the new hospital wing. Many of them would prefer to continue to insist on higher unearned wages and would keep their productive efforts to a minimum. But the mere realisation of the principle which is at present ignored that there is, or there should be, some sort of relationship between what they receive from the community and what they give to the community might be an immensely important step in the right direction.

CHAPTER ELEVEN

'WE'VE NEVER HAD IT
SO GOOD'

THE much-quoted Conservative slogan in the 'fifties, 'We've
never had it so good', has been ever since a source of much
criticism. Yet there is nothing wrong with having it good. It
is true recent experience in countries with the highest standard
of living unfortunately shows that increase in material welfare,
if unaccompanied by an increase in the appreciation of spiritual
values, is apt to produce gravely demoralising effects. Even in
countries where it has not bred 'English disease' to any noteworthy extent, it has bred unwarranted discontent, boredom
with unadventurous life, decadence in various forms, crime
waves, increased rate of suicides, violent demonstrations on the
flimsiest excuse, defiance of authority, drug-taking, alcoholism,
etc. Even so, the achievement of a higher and ever-higher
standard of living is, and must remain, one of the supreme tests
and supreme ends of statesmanship. Any Government which
has succeeded in bringing about *genuine* progress towards a
higher standard of living has indeed every right to claim credit
for its achievement.

It indicates a perverse puritanical mentality to favour austerity for its own sake in the strange belief that we simply must
have a thoroughly lean time in this world in order to qualify
for a happier time in the next. It is more difficult to shrug off
criticism of the cult of affluence made on the ground that it
is easier to make people appreciate spiritual values if their
material welfare is less satisfactory. There must surely be an
answer to that argument but its discovery and examination is
outside the scope of the present book.

The author's own criticism of the popular slogan is on totally different grounds. A Government certainly deserves credit for making genuine progress towards raising the standard of living of its nation, but the accent must be on *genuine*. Progress must not rest on false foundations. It must not be achieved by an advanced country at the cost of becoming indebted to foreign countries — a view which was firmly held already in Biblical times, as indicated in the quotation from Ecclesiasticus at the beginning of this book — or at the cost of realising previously acquired foreign assets to be kept for emergencies, or at the cost of selling out national assets to foreign enterprise or foreign investors. Nor must progress be the result of unduly sudden expansion, inspired by the prevailing fashion of growth-hysteria, carrying the risk of advanced inflation and of disastrous setbacks.

Genuine progress cannot be maintained in the long run if an over-expanded economy is balanced so precariously that it is liable to become unbalanced even by relatively moderate disturbing influences. If unduly rapid increase in consumption in a country is not justified by an at least equal increase in production, the result is an adverse balance of payments and the economy is exposed to frequently recurrent foreign exchange crises. Unless it possesses adequately strong gold and foreign exchange reserves to ride such crises, they are liable to reverse its progress towards a higher standard of living. Progress which is too much exposed to such reverses, because it has been achieved at the risk of unbalancing the economy and through neglecting essential precautions to reinforce the technical defences of monetary stability, cannot be regarded as being genuine.

Admittedly a free economy is always exposed to ups and downs. According to one economist, the main cause of crisis is prosperity. To renounce prosperity for the sake of avoiding the risk of crises would mean condemning mankind to stagnation. A system under which progress is never interrupted by setbacks has yet to be invented. The Americans had imagined during the 'twenties, and again during the 'sixties, that they had succeeded in inventing it. Their attitude reminds one of

'The Gospel of the Brothers Barnabas' in Shaw's *Back to Methuselah*, Part II, according to which longevity could and should be achieved by the simple device of being firmly convinced that its achievement is possible. In a similar way, American politicians, economists and the public came to believe, during the two periods referred to above, that it would be possible to achieve everlasting business expansion by firmly believing in its possibility. They came to know better after 1929. They became disillusioned once more — fortunately in much less dramatic circumstances — less than forty years later.

Judging by the experience of the Soviet Union and other Communist countries even strictly controlled totalitarian economies have their ups and downs. But even admitting that setbacks cannot be avoided altogether progress cannot be claimed to be genuine unless it is sufficiently consolidated not to be at the mercy of any adverse change in the situation at home or abroad. A country which is forced into devaluation by a major strike or by a war between third countries cannot claim to have achieved genuine progress.

A reason why the Conservative claim to have achieved affluence during 1951–64 is open to criticism is that it had been achieved largely at the cost of neglecting to make adequate provisions for safeguarding the economy against adverse changes. The external stability of sterling was maintained precariously with the aid of reserves which, having regard to the growing volume of Britain's foreign trade, the formidable size of foreign short-term claims in sterling, and the extensive use of sterling as a currency in international trade and finance, had been most inadequate. Admittedly, it had been in accordance with British traditions to manage the gold standard on a shoestring. At no time, not even during the heyday of the gold standard in the 19th century, did Britain possess a really sufficiently large gold reserve to safeguard her domestic economy against unsettling reprecussions caused by developments in the international field. But one would have thought that a Conservative regime would heed the lessons taught by the crisis of 1931. Besides, the abnormally large size of foreign short-term claims after the last War had called for a reconsideration of Britain's minimum reserve requirements.

The need for a reinforcement of sterling's defences became evident again and again after the end of the second World War. The inadequacy of the reserve became only too painfully obvious at frequent intervals under Socialist and Tory Governments alike. The Attlee Government faced three sterling crises during its six years' existence, in spite of the generous financial assistance it had received from the United States. The Conservative Governments that succeeded each other between 1951 and 1964 had also several stern warnings indicating the imperative need for reinforcing the technical defences of sterling. But their success in dealing with these crises swiftly and effectively during the 'fifties appears to have lulled them into a false feeling of security. The authorities deemed it safe to keep the gold and dollar reserve at a low level on the assumption that a 7 per cent Bank rate would always restore the position.

The abnormally increased overseas sterling balances inherited from the War were neither reduced with the aid of a series of genuine balance of payments surpluses nor consolidated into long-term obligations during the years when the situation was sufficiently favourable for such operations. In 1932 the National Government took full advantage of the first available opportunity to reduce the burden Britain had inherited from the first World War, by converting the big 5 per cent War Loan. It did not seem to have occurred to the Conservative Governments of the 'fifties to emulate the sound policy of their predecessor of the 'thirties by reducing the heaviest burden inherited from the second World War — the excessive amount of foreign-owned sterling balances which were liable to be recalled at short notice.

It is only fair to confess that in criticising this omission the author is jobbing backward. Notwithstanding the recurrent sterling crises, the basic technical weakness of sterling did not become sufficiently evident at the time, so long as it appeared to enjoy widespread confidence most of the time in spite of its inadequate technical strength. But those who had access to all official information relevant to judging the situation ought to have realised how precarious the stability of sterling and the equilibrium of the British economy was bound to be so long as the sword of Damocles was hanging over it in the form of gigantic foreign sterling balances. It would have been more statesmanlike even to forgo some progress, for the sake of a higher degree of well-established stability, if a genuine consolidation of the external floating debt by means of long-term issues — as distinct from the phoney consolidation resorted to by the Labour Government in 1968 — had been found to be impracticable without cutting down home consumption for the sake of securing a series of big export surpluses. This had been vitally important in spite of the fact that under Tory rule over-seas holders had trusted sterling, because they had taken it for granted that in case of a crisis the authorities would not hesitate to adopt harsh measures in order to safeguard the exchange.

Foreign holders of sterling did not have the same confidence in the Labour Government that assumed office in 1964, partly because of the memories of the devaluation fifteen years earlier, and partly because some of the new Government's initial measures inevitably inspired distrust. It is arguable that, even if the previous Conservative Governments had left an impregnably strong reserve and a strongly reduced external short-term debt behind, this strength would have been quickly dissipated by the Labour Government. It would have simply enabled Mr. Wilson to carry out in full his programme planned for the 'hundred dynamic days', by the end of which the technical position of sterling would have become in all probability as weak as it had actually been in October 1964, owing to the absence of any consolidation under Tory rule. Even acceptance of this argument does not mean that it exonerates the Conservative Governments from the blame for omitting to pursue the sound policies traditionally associated with Conservative rule in Britain.

The difference between the response of the 'gnomes' to a 7 per cent Bank Rate under Tory rule and under Socialist rule

E 2

indicated the degree to which sterling's stability had depended
on the confidence of foreign holders in the Government of the
day. The 'gnomes' had of course been right in distrusting the
Labour Government. They had not been quite so right in
trusting the Tory Government, judging by the latter's omission
to take advantage of their confidence in sterling to strengthen
its technical position instead of relying almost exclusively on
the psychological factor, which had been in their favour, as
the permanent influence in defence of sterling.

Another reason for qualifying the Tory claim for having
achieved affluence is that to a large extent it had been achieved
through tolerating the rise in the cost of living as a result of
creeping inflation. As pointed out earlier, initial stages of
inflation are always accompanied by a widespread feeling of
prosperity. Had the Governments that succeeded each other
in office after the War resisted inflation more effectively, they
might have risked a slowing down of progress towards a higher
standard of living. But judging by the fact that in various
countries of Western Europe where inflation had been resisted
more effectively than in Britain progress has been more impressive than in Britain, it is possible and even probable that the
net result of a policy of resisting inflation over a number of years
would have been more prosperity and not less prosperity. In the
absence of the non-stop creeping inflation that had been tolerated
in order to be able to abstain from impeding expansion, trade
unions and their members might have been more manageable.

The inflationary implications of 'We've never had it so good'
are evident in Goethe's *Faust* (Part II). When the emperor was
handing out paper money to all and sundry as a free gift, one
of the lucky recipients was asked whether the emperor's gift had
saved him. '*Geschieht mir oft, doch nicht so gut als jetzt*', was his
answer. Gifts without reciprocity, enabling their recipients
to claim that they had never had it so good, caused the currency
to depreciate.

But even if a policy of resisting inflation more firmly had
yielded no gain in the form of a higher standard of living in the
long run, progress would have been better founded and less

precarious. British Governments, more than other Western European Governments, had come too much under the influence of temptation and pressure to pursue growth with little regard to its cost in terms of rising prices. Expansion and more expansion was the supreme end, and no time was wasted on intervals during which to consolidate from time to time the progress achieved. Since Britain had had no experience in advanced inflation, she was only too willing to pay the price for growth in the form of creeping inflation.

Germany, with her painful experience in extreme inflation after the first World War, had been considerably less willing to pay that price. Her creeping inflation was interrupted from time to time by spells of disinflation even though, unlike Britain, she was not forced to adopt such policies by any weakening of the D. mark. The West German experience since the War shows that it is by no means impossible to achieve progress while upholding stability. In spite of repeated and at times drastic interruptions of the moderate creeping inflation in Germany — or perhaps because of them — growth in Germany has been much more impressive than in Britain.

British Governments resorted to deflation only when they became alarmed by the decline of the gold and dollar reserve. The author can only recollect one single instance in which effort was made in Britain to check the creeping inflation not because sterling was under acute pressure but for the sake of achieving stability of the cost of living — the 'plateau' of prices achieved during Mr. Macmillan's term of office.

Acceleration of growth, by causing the cost of living to increase, had victimised the classes whose incomes could not keep pace with the rising trend of wages and prices. A great many people failed to benefit from growing prosperity under Tory rule, and were, on balance, worse off in 1964 than in 1951. For many others the extent to which they shared in it lagged very far behind that of the gains of other classes.

But the main criticism of the slogan 'We've never had it so good' is that, in its result if not in its intention, it had encouraged trade unions and their members in their belief that, since everything was going wonderfully well, they were fully entitled to claim the maximum of wage increases that they were able to secure without risking a prolonged major strike. Instead of pursuing its all too popular line, the Government ought to have made the utmost effort to ensure that the public realised the essentially precarious character of its prosperity unless and until it comes to be justified by harder work to enable the country to earn large export surpluses and to consolidate its external short-term debt.

It would of course be easy to quote, in refutation of the above point, many scores of isolated official pronouncements exhorting workers to work harder and to moderate their wage demands. But what really mattered was the overall impression conveyed by the basic trend of official pronouncements. The emphasis was distinctly on the side of claiming credit for enabling the public to have a good time. Tories were by no means alone in making that claim. Their Socialist critics, too, adopted the same slogan with only minor verbal alterations — and with considerably less justification. It was restated, among other occasions, at the Labour Party Conference in September 1968.

It is of course very tempting for politicians of all parties and of all countries to claim the maximum of credit for their Government's achievements. This claim is apt to conflict with the unpleasant but necessary task of warning trade unions and others about the imperative need for increased effort and for restraint. Conservative Governments of the period are open to criticism for failure to perform that task adequately. It would be of course gross exaggeration to suggest that, had it not been for the optimistic atmosphere created by Tory pronouncements in the 'fifties, there might have been a British miracle rivalling other national miracles. But the possibility that amidst a less complacent atmosphere trade unions might have been more induced to co-operate towards the achievement of sounder basic economic conditions cannot be ignored. Their present intolerably non-cooperative attitude developed and became firmly established during the 'fifties and early 'sixties, even before the advent of Socialist rule.

CHAPTER TWELVE

'WE ARE THE MASTERS NOW'

HARD things have been said in this book about British trade unionist workers, because these hard things needed saying. But British workers deserve profound respect for the way in which they bore the prolonged hardships inflicted on them by inexorable economic trends and ill-advised policies between the Wars. As for the way in which they responded to the country's desperate need in 1940, it deserves the highest tribute. Aircraft workers are entitled to share with R.A.F. fighter pilots the credit for winning the Battle of Britain. It is therefore with great regret that one is forced to reach the conclusion that the increase of the workers' prosperity since the war has been accompanied by a deterioration of those of their qualities for which they deserve admiration.

Even criticism of their behaviour since the War must necessarily be tempered by the realisation that they have been placed in a position in which there has been a maximum of temptation to abuse a strong bargaining position, coupled with the maximum of opportunity for doing so. We saw in earlier chapters that there had been no adequate efforts to make them realise either the precarious character of the improvements achieved or the extent to which the improvements were due not to their own exertions but to those of their employers and of the community. The result was the development of an arrogant attitude, but for which the rate of economic progress would certainly have been much higher.

That arrogance can best be characterised by the all too familiar slogan 'We are the masters now'. Although the originator of that slogan has long ceased to be a Labour spokesman, the slogan itself continues to characterise the trade

unionist workers' attitude, irrespective of whether the Labour
Party is in or out of office.   It is admittedly in accordance
with human nature that, having been downtrodden underdogs
for so many generations, industrial workers should now feel
entitled to have their own back and to treat the other classes
with the same intolerable arrogance with which they themselves had been treated in the past.   It is also in accordance
with human nature that, while they had keenly resented the
arrogance with which they had been treated in the past, they
are now completely unaware of their own arrogance when
inflicting it on other people.   An explanation is not an excuse,
however, and the validity of the saying *tout comprendre c'est tout
pardonner* is open to doubt.

The theoretical foundations of the quasi-religious belief
that, since physical labour alone can create goods, physical
labourers are to be worshipped as the ruling classes, were laid
down by Ricardo in his theory of value which was adopted and
greatly reinforced by Karl Marx.   Even if one were to accept
this theory — and it is a big 'if' — that the value of goods and
services depends on the quantity of labour expended on their
production, it would not justify the contention that only
physical labour directly employed on their production counts.
But it suits Socialists to base their attitude on that fallacious
interpretation.

Most workers, at any rate in Britain, are barely familiar with
theoretical Marxism.   Their arrogant assumption that physical
labourers alone are the ruling classes and are entitled to dictate
to the rest of the community is the result of the essentially
practical influence of labour scarcity due to the high degree of
employment that has prevailed since the War.   It has made
them realise that in such a situation they hold most of the
trumps.   They are aware of their nuisance value because of
their power for damaging the interests of their employers, of the
Government and of the public depending on the goods and
services they produce.   They know they can inflict heavy
financial losses on their firms by slowing down, because under
contracts the firms have to pay penalties for failure to deliver

the goods by the date fixed in the contract. No wonder many firms, instead of announcing the imminence of an important delivery date in order to spur their men to an extra effort, keep such date a closely guarded secret. It is a favourite trick to slow down constructional work on the eve of the opening of exhibitions, the dates of which cannot be kept secret. Dock labourers can make ships miss the outgoing tide. They can make their country lose vitally important foreign markets. This list of situations in which workers are in a position to hold the nation to ransom could be prolonged indefinitely.

The realisation of their ability to inflict crippling losses on their employers and on their country has made many workers drunk with pride in their power. They must derive immense satisfaction from their feeling of being in a position to bring the wheels of an important industry to a halt, to be able to cause grave inconvenience, losses and hardship to millions of people; to be able, if their demands are not met, to damage the economy of their country. It is alleged that dockers were heard in public houses to boast of having been able to force Mr. Wilson to devalue in 1967. Even a handful of men in key positions are in a position to stop the entire production of their firms. They derive pride from being able to abuse such a position, not only for the sake of the financial advantages derived from it but even for the sake of the sheer satisfaction derived from feeling their power.

It is of course understandable if the workers felt an urge to reassert themselves after the change in the balance of power in their favour. They had been pushed about far too long between the Wars, and they had admittedly a great many genuine grievances in the past when it was many employers who had misused their power. Yet even before the change in the balance of power in favour of the workers there had been innumerable employers who had treated them in the right spirit, without being forced to do so by threats of wildcat strikes or by fears that they might be unable to recruit or retain adequate manpower unless they met the workers' demands.

But now the pendulum has swung very much in the opposite

direction. All employers, good and bad alike, have to put up with the high and mighty attitude of their workers, many of whom now feel that in their strong positions they can do as they please. They are fully aware that they are able to resist any attempt to penalise offensive behaviour, indiscipline, inefficiency, sabotage by neglect or even active sabotage. They can retaliate, by lightning strikes or by other industrial action, even to mild reprimands or to reasonable criticism of their work.

Even when strikes begin by being unofficial, started against the advice of trade union officials — we have already quoted the Donovan Report as saying that 95 per cent of the strikes are in fact unofficial — the strikers know that, right or wrong, they can rely upon being supported by the whole might of the Labour movement. 'No victimisation' is a magic formula that secures immunity from having to suffer the consequences of even the most flagrantly irresponsible and mischievous of unofficial strikes. It means that while firms and their shareholders, and indeed the entire community, can be made victims of malicious troublemaking, those who cheerfully inflict such losses on them are safeguarded against being penalised for their anti-social behaviour.

The 'we are the masters now' attitude has led to considerable deterioration in industrial efficiency. The standard of workmanship has declined in many factories, because the workers simply refuse to tolerate any criticism of their work. This is particularly the case with firms which operate the system of piece-work payment, so that attempts to maintain and improve the quality of the manufacture are resented not only because they imply criticism but even more because they are bound to slow down the output and to reduce earnings. In the past workers took genuine pride in the quality of the goods they had produced and in the reputation of their firm. In many factories that spirit is almost completely gone. Most workers are now only interested in their pay packets.

The author chanced to come across a striking piece of first-hand evidence of the way in which the workers' attitude has deteriorated and is still deteriorating. During the late

'forties, when a new boiler was installed in the basement of the
Palace of Westminster, some of the workers acquired the habit
of having half a pint in the Lords' Bar after finishing their
day's work. (This may sound strange to those who are unaware
that the Lords' Bar, in spite of its aristocratic-sounding name,
is probably the most democratic and egalitarian institution
of its kind in existence. Peers and postmen, Ministers and
messengers, Members and mechanics rub shoulders in its
crowded premises. Once on a New Year's Day the author
had a drinking session there with a senior Cabinet Minister
and with Bill, the lift attendant.) On one occasion the author
got into conversation with one of the boiler workers. He was a
young man and this was his first job in London. He was a
loyal member of his trade union and an enthusiastic member
of the Labour Party. Nevertheless he was very proud of his
firm which, he said, made the best boilers in the world. And
he was proud of the part he was playing in installing the best
boilers in the world in the basement of the Mother of Parliaments, under the Victoria Tower. He was thoroughly enjoying life. It was indeed a pleasure to talk to him, because
he was contentment personified. But when we met again
a few weeks later, he was a different man altogether. He
grumbled and groused about hard work, long hours and
inadequate pay. He was as thoroughly disgruntled as he had
been content a few weeks earlier. When asked about the
change in his attitude he became rather embarrassed and
ended by admitting with some reluctance that his fellow-
workers reprimanded him for having expressed praise of his
employers and satisfaction over his work. They told him there
was no hope for improving their conditions unless everybody
shared their own attitude. So he felt obliged to toe the line
and to join the chorus of discontents. It is doubtful whether, if,
because of this change, he got a rise, his additional earnings
really compensated him for the spirit of dissatisfaction that had
taken the place of his previous contentment with life and with
his work.

Mr. Shinwell once expressed the trade unionist attitude by

his oft-quoted remark — which is believed to have cost the
Labour Party many votes and seats at the elections of 1950 and
1951 — that only organised labour counted, the rest did not
matter 'a tinker's cuss'. Yet that was at an early stage of
overfull employment, the progress of which in later years
has gradually accentuated the arrogance of the working classes
as and when it increased their near-dictatorial bargaining
position.

Is this arrogance really necessary? To a large degree it only
serves subconsciously the desire of the workers to reassure
themselves again and again that they are really the equals and
more than equals of the former ruling classes and of the middle
classes. Every now and again a good many of them evidently
feel the need for reassuring themselves on that score by deriving
satisfaction from being rude and insulting to foremen in factories, to people they serve in buses or in restaurants, etc. One
of the reasons why it is pleasant to spend holidays in Switzerland
or in Norway is that working class people there have long
reached the stage at which they are able to take their equality
for granted without feeling the need frequently to reassure
themselves that they are really equals by being rude to the
public. Perhaps that stage will be reached also in this country
sooner or later, but by the look of things one hardly dare to
hope that it will be in our lifetime.

Another manifestation of the 'we are the masters now' spirit
is the frequent attempt by trade unions to overrule the verdict
of the electorate by defying Government policies endorsed by
the electorate and by trying to dictate policies in a sense that
differs from the intention of the Government in office. Trade
union Members of Parliament are a powerful pressure group
in the House of Commons. They receive guidance from trade
unions that had financed their election. Many of the Members
are still on their payroll or their former jobs as trade union
officials are kept open for them. Since most decisions at
trade union meetings are taken by a small fraction of the
membership because the majority never attend such meetings,
this influence is far from democratic. Occasionally our new

masters even went so far as to defy the judiciary, for instance in the notorious case of Smithfield porters. In another instance a certain trade union threatened a strike because one of its members was convicted of theft. Another group of workers threatened to strike on one occasion in protest against the reinforcement of measures against pilfering.

It is a thousand pities that trade unions are unable to make better use of their power for good, even though it has increased to the same extent as their power for evil. They fail to render the immense service they are in a position to render, not only to the community but in the first place to their own members, by encouraging an increase of productivity rather than preventing it. Instead of doing their best to discourage indolence and selfish greed that is a grave obstacle to progress, they organise such anti-social attitude systematically. If only they adopted constructive policies they could enable Britain to achieve expansion without inflation, or at any rate with the minimum degree of inflation, so that there would be no need for the Government to resort to deflationary measures from time to time, thereby delaying progress and bringing about setbacks. No matter how powerful trade unions may be, they are unable to safeguard their own members in the long run from the disadvantages inflicted on them by the inexorable economic trends generated by their own indolence and greed.

Workers who do their job really well and contribute according to their means towards the welfare of the community have no need to display arrogance. They can indeed take it for granted that they are absolutely equal to any class in the community. They have every reason to feel genuine and justified pride for being useful and indispensable members of society. Instead of unwarranted conceit, they would have the respect of the community they serve. Why must they live on the memories of past insults and grievances? Even workers of the post-war generation, possibly more than pre-war workers, seem to feel impelled to get their own back for those insults and grievances, although they date from another world which will never return.

CHAPTER THIRTEEN

TOLPUDDLE IN REVERSE

In 1834 six Tolpuddle farm labourers were sentenced to transportation to Australia for the offence of 'conspiring against trade' by forming a trade union. The victims of this cruel attempt to strangle the trade union movement have gone down in history as 'the Tolpuddle Martyrs'.

In 1968 one of the trade unions took drastic action to strangle likewise a new movement initiated by five typists employed by a Surbiton industrial firm, threatening them and those who followed their example with grave penalties, because of their offence of trying to 'back Britain' in flagrant disregard of the basic trade unionist principle to give employers and the community as little as possible in return for getting as much as possible out of them.

Had the typists and their fellow-workers who shared their desire to 'back Britain' persisted in their attitude they might have had to pay a heavy penalty for their public-spirited action and might have gone down in history as 'the Surbiton martyrs'. Nobody could possibly contest that the attempt to work longer hours for the same pay was at least as much in accordance with the public interest in 1968 as the attempt to form a trade union had been in 1834. Both attempts were checked, nevertheless, by the respective ruling classes of the day.

The successors of the oppressed of 1834 have become the oppressors of 1968. Although they did not possess the power to sentence the typists of Surbiton to transportation for their offence of 'conspiring' against a sacred trade union principle, they certainly conveyed the impression of being prepared to go to the limits of their present-day power, just as the oppressors of 1834 had gone to the limits of their much more formidable power. It is only fair to admit that in both instances the oppressors acted in good faith according to their lights. They acted in defence of the classes whose sectional interests they conceived it to be their duty to serve, by using means which they conceived to be justified, to serve the end they deemed to be justified. Both magistrates of 1834 and trade unionists of 1968 acted simply in accordance with the spirit of their respective times.

Thank goodness the spirit that prevailed in the early 19th century changed soon after the Tolpuddle judgment of 1834, to such an extent that in response to a national outcry the victims were pardoned two years later. Their 'martyrdom' had been of brief duration. There is unfortunately no likelihood of a repetition of that aspect of history in case anyone should be brave enough to emulate the Surbiton would-be backers of Britain. For this time there was no nation-wide outcry against the threat of victimisation. Possibly if they had defied the trade union and if they had lost their jobs in consequence, there might have been a wave of protests. As it was, their eventual acceptance of the ban on 'backing Britain' seems to have firmly established the principle that members of trade unions are forbidden to try to serve the public interest if it conflicts with the immediate interests of the trade union concerned.

Needless to say, the Donovan Report ignores the Surbiton incident altogether. Dealing with the broad principle of trade union members' right to appeal against expulsion from their unions or against other penalties, the Royal Commission admitted that there was a case for setting up an independent review body to enable the victims to appeal. But, having regard to the present spirit of the times, it is very much to be doubted whether such a body would be sufficiently independent-minded ever to risk antagonising the entire trade union movement by upholding the right of members to disregard trade union principles merely because those principles conflict with the public interest.

The same ruthless despotism that aimed at strangling the primitive trade union movement at Tolpuddle is now applied in reverse by that self-same trade union movement, having long passed the stage at which it changed its role from that of the oppressed victim to that of the despot. No doubt the trade unionists who have intervened so effectively to strangle the 'I'm backing Britain' movement are satisfied that they have done what they conceived to be their duty, in preventing some employees from trying to help their country in a modest way by giving their firm extra work without extra pay. Likewise, the Tolpuddle magistrates must have felt self-righteous for having succeeded in checking a movement which appeared to be against the interests of the class whose interests they represented.

Historians dealing with the Tolpuddle incident and contemporary commentators dealing with the Surbiton incident are wrong in pillorying individuals who simply acted in accordance with the spirit of their times. Viewed in retrospect, the judgment delivered by the magistrates in 1834 now appears to be shocking. We can only hope that, in a century or much less, the intervention of trade unionists in the Surbiton incident will appear to be equally shocking, thanks to the change in the spirit of the times that might, and should, take place.

Meanwhile the extent to which such despotic acts by trade unions enjoy immunity from criticism is really amazing. They are indeed the new privileged class. In Parliament very few Members on either side of the House ever dare to be outspoken in their criticism of trade union policies and behaviour. Even many Conservative Members of rural constituencies, who do not depend on the trade unionist vote, hesitate to offend trade unions. The way in which some members of the Donovan Committee, who surely ought to know better, have lent their authority to a report amounting to an apologia for the unions and an indictment of employers speaks for itself.

Although trade unions are subject to occasional criticism in the Press, the sum total of such criticism falls considerably short of what their behaviour and that of their members deserves. Two or three industrial firms had been subjected to a torrent of abuse in Parliament and in the Press for having overcharged on their contracts with the Government. But the sum total of the amounts involved is an infinitesimal fraction of the losses suffered by the Government and by nationalised industries as a result of overcharging by means of unearned wage increases forced upon them by trade unions.

Apologists for trade union tyranny claim that, since trade union members and their families represent a very high percentage of the total population, their dictatorship has democratic foundations. Like Louis XIV they claim that they *are* the State. Nothing could be further from the truth. It is true, trade union decisions are usually taken by majority vote. But on most occasions the large majority of members just can't be bothered to attend meetings and to exercise their rights to vote on resolutions. Vital decisions are usually taken by an insignificant minority of the members. To give an instance based on first-hand experience, during the seventeen years of the author's membership of the Parliamentary branch of the National Union of Journalists he only attended a single branch meeting. He voted against the official resolution, which was passed by two votes against one.

Since militant members are more likely to attend meetings than moderates, the chances are that decisions which are binding for all members are very often taken by a militant minority representing a negligible fraction of the total membership. They don't even represent their own union, let alone the workers affected by their decision or the people as a whole.

The militant wing of trade unions is strongly represented on their Councils and Committees and their nominees stand a better chance of being chosen as union officials. The officials, once elected, have in many situations much more influence on the affairs of their unions than Government officials have on public administration. It is to the interest of trade union officials to press for the maximum of concessions for the benefit of their unions even if they are intelligent and fairminded enough to realise that their demands are not warranted by the earning capacity of the firms or industries concerned, or by the general economic situation. But unless they are tough bargainers they cannot depend on the support of the active militant minority on which their position and promotion prospects largely depend.

Moreover, membership of trade unions depends largely on the extent to which they are capable of obtaining satisfaction for exaggerated claims. As in many instances workers are in a position to choose between joining alternative unions, in such situations the rival unions seek to outdo each other in pressing employers to grant the maximum of unwarranted advantages. The trade union that behaves in a reasonable and public-spirited manner is liable to lose members in favour of the more militant and less public-spirited union. And, if unions are unable to extort from their firms more concessions than the firms would be prepared to concede on the merits of their case, the employees may not deem it worth their while to pay trade union subscriptions — unless of course the firm is a 'closed shop'.

What a complete change within the space of 130 years! At the time of the Tolpuddle trial workers were at the mercy of the ruling classes of the day, who felt justified in misusing their strong position at the expense of the weaker section of the community. Today the trade unions *are* the ruling classes in an economic sense and to a very large degree in a political sense too, and they feel equally justified in misusing their strong position at the expense of weaker sections of the community which are very largely at their mercy. Their influence on the Government of the day is considerable, because of the pressure group of trade union Members of Parliament referred to in earlier chapters. The influence of the Parliamentary Industrial Group during the 'twenties — popularly known as 'the forty thieves' — representing employers under the Tory Governments, was negligible compared with the influence of this well-organised group under any Government today. Under a Labour Government even Ministers are liable to be influenced subconsciously by their hopes that, should they lose their Ministerial posts, they could return to their former trade unions.

Beyond doubt in the past a great many industrialists and other employers had grossly misused their power over the workers they had employed, and the Governments and Parliaments of that period had unpardonably failed to provide them with adequate safeguards against such abuses. Today bosses are no longer in a position to abuse their power, indeed they are hardly even masters in their own firms. To the extent to which they had abused their power in the past this change has been unquestionably in the right direction. Unfortunately the new despotism is no better than the old one had been, only its burden now falls on different shoulders — not only on the shoulders of employers directly concerned but also on those of the public which is very often the ultimate victim of trade union tyranny.

The *raison d'être* of trade unions is to defend the legitimate interests of their members. If only they confined their activities to this they would render a valuable service not only to their members but to the community as a whole. But they act on the principle of 'my union right or wrong' or even 'my union can do no wrong'. They aim at extorting the maximum of advantages for their members at the expense of the community regardless of whether their claims are justified or not. They now interfere with the functions of managements to an extent that is gravely detrimental to productivity. The indiscriminate support they give to their members in conflict with managements is detrimental to the minimum degree of industrial discipline required in the interest of efficient production. And the feeling that workers can always depend on being backed up by their unions encourages bloody-minded attitudes.

In former days there used to be a favourite saying of employees: 'If only I could win the football pool I could afford to tell my boss exactly what I think of him.' Recently a factory-owner, exasperated by the bloody-minded behaviour of his workers and by their aggressive reactions to even the mildest degree of criticism, exclaimed: 'If only I could win the football pool I could afford to tell my workers exactly what I think of them.' He explained that to reprimand them, or even to criticise their work, is liable to prove to be an expensive luxury, for their response to the slightest real or imagined affront is apt to be a wildcat strike. When the owner of a small industrial firm made a mildly critical remark about his workers turning up half an hour or an hour after the time they were supposed to start work they all downed tools and refused to resume work unless their boss apologised to them. Every day employers or their representatives have to take decisions balancing the certain losses suffered through slack working against the possibly bigger losses that would result from a lightning strike in response to their criticism of slack working. Very often unofficial strikes are actually encouraged by trade union officials who are reluctant openly to dishonour recently signed agreements.

Trade unions impose their tyranny on workers who are forced against their will to join the unions and to submit to decisions which they consider to be wrong from the point of view of the public interest and, taking the long view, also from the point of view of their own interests. In many instances the principle of the 'closed shop' is enforced — an attitude encouraged by the Donovan Report, which is also firmly opposed to reinforcing existing inadequate measures against unofficial strikes. As the experience of the five Surbiton typists shows, a trade union is well in a position to stop any action by its members — or even by non-members through pressure on their employers — if they do not conform to its policy. For instance, any worker who refuses to join in an official strike is liable to be expelled and declared 'black' which might make it difficult for him to find future employment.

Needless to say, trade unions are not always keen on enforcing compliance with their decisions by their members. Those who refuse to strike are liable to be subjected to strict disciplinary action even if they are not actually expelled. But those who disobey their union by engaging in unofficial strikes in defiance of instructions from the union need never lose any

sleep through worry over the consequences of their dis-
obedience.

Unions unhesitatingly inflict major hardships on the public
even for the sake of securing minor concessions for their
members. Very often the extent of the advantages gained as
a result of a strike is quite negligible compared with the extent
of the inconvenience and of the losses suffered by the ultimate
victims who are no party to the dispute and are not in a position
to influence its outcome one way or another. More often than
not it is the public that pays the cost of labour disputes, not
only because of the hardships it has to suffer during strikes
but also because the increase of costs resulting from the settlements of labour disputes is almost invariably passed on nowadays to the consumer. Indeed their ability to inflict grave
hardships on the public is the principal bargaining weapon
of the unions. They seek to enforce their anti-social claims
with the aid of anti-social means.

Trade union tyranny determines major trends in the national
economy. It sets the pace of wage inflation, for the relative
importance of wage claims has increased to such an extent that
it has become the dominant factor in the trend of prices. In
the past monetary policy, by restricting the volume of funds
available for wage increases and by discouraging employers
from giving way too easily, was in a position to restrain wage
inflation. But amidst conditions prevailing in the 'fifties and
'sixties, as a result of the adoption of the policy of full employment, monetary policy has been subordinated to requirements
created by wage increases.

In a Presidential address delivered to Section F of the British
Association in Bristol in September 1955, Professor Sir John
Hicks stated that since the last war Britain has been on what
he called the 'labour standard'. The author would prefer to
call this system the 'wage standard', but the name is im-
material. What matters is that the value of money is no longer
determined by the quantity of gold or by that of bank credit,
but by the trend of wages. Professor Hicks warns against the
evil effects of a rapid rate of wage inflation resulting from the

operation of the system in which the operating forces have a
strongly one-sided tendency.   Monetary policy simply adapts
itself willy-nilly to changes in the wage level resulting from
wage bargains.

It is true, on repeated occasions in recent years this process
was interrupted by credit squeezes leading to temporary unemployment and discouraging, for the time being, excessive
wage demands, without checking them altogether.   But since
such credit squeezes, and also wage restraints, are always
abandoned as soon as they are beginning to become effective,
it remains true that the trend of prices is dictated in the long
run by the increased bargaining power of the trade unions
and by the increasing misuse of that bargaining power to
secure anti-social unearned wage increases.

The caprices of nature which, by largely determining the
volume of the current gold output, determined the volume of
currency in the past, no longer dictate the trend of prices.
Nor is the power of bankers, or of the Central Bankers and
Treasury officials, to regulate the volume of bank credit able
to override the power of trade unions.   It is the latter who
determine the trend of prices, and the authorities and bankers
have to adapt the volume of bank credit to the increased credit
requirements resulting from the increase of wages.   Politicians
who want to keep on the right side of the unions would think
twice before attempting to curtail their power to determine
the pace of inflation in the long run by keeping the volume of
credit short of requirements.   That power is only limited by
the operation of economic laws.   No doubt, if they could, trade
unionists would follow the example of the petty African despot
in Evelyn Waugh's *Black Mischief*, who issued a decree abolishing the law of supply and demand, or of King Canute calling
a halt to the incoming tide.   Their action would be equally
ineffective, however.

One of the things against which trade union tyranny is
powerless is the development of discrepancies between wage
levels in this country and abroad, leading to balance of payments deficits.   What matters is not the arithmetical difference

between the actual wage levels which might well be lower here than in some other countries. Allowance must be made, however, for the difference between the productivity of labour. British labour is less productive partly because capital equipment is inferior to that used in the United States and, to a much less extent, in some other countries, but mainly because the British worker is less inclined to give a fair day's work for his pay.

Trade union tyranny is responsible for both causes of the relative unproductivity of British labour. We saw in earlier chapters that modernisation of capital equipment in Britain is delayed by the attitude of trade unions towards it. As for the relative inadequacy of the British worker's contribution towards the productive effort, it is attributable almost entirely to the trade unions.

The attitude of unorganised labour is necessarily influenced by that of organised labour. Wage levels achieved by the latter thanks to their superior bargaining power come to be applied more or less to workers who don't belong to trade unions. Nor is trade union tyranny confined any longer to unions representing physical labour. White-collared workers had been for a long time at a disadvantage, but now the increase of salaries keeps pace more or less with that of wages. Even bodies representing technicians and senior employees in key positions have acquired a taste for holding the community to ransom, having discovered that in spite of their small number they are in a position to interrupt production. In recent years we have witnessed strikes by employees who are in the surtax-paying class — such as airline pilots — or very near to it. The behaviour of all these classes has become demoralised by the greed of industrial workers.

However, in spite of the gross abuse of power by trade unions, the present position is infinitely preferable to that of the old days when workers were at the mercy of their employers. Bentham's principle that the supreme end is to ensure the highest degree of happiness to the largest number is still fundamental. But precisely because one believes in this, one must condemn trade unions for misusing their power to secure minor temporary advantages instead of taking a broader view and co-operating whole-heartedly with employers and with the Government in the interest of greatly accelerated expansion for the permanent benefit of all. Their attitude hinders the achievement of the highest degree of happiness by the largest number, instead of assisting it. At times it is even gravely detrimental to the welfare and happiness of their own members.

In 1968 a trade union took action that conceivably torpedoed the attempt made by employees of the British Eagle International Airlines when it got into financial difficulties. Being desperately anxious to save their jobs as well as to save the firm they were genuinely fond of, they declared themselves prepared to work for a greatly reduced pay. But their trade union firmly objected to this generous gesture. Rigid observance of the rules was apparently more important to it than the welfare of its members.

Possibly even the sacrifice offered by the staff might not have saved the firm. But the trade union went out of its way to ensure that it is not saved at the cost of permitting its members to cut temporarily trade union rates of pay. No doubt the trade union leaders concerned felt as self-righteous as the Tolpuddle magistrates that they were doing what they conceived to be their duty, by acting in accordance with the spirit of their times. Whether the employees, as they were queuing for jobs at the Labour Exchange, shared their elected leaders' satisfaction over their success in forcing the men whose interest they claimed to represent is quite another question.

CHAPTER FOURTEEN

ANTI-SOCIAL SOCIALISTS

THE title of this chapter may appear to be, on the face of it, a contradiction in terms — something like 'anti-Catholic Popes' or 'anti-Royalist Kings'. What this paradoxical title is trying to convey is that, although Socialism aims at securing absolute priority for social considerations over economic considerations — to the detriment of both in the long run and sometimes even in the short run — British Socialists very often disregard even social considerations proper. They want to accelerate the trend towards a higher standard of living of the masses with the aid of policies which are gravely detrimental to economic progress. Even though their policy may appear to gain temporary advantages for the masses, by slowing down expansion it does not serve their true interests.

To suggest that Socialists — at any rate the British variety of them — are anti-social is like suggesting that Socialists, in their capacity of representatives of the interests of the masses, are against themselves. But that is precisely what the title of this chapter and its argument deliberately mean to convey. Socialists, by subordinating economic considerations completely or at any rate unduly to social considerations, render a grave disservice to all social classes, including the working classes and lower income groups, the interests of which they profess to serve at the expense of all other social classes by aiming at an increase in their standard of living. But that aim cannot be achieved without an increase in production.

Socialists often accuse non-Socialists of being 'anti-social'. It is high time to fling that accusation back at them.

There are four methods of ensuring the working of an

economy and promoting its progress towards achieving a higher standard of living:

(1) The method under which workers feel impelled to exert themselves for fear of losing their jobs and of being unable to find other jobs.

(2) The incentive method under which workers increase their output, for the sake of obtaining higher wages.

(3) The totalitarian method under which workers are forced to exert themselves for fear of severe penalties for slackness and inefficiency.

(4) The method under which workers are persuaded to do their best for the benefit of the community even in the absence of totalitarian compulsion or of a risk of unemployment or of special incentives.

There are of course many intermediate methods combining the four formulas to a varying degree. In a democratic country the choice is between inducing workers to exert themselves because of their fear of unemployment, or in return for higher pay, or because they are made to realise that it is to their own interests to contribute towards the welfare of the community. We propose to deal with incentive in the form of higher pay later in this chapter and also in Chapter 16. It will be seen that mere promises to increase output in return for higher wages do not produce satisfactory results. Unless workers respond to exhortations or are prepared to conclude and carry out productivity agreements the only effective way in which they can be induced to put in a fair day's work for their pay is actual or potential unemployment.

If we lived in an ideal world the method of persuasion would work satisfactorily. It is a pity human beings are not like bees or ants who work, presumably even without exhortation, selflessly and with the utmost zeal for the good of their communities. That inclination to work does exist in some countries, if not to the same extent as in beehives or antheaps, at any rate to a reasonable degree. Unfortunately the British are not among these peoples. If we disregard at this stage the complex problem of productivity agreements, the only way in which to ensure adequate economic progress in Britain is to persuade British workers that it is to their interest to be public-spirited, and to make them realise that inadequacy of their efforts is detrimental to their standard of living and might even entail large-scale unemployment, not because of any deliberate policy to that end but because of the economic consequences of their own behaviour.

The success of a democratic country in maintaining full employment permanently depends on the extent to which it is possible to persuade workers, not to sacrifice their self-interests for the common good, but to adopt an attitude of *enlightened* self-interest instead of continuing their present attitude of *unenlightened* self-interest. Surely there ought to be a way to make them realise that it is in accordance with their true interests in the long run, in the medium run, and sometimes even in the short run, to do their best to ensure an increase in output to the utmost limit of possibility. This might appear to them to conflict with their apparent self-interest in the short run, which makes it appear convenient for them to work as little as possible in return for the highest possible pay.

In order to realise that it is to their interests to subordinate such short-run considerations to the interests of increased production they need not even become unselfish and patriotic. It would be amply sufficient if they were to become intelligently selfish instead of remaining unintelligently selfish. The reason why the economic effort of the Labour Government during 1964–68 was an almost unmitigated failure is that exhortations addressed by official spokesmen to trade union leaders and to workers in general have failed to produce the desired results. This was because most of the millions who voted for Labour in 1964 and in 1966 had done so not because they were eager to do something for the community but because they were eager to get something out of the community — more pay for less work or for no work at all, increasing dependence on the community for providing them with increasingly good living.

F

There is indeed very little idealistic Socialism in the British Labour movement today. Yet in the absence of idealistic or materialistic willingness to serve the community fears of unemployment are the only effective incentive to work. In the absence of such fears very few Socialists are prepared to make sacrifices in the form of intensified efforts or self-restraint in order to serve the interests of the community. It is disappointing that so many young people in Britain are enthusiastic supporters of the British brand of Socialism the aim of which is to scrounge on the State, to quote the term coined by a Socialist Minister. If even youth has ceased to be idealistic to such an extent how can one expect the older generation of Socialists to want to serve the community?

In the present-day Britain trade unionists behave like the 'economic man' of the classical economists. The *homo oeconomicus* is an abstract human being invented by early economists, who pursues his economic self-interests, in total disregard for any other considerations, by aiming at obtaining the maximum of benefit in return for a minimum of effort. In more recent economic literature this concept came to be denounced and ridiculed as being utterly absurd and unrealistic. It was contended that in real life most people are apt to depart from the rule for some non-economic consideration for the sake of which they are apt to be content with less than the maximum reward in return for more than a minimum of effort. Yet if classical economists who based their theories on the assumption that all human beings are 'economic men' lived today they would find their theory completely vindicated. For a very high proportion of British trade union members are perfect living examples of the theoretical 'economic man'.

The existence of such specimens would only be justifiable on the assumption made by classical economists that the unrestricted pursuit of self-interest by all members of the community necessarily works out for the benefit of the community. That assumption is certainly not shared by Socialists. Yet they share with Conservatives the responsibility for the conversion of the British worker into the perfect 'economic man' during the 'fifties and 'sixties, as a result of two decades of pampering by politicians.

Trade unions organise individual selfishness and greed into collective selfishness and greed. Their members may be willing to subordinate — or, to be more exact, to co-ordinate — their personal interests with those of their fellow-members of the same union. Beyond that they are utterly indifferent even to the welfare of their fellow-workers in other unions, let alone to that of workers outside the unions, or of the public at large, including old-age pensioners — whose interests they are only prepared to further at the expense of other classes — or of their country. They aim at contracting out of any reverses that their community is liable to suffer as a result of their behaviour, and they are short-sighted enough to believe that it is possible for them to do so.

This attitude is utterly anti-social. The author cannot claim credit or take the blame for inventing this unconventional use of the term 'anti-social'. He first came across it years ago in an article condemning the workers of one of the London docks as anti-social, because they had not been interested in the least in the effects of their unofficial strike on the community, and because they just could not care less about anyone apart from themselves, their families and their trade union. The article appeared in the *New Statesman*, not exactly a reactionary publication.

Group selfishness is even more anti-social than individual selfishness, because it is incomparably more effective. In Communist countries group-selfishness of trade unions is not permitted. Their sectional interests are ruthlessly subordinated to the overriding interests of the State. This result is achieved by totalitarian methods of intimidation, fortunately unacceptable to democratic peoples. It is very much an open question whether by forcing totalitarian discipline on trade unions in Britain it would be possible to increase production. The fact that it has proved to be possible in countries with a low

standard of living such as Russia and China does not prove
that it would be possible in countries which have already
attained a much higher standard of living.

In any case it seems to be the opinion of the overwhelming
majority of British workers — judging by the diminutive size
of the British Communist Party — that they would not be
prepared to achieve an increase of their standard of living at
the cost of sacrificing their individual freedom. Even if they
were certain that their material well-being could be improved
to a higher degree under a totalitarian regime — which is
indeed doubtful — it is certain that they would be less happy
than they are under freedom, if they had to tremble each time
they would hear the approach of heavy footsteps outside their
front door. After all, a high standard of living is not an end in
itself but merely a means to the supreme end of human happiness.

One of the main reasons why the Government finds it so
difficult to persuade the workers to be less anti-social lies in
the basic character of traditional Socialist propaganda. For
many generations the workers have been told that their
welfare depends on their success in achieving a more equitable
distribution of the national income. Admittedly, it is possible
up to a point to increase the workers' share in the national
income without increasing the size of the national income.
But redistribution has limits beyond which it is bound to act
as a disincentive, thereby handicapping increases in production,
and it might even cause its reduction. A really substantial
increase in the workers' share could only be achieved through
a substantial increase in the size of the whole national income.
But British Socialism is essentially redistributionist and pays
scant attention to the possibilities of securing benefits for
workers through an accelerated increase in output instead
of depending on further redistribution of a slowly-increasing
national income.

Unfortunately the idea of redistribution has an infinitely
stronger popular appeal than the idea of higher productivity.
For recipients of additional income through redistribution

have not only the satisfaction of getting more for their unchanged or diminished work but the additional satisfaction that their employers are getting less. It is sad but true that the attitude of far too many Socialists is 'It does not matter so much if I can't get it so long as nobody else can'.

Since the War redistribution has made considerable progress and there is much less scope for its further progress. But Socialists refuse to admit this. They believe in 'soaking the rich' instead of contributing their share to the increase in productivity. Of course promises to increase productivity have been found a very useful bargaining counter with the aid of which it is possible to induce employers to concede wage increases and to make other concessions. But in practice the large majority of agreements to that effect proved to be worth less than the paper on which they were written. Undertakings to increase productivity in return for wage concessions are only too often dishonoured. Yet many employers are unable to resist the temptation of accepting such promises, if only as a face-saving device by which they can justify otherwise un-warranted concessions before their shareholders, their customers and even before their own selves.

The additional inflation created by wage increases granted in return for paper promises of future increases of productivity instead of making the wage increases conditional on actual accomplished increases in output recalls the inflation in Goethe's *Faust* (Part II) when Mephistopheles persuades the Emperor to solve his financial difficulties by issuing paper money that is to be redeemed by gold that is at present in the bowels of the earth and is to be mined in the future. The following is a free translation and adaptation of Goethe's text to our present-day conditions:

> Let it be known by all this may concern:
> Ask for a rise, more money you shall earn.
> You just promise to raise your output sure,
> Your money's worth your promise will secure.
> Just spend the new cash now, it is the scheme
> Some day the goods might come, it to redeem.

To quote a historical example nearer home, the French revolutionary Government during the 1790s issued *assignats* secured by the proceeds of the confiscated estates. Although the value of that money had more realistic security than the money spent by workers in anticipation of a dubious future increase in their output, it ended by depreciation of the notes to next to nothing.

Understandably, workers don't like increases in productivity, because they are afraid that it might lead to redundancy. Hence the restrictive practices with the aid of which productivity is kept down deliberately. But the price paid for avoiding temporary unemployment caused by redundancy is a considerable and permanent slowing down of progress. This result is produced by the unions also through preventing modernisation — for instance by resisting the use of fork lift trucks. If resistance to automation in Britain at a time when it proceeds unhampered elsewhere is not anti-social, it is difficult to understand what the meaning of the term is. Although urging employers all the time to modernise their plants, at the same time trade unions have been fighting stern rearguard actions against modernisation.

This prevention of modernisation is almost as anti-social as the destruction of machinery by Luddites had been, with considerably less justification. During the early part of the 19th century the workers displaced by machinery had been virtually condemned to starvation. Today they are given a 'silver handshake' out of the Redundancy Fund. The author claims to be among the first to advocate such compensation in his *Economic Consequences of Automation* published in 1956, and he still feels that there is every justification for it, in spite of the fact that it is not difficult in existing conditions of full employment for the victims of automation to find alternative employment long before they have spent the compensation.

Attempts to justify resistance to redundancy with the aid of restrictive practices on the ground of the moderate increase of unemployment in 1966–68 carry little conviction in the light of the fact that during the long years of overfull employment those restrictive practices were fully maintained and even reinforced.

The most important anti-social way in which trade unions are responsible for delaying progress is by enforcing demands for unearned wage increases. The inflationary effect of creating additional consumer purchasing power without creating a corresponding amount of additional goods, and the resulting diversion of goods from exports to domestic consumption, compels the Government from time to time to adopt deflationary measures leading to stagnation of production or even to actual setbacks. Surely it is anti-social to create situations in which progress must be interrupted. It would be highly beneficial from both economic and social points of view if this could be avoided by keeping wage increases from exceeding increases in productivity.

It is of course even more important that wage increases should not be allowed to lag behind increases in output, because otherwise the experience of the inter-war slump, which was incomparably worse than the post-war inflationary boom, might repeat itself. For this reason the increase in the bargaining power of the trade unions is in a sense a blessing in disguise, provided that it is not abused, because its normal use is the best safeguard against the recurrence of the slump experienced in the 'thirties as a result of under-consumption. But if it is grossly abused, as it is in Britain in the 'sixties, it is liable to create a situation in which deflationary measures might lead to a slump.

This is a consideration which appears to be ignored by industrial workers and by their leaders. Since relapse into mass-unemployment is the worst evil that can befall the workers any behaviour that is liable to produce such a disastrous result is anti-social. It is not economists who favour a permanent unemployment pool, or those who favour deflationary measures in face of inflated consumer demand, who menace full employment. It is the potential victims themselves, who, by their anti-social behaviour, expose themselves and their fellow-workers to the risk of a return of large-scale unemployment, who are their own worst enemies.

Wage inflation is anti-social not only because it forces the Government to resort to deflationary measures from time to time but also because the resulting rise in the cost of living hurts the most defenceless sectors of the community — old-age pensioners and others with fixed or inelastic small incomes.

Another manifestation of the anti-social attitude of trade unions is the frequency of clashes arising from inter-union rivalries, which are often fought with utmost bitterness. Relationship between employers and employees is positively affectionate compared with relationship between rival unions. Borderline disputes lead to prolonged strikes in face of which employers are quite helpless. The terms of their settlement, under which two or more men belonging to the rival unions are allotted to do one man's work. This increases the cost of production, in addition to aggravating the scarcity of labour. It prevents or slows down the increase of output. The unearned incomes resulting from the settlement of borderline disputes constitute sheer inflation. In shipyards and elsewhere employers have to accept arrangements under which one man is doing the work while two men, belonging to different unions, are watching him on full pay. One hears of instances in which the adoption of modern machinery would have made it possible for two men to do the work formerly done by eight, but the union insisted on retaining all the eight and were opposed even to transferring the superfluous six men to other parts of the factory which were short of labour. As the new equipment occupied more space, additional space had to be provided at considerable expense to make room for the six idlers.

At Stewarts & Lloyds the application of a labour-saving method of handling steel tubes was held up for some eighteen months by a borderline dispute. Such examples could be multiplied; they are encountered all too frequently by regular readers of newspapers.

One has yet to hear of a trade unionist or a Socialist who is decently ashamed of himself for such a disgraceful anti-social abuse of trade union power. While reluctantly admitting (in private conversation) that such waste of labour is perhaps not quite right, they usually add that the men's desire to safeguard themselves against redundancy is perfectly understandable and legitimate. It would have been understandable during periods of large-scale unemployment, when the loss of job might have meant years on the dole, but even then it increased the difficulty of emerging from the depression, so that, taking a long view, it was against the best interests of the industrial workers. But amidst conditions prevailing most of the time in the 'fifties and 'sixties, when in most instances redundant workers had only to cross the road to find another job, and when increased social service benefits safeguarded them against the worst consequences of unemployment during the short time while it lasted, the practice has been absolutely anti-social.

If the mental effort expended on finding excuses for the inexcusable had been expended on finding a solution no doubt a solution would have been found long before now. What is wrong, for instance, with a formula under which the unions concerned in a borderline dispute would agree that members of one union should do the disputed job in one shipyard, members of the second union in the second shipyard and members of the third union in the third shipyard? But when the author tentatively suggested this solution to a trade unionist he was told that its application might necessitate changes of residence by many of the men to other districts. He was severely rebuked for his inhumanity for wanting to inflict such grave inconvenience on the 'victims' of such an arrangement. No doubt in order to spare them such inconvenience his critic would prefer the men concerned to continue to receive their wages without doing a stroke of work for the rest of their lives, or until they retired on a well-earned old-age pension provided for them by the grateful community as a reward for their services rendered to it by keeping down output and causing an increase in the cost of production.

The anti-social solution of anti-social borderline disputes places British shipyards and other industries at a grave disadvantage against their foreign rivals. For in no other country

F 2

does such an amazing practice exist. It is looked upon abroad as a typically British practice and as one of the most flagrant manifestations of the 'English disease'. The way in which such arrangements are accepted over here as a matter of course is yet another indication of the debasement of the British character.

> Would you be kept in idleness?
> Would you give up work for good?
> Why ask such a silly question?
> By my blooming oath, I WOULD!

British industrial workers during the 'sixties — to be fair, no Gallup Poll has ever been taken to find out what proportion of them — would gladly perpetuate the state of affairs under which they draw wages without doing a stroke of work. They don't find this degrading. They don't have the least urge or even the least inclination to make themselves useful to the community. Trade unions are largely to blame for that mentality.

Another way in which the anti-social attitude of British trade unions has handicapped progress is through its discouraging effect on capital investment. Excessive redistribution of income — which they have succeeded in enforcing just at a time when other industrial countries have stepped up the pace of modernisation of their industries — increases the relative proportion of consumption and reduces the relative proportion of investment, not only by reducing profits available for ploughing back into the firm but also by discouraging modernisation. Narrower profit margins resulting from higher unearned wages and from higher direct taxation favoured by Socialists generate a feeling of growing reluctance to take a risk by investing in unproven enterprise and in innovations. Trade unions and Socialists in general criticise employers for the inadequacy of the amount of capital per man employed, which is admittedly much lower than in the United States, and, according to the Brookings Report, in many other countries. But who is to blame for the reluctance of British firms to sink more capital in their factories? American trade unions, while determined to safeguard the interests of their members, are intelligent enough to realise that it is to their interest to give employers a chance to make enough profit to provide an incentive for increased investment. Above all, as we saw earlier, trade unions in Britain actually resist the installation of labour-saving machinery.

The way in which British trade unions endeavour to create artificial scarcity of manpower is nothing if not flagrantly anti-social. Millions of men and women are under-worked because of restrictive practices on their individual output and especially on the activities of mates, as admitted even by the Donovan Report. Restrictions on the intake of new labour prevent employers from increasing their output even through the employment of more hands. Limitation on new entrants, prevention of men and women qualified for retirement benefits from continuing in their jobs without forfeiting the whole or part of their pensions — a rule forced by the trade unions on the Attlee Government, it is claimed, in the pensioners' own interests — are some of the ways in which trade unions deliberately accentuate the scarcity of labour for the sake of exploiting the scarcity-value of their members.

Surely it is anti-social for trade unions to resist the employment of women in some factories. Surely it is anti-social to pursue policies resulting in a slowing down or limitation of production, and at the same time to increase the share of those responsible for preventing the increase of production. Surely it is anti-social for the majorities within the unions to secure special advantages for themselves, thereby forcing the victimised minorities to form splinter unions to safeguard their special interests. The multiplicity of trade unions with which British firms have to deal is one of the major sources of difficulty, because a strike by any one of the splinter unions is liable to bring the work to a halt.

Whenever the Government of the day feels impelled by wage inflation, because of its effect on the balance of payments and on sterling, to resort to measures which cause unemployment, the arrogance of trade unionists becomes curiously mingled with self-pity. They are surprised and shocked at the absence of evidence of much public sympathy outside their own circle for the victims of the measures which their own behaviour forces the Government to adopt. But there is always ample evidence of public sympathy for the men who lose their jobs through inevitable redundancy resulting from progress towards more efficient methods of production. Yet trade unions have to a large extent usually only themselves to blame even for the hardship caused to their members by redundancy resulting from automation or the adoption of other forms of labour-saving devices. They exert the utmost pressure on employers even during periods of full employment to prevent them from releasing workers made redundant by such modernisation. As a result the workers have to be released on the occasion of the next recession when employers can no longer afford to continue to 'hoard' them. While the redundant men could have easily found alternative employment if they had been dismissed during a boom, they might find themselves condemned to prolonged unemployment if, as a result of trade union pressure, their dismissal is deferred until a recession.

This attitude of the trade unions has greatly increased the difficulty of finding a solution of the problem of reconciling the interests of progress with humanitarian considerations. Although trade union pressure to delay the dismissal of men displaced by machines is exerted in order to serve the immediate interests of the men concerned, it is nevertheless anti-social from all but the narrowest point of view. The men have no cause for thanking their unions for ensuring a deferment of their dismissal by a few more months, as a result of which they feel forced eventually to accept re-employment under much less satisfactory circumstances.

CHAPTER FIFTEEN

SANTA CLAUS WORKING OVERTIME

IF only the British worker could be made to realise the full extent to which his conditions have improved during the last twenty years he would duly appreciate the long list of his blessings received instead of taking his present conditions simply for granted. There would then be some hope that his appreciation of what the community has done for him might find expression in the adoption of a less anti-social attitude. As a result, the progress of Britain would be certain to cease to lag behind that of other countries and further improvement of the worker's conditions could be stepped up. There would then be no setbacks at frequent intervals because of the inadequacy of the worker's contribution to the national economic effort. Unfortunately, owing to his lack of realisation or appreciation of the amazing improvement of his conditions, the more the community is doing for him the less he is doing for the community.

The British worker's present attitude towards his employers and towards the community can best be described as one of sullen malevolence that goes at times beyond mere short-sighted selfishness. Before the War such an attitude might have been understandable. Having regard to the harsh treatment of the workers by many employers and by the community itself, he had good reason for feeling bitter and bloody-minded and very little reason for feeling grateful and co-operative. But meanwhile the improvement of their conditions has been truly spectacular.

While younger workers can hardly be blamed for being

unaware of the extent of that improvement, there can be no excuse for survivors of the pre-war generation not to realise or admit the changes compared with pre-war days. It may not be superfluous to remind workers, young and old, of the improvements that have taken place in their conditions during the brief span of three decades:

(1) Real wages have increased very considerably.
(2) There are now more fringe benefits to supplement wages.
(3) Social services have improved beyond recognition.
(4) Much shorter hours are now worked.
(5) The risk of unemployment has become greatly reduced.
(6) Modern equipment has reduced the extent of physical exertion.
(7) Factories and other premises are much more hygienic.
(8) Workers are now entitled to paid holidays.
(9) They now work in more congenial surroundings.
(10) They are entitled to longer notices of dismissal, and their dismissal is not nearly as arbitrary as it had been.
(11) They are now entitled to compensation payments for redundancy.
(12) They have more influence on managerial decisions relating to them.
(13) Their social status has greatly improved.
(14) A great many workers benefit by controlled or subsidised rents.
(15) Hire-purchase facilities and mortgage facilities are now more easily available to them.

This list is by no means complete, but it is sufficient to give an idea of the wide range and considerable extent of the improvements in working-class conditions. To recall the wide variety of ways in which industrial workers are now better off than before the War calls for no apology, because, as pointed out above, judging by their behaviour most of them are either oblivious of the improvements or simply take them for granted in the way they take for granted the air they breathe. It does not occur to them that all these improvements are far beyond the maximum of improvements which even the most optimistic amongst them would have dared to expect to achieve in the lifetime of our generation. Nor does it occur to them that employers, or the community, or consumers, have to bear the costs of these improvements.

The British industrial worker has grown used to receiving everything without any *quid pro quo*. He seems to have come to take it for granted that the Government, the community and the employers have assumed the role of Santa Claus who gives away everything and does not expect anything in return. Indeed, in accordance with the prevailing fashion, Santa Claus has been working overtime in recent years. The British worker has come to assume that all these benefits are due to him, that they are his birthright, so that he does not even have to go through the formal gesture of thanking Santa Claus, let alone trying to reciprocate the benefits. It is his basic attitude to be always dissatisfied with any concession — even if his full demands of the moment are conceded — and to press for additional concessions as soon as his latest claim is met.

Another principle is that British workers are entitled to stipulate that no strings must be attached to the concession. This is strictly in accordance with the spirit that has prevailed since the War — that workers have only rights and no duties towards the community — whenever they put forward new demands. Indeed, incredible as this may sound, it has come to be regarded as something humiliating to have to agree to submit to 'strings'. As a matter of prestige, trade unions want to be in a position to dictate terms of unconditional surrender. They often refuse to allow employers even to save their face by agreeing, purely as a matter of form and with their tongues in their cheeks, to the inclusion of clauses relating to higher productivity or to more constructive behaviour. In a number of instances, however, practical considerations prevailed over arrogance, false pride and prestige — trade unions were willing to accept strings if as a result they were able to secure extra concessions, without the least intention of carrying out their part of the bargain.

Admittedly the greater part of the increase in money wages obtained since the War has been offset by the rise in the cost of living. Even so, the rise in real wages has been quite appreciable in the majority of industries. In any case, workers have themselves to blame if the rise in the cost of living has deprived them of a large part of the benefit derived from higher money wages. If only they had been doing a fair day's work for their increased pay they could have retained the whole of the benefits from the increase in their money wages, or at any rate a very considerable part of it, because the rise in prices — if any — would have been much more moderate.

Wage increases as a result of national agreements and of local 'wage drifts' are by no means the sum total of the unilateral free gifts workers have received from Santa Claus. They have obtained a wide variety of fringe benefits, very often on the initiative of their employers anxious to attract or retain labour. Canteen facilities have greatly improved and prices charged in canteens are kept well under commercial level. Alternatively, firms issue lunch vouchers to their employees and subsidise their meals. Many firms provide extensive recreation and entertainment facilities. The value of such increased benefits should also be borne in mind when comparing present wages with pre-war wages.

Nor indeed should the greatly improved social service benefits provided by the Welfare State be overlooked in connection with such comparisons. Although the workers contribute towards the cost of National Insurance, the bulk of it is provided by the employers and by the Exchequer between them. And increases in the workers' own contributions are also paid ultimately by employers and by the public in the form of wage increases, so that in practice the workers receive the social service benefits without really contributing towards their cost. The National Health Service alone is worth to workers a great deal in terms of saving medical expenses. If they had to pay commercial insurance premiums to cover the benefits they are entitled to under National Insurance it would cost them a great deal.

Likewise the increased cost of the education of their children to the Government and to local authorities must be taken into consideration. Children of working-class families are now given a better start in life and have incomparably better opportunities for advancement than their parents had before the War. Surely that is worth something to industrial workers. The large and increasing number of scholarships to universities and other higher educational establishments provide greatly improved opportunities for men and women of working-class origin to assume professional status or to rise to executive positions. Their close association with students of the middle classes and upper classes goes a long way towards demolishing barriers that had separated classes in the past.

Thanks to the policy of full employment, the risk of unemployment is now incomparably smaller than it was before the War. Apart altogether from the increased unemployment benefits which make unemployment less unbearable if and when it does occur, sharp falls in the workers' incomes through a loss of their job and inability to find another job are much less likely to occur now. This means that even the prudent amongst them do not feel the same degree of need for putting aside part of their earnings in order to build up a reserve for the contingency of unemployment. Likewise, they do not feel the same need for curtailing their current spendings in order to provide for illness and especially for old age. Workers need not necessarily spend now nearly as much, if anything at all, on subsidising their aged parents. As we saw in Chapter 10, a great many of them don't spend anything on it. Children's subsidised school meals also help.

The working week has become reduced quite considerably since the War. Each time there is yet another reduction trade unions ensure that it is not accompanied by any cut in the basic pay, which means that there is an increase in the basic pay per hour. It is true, in a great many instances the shorter working week only means that more overtime is worked, but this means receiving much higher wage rates for the extra hours. Moreover, the basic pay is supposed to suffice for meeting the essential requirements of those who prefer more leisure to more money. This enables workers to take very effective industrial action without having to suffer undue hardship, by banning overtime when they know that their employers are under obligation to complete contracts without delay.

The practice of paid holidays has become all but general during recent years, and the length of paid holidays tends to increase. This, together with the reduction of physical exertion thanks to the adoption of modern equipment in many factories, and the increasingly hygienic conditions in factories, has gone very far towards providing better safeguards to workers against sickness. Safeguards against accidents, too, have greatly improved, even if there is much scope for their further improvement. Apart from other considerations, this means that losses of earnings by workers through illness or through enforced premature retirement have been materially reduced. In addition to improved working conditions, many modern factories are incomparably more cheerful places to work in than most of the gloomy and dingy pre-war industrial premises had been.

The Contracts of Employment Act provides for minimum notices of dismissal. Apart altogether from the more favourable legal position it has created, the trend is in any case towards a change in the attitude of employers, who are now not nearly as arbitrary — indeed they cannot afford to be — in dismissing their workers as they were before the War.

It is true to say that in practice the freedom of workers to withdraw their labour has no longer as corollary a corresponding degree of freedom of employers to dismiss their employees. According to the Donovan Report the freedom of workers to withdraw their labour — even though it means freedom to dishonour agreements freely entered into by their elected representatives — must be upheld and even reinforced while the freedom of employers to exercise similar rights must be reduced by enabling the workers to appeal against what they consider to be 'unfair' dismissal. In any case, apart altogether from the legal position and from the change in the balance of power which enables trade unions to protect their members, the despotic type of employer is dying out. Indeed the pendulum has now swung in the opposite direction. On the other hand, the power of trade unions is very often misused in securing for workers immunity from dismissal in entirely undeserving cases.

Redundant workers have no longer to face immediate hardship. The nightmare of mass unemployment through automation or through other methods of reducing labour requirements has been greatly mitigated by recently introduced legislation under which redundant workers are compensated out of a Redundancy Fund, the amount of their compensation depending on the length of their service. They receive, if not a golden handshake, at any rate a silver handshake. As in the circumstances prevailing most of the time since the War a high proportion of redundant workers can step immediately into another job, the redundancy payments really amount to a free bonus. This does not mean that there is no scope for further improvement. Retraining and the provision of housing facilities for redundant workers who have to change their occupation and/or their residence are absolutely essential.

A large and increasing number of firms have established private superannuation schemes under which employees with more or less long service with them are able to supplement quite appreciably their National Insurance retirement benefits. One of the objects of such schemes is to ensure the loyalty of workers to their firm. But there is considerable pressure — oddly enough mainly from the Conservative side — in favour of legislation to make such private pensions transferable if the workers choose to change their jobs. Employers bear a substantial part of the costs of the Welfare State, and such private insurance schemes involve substantial additional burden for them, so that it is hardly fair to deprive them of the benefit they hope to derive from such pension schemes in the form of discouraging workers to change their employment for trifling reasons

There is a curious kind of conspiracy between employers and their older employees in respect of redundancy payments. As they are not made directly out of the employers' own resources but out of the pool towards which all employers have contributed, they are often willing to confine redundancy, as far as possible, to older workers who are in any case on the eve of retirement, instead of adhering strictly to the rule of 'last in first out'. By such means they secure a silver handshake for their old employees. No doubt in many cases such a parting gift is well deserved. But it is not the purpose for which the Redundancy Fund was set up.

A high proportion of workers live in rent-controlled privately owned dwellings or in subsidised council houses. Having regard to the substantial difference between the artificially low rents they pay and current commercial rents, this means quite a substantial addition to the spending power of the millions of workers who benefit by this system. And since employers cannot discriminate between those who pay high rents and those who pay low rents wages are established at a level at which even those who have to pay high rents can get by reasonably well. This means that those who pay low rents receive what amounts in practice to an extra unearned bonus.

Although hire-purchase existed before the War, the facilities now available for working-class borrowers have improved considerably. So have mortgage facilities. It is true from time to time credit squeezes make it more difficult to borrow for the purchase of houses and of consumer durable goods, and the perennial high Bank rate makes such borrowing very costly. But whose fault is this? Were it not for unearned wage increases and the unwillingness of workers to give a fair day's work for their pay, there would be no need for resorting to such frequent and prolonged credit squeezes and interest rates could be kept down to about half the existing high level at which they have been maintained most of the time during the 'sixties.

Workers are now in an incomparably better position to influence management decisions affecting them. There are much more frequent consultations before decisions are taken, instead of presenting the employees with a *fait accompli*. This is considered essential in order to avoid conflicts arising from arbitrary action. Such consultations do not mean simply that the workers are informed in advance what action will be taken. They are in a position to present their objections and to make counter-proposals. Employers are usually prepared to meet to a considerable degree reasonable demands of their employees relating to working conditions. One of the executives or a senior official is in constant touch with their representatives to deal with grievances before they develop into a conflict.

Industrial workers are now regarded much more as equal partners in industry than they were before the War. Their status, compared with that of managements, and also compared with other social classes, has greatly improved. The old-fashioned belief in the superiority of 'white-collared workers' has all but disappeared. Anyway most factory workers can well afford to wear a white collar — that status symbol of 'respectability' — when they are off duty. Very often office workers apply to be transferred to the factory, owing to the higher pay.

Were it not for the unwarranted inferiority complex from which so many industrial workers still suffer and which impels them to assert themselves in an aggressive manner — a subject that was discussed in Chapter 12 — they would find that they are willingly and gladly accepted by people of all classes on an equal footing.

The above list of the advantages gained by workers since the War is far from exhaustive. No fair-minded human being could possibly begrudge them these gains. Most changes have been in the right direction and it is to be sincerely hoped that they will go much further. They could have gone much further already if only the workers, instead of aiming at confining to a minimum their contribution to the productive effort, had exerted themselves to enable the community to earn the cost of the changes instead of accepting them as gifts from Santa Claus.

Of course things are still far from being ideal. But then this is not an ideal world. Conditions in schools and hospitals leave much to be desired. Retirement pensions are still barely sufficient to cover necessities. In many industries workers still have to carry out unduly heavy, dangerous or unhealthy work. Their existence is still precarious to some extent, even if it is incomparably less so than before. Some old-fashioned employers — including some nationalised industries — are still inclined to be too autocratic. Housing conditions are often still far from satisfactory, especially for workers who have to change residence because of voluntary or enforced change of employment. What matters is that the improvement during the last twenty years has been truly spectacular, far beyond anything anybody would have dared to hope twenty years ago. Nobody could reasonably expect the advent of the millennium in such a short time.

In return for all this, what has the worker given to the community? Considerably less than nothing. If only the worker had simply abstained from contributing more than before the War towards the process of production, the community would be in a position to derive full benefit from the management's substantially increased contribution in the form of modern capital equipment. But since the worker's contribution has actually declined very considerably the community is only able to benefit by part of the management's increased contribution. In many known instances the modernisation of factories has not even been able to offset the decline in the worker's contribution. In some factories the output per man hour is now actually lower than it was before the installation of all the costly labour-saving devices.

So long as the workers continue to regard all the concessions listed above as the gifts of Santa Claus which need not be reciprocated their attitude is not likely to change. It is only if and when they come to be made to realise that they have duties as well as rights in relation to the community that it might become possible to hope for a basic change in their attitude. In fairness to them, they are not altogether to blame for their present anti-social behaviour. So long as the Government, employers and public opinion don't insist on a *quid pro quo* for favours conferred, it would be too much to expect the workers voluntarily to reciprocate the gifts of Santa Claus. And in existing circumstances the trade unions can hardly be blamed if they abstain from pursuing policies based on *quid pro quo*. Their members would take a dim view of any effort on the part of their elected representatives to insist on reciprocating the new benefits, so long as the community itself does not appear to insist that they should reciprocate them.

CHAPTER SIXTEEN

UNEARNED WAGE INCREASES

'UNEARNED wages', like 'anti-social Socialists', might at first sight seem to be a contradiction in terms. According to the popular conception, which has never been challenged up to now, wages are by definition earned incomes. They are taxed as earned incomes even if their recipients have not done a single stroke of work in return for receiving their pay. It would be of course a most unenviable task for any Inspector of Taxes or for anyone else to try to assess the extent to which most wages or any other forms of incomes are really earned. Although there are many flagrant instances of entirely unearned wages, there are bound to be innumerable grades of borderline cases. To a large degree it is often a matter of opinion whether a certain income should be regarded as earned or unearned.

Opinions on this highly controversial subject are inevitably affected by ideological or political considerations. For instance most Socialists would indignantly reject any suggestion that men in shipyards who watch other men work under terms of settlements of borderline disputes, while they themselves abstain from working, are recipients of unearned incomes. They would be doubtless equally emphatic in rejecting a suggestion that if a man risked his life's savings by financing the production of a medicine that would cure cancer, and if a success of his venture brought relief to millions of sufferers, he would be entitled to expect that his resulting dividends should not be taxed as unearned income.

Volumes could be written about the economic, social and moral aspects of the differentiation between earned and unearned incomes. All the author intends to do here is to indicate

personal views which are fully expected to be sharply condemned by those who are convinced that all workers are saints,
and that all employers are devils. To their minds all wages
(and perhaps salaries, provided they are within the lower
income groups) are unquestionably earned, even if the social
utility of the activities or inactivities of the recipients is nil or a
negative quantity.

Without going into this controversy about the earned or
unearned nature of various types of incomes, it is contended in
this chapter that any wage *increase* which is not the result of a
previous or simultaneous increase in productivity is necessarily
unearned. It creates a fictitious purchasing power with no corresponding increase in the volume of goods and services available to the community. It is, therefore, obviously inflationary.

During the last twenty years or so we have witnessed year
after year the creation of a more or less substantial amount of
fictitious purchasing power through wage increases unaccompanied by corresponding increases in the volume of purchasable
goods and services. This was due to the exploitation of the
scarcity value of labour resulting from full and overfull employment, which enabled the workers to force the community to
increase their money wages in excess of the increase in the
output of goods and services.

Exploitation of scarcity values of goods and of monopolistic
situations in production or trade enjoyed by industrial and
commercial firms has always been severely condemned by
Socialists, and rightly so. Yet the industrial branch of the
British labour movement — trade unions and industrial workers
in general — of which the Labour Party is the political
spokesman, has been engaged during the past twenty years in a
most ruthless exploitation of the community by a systematic
abuse of the scarcity value and monopolistic position of labour.
The term 'obscene plundering', which was coined by Aneurin
Bevan in the early 'fifties to condemn the earning of profits by
speculators, applies perfectly to the way in which the community has been held to ransom by trade unions on innumerable occasions. Indeed while the chief victims of successful

speculators are usually unsuccessful speculators — not a particularly deserving section of the community — the chief victims of the exploiters of scarce labour supplies and labour monopolies are the most defenceless sector of the community — people struggling on small and inelastic incomes.

The same deserving classes are of course also the victims of price increases caused by monopolistic practices and exploitation of scarcity value by business firms. What is the difference, one may well ask, between the two types of exploitation which would justify condemning the one and accepting the other as a matter of course? Are old-age pensioners victimised to a less extent by the effect of unearned wage increases on prices than by the effect of increased rents due to scarcity of houses or of increases in prices due to the monopolistic position of producers or merchants? They would hardly derive much comfort from discovering that an increase of their weekly grocer's bill by, say, 10 per cent was due to higher undeserved wages and not to profiteering by manufacturers, wholesalers or retailers.

As already admitted, it is in accordance with human nature to exploit a strong bargaining position, unless this is prevented either by legislation or by strong pressure of public opinion, or by a realisation on the part of monopolists that in the long run they might have to pay heavily for the short-term gains secured by their selfishness and greed. There has been in force for some time a certain amount of legislation against the exploitation of monopolistic and quasi-monopolistic situations by business firms and by landlords. But there was until recently no legislation to prevent the monopolistic exploitation of labour shortages. Nor has there been adequate pressure by public opinion against the systematic exploitation of consumers through the unearned wage increases witnessed in the 'fifties and 'sixties. As for any relief through a realisation by the monopolists in labour that in the long run it would be against their own interests to exploit their bargaining strength at the expense of the community, there has been, alas, no sign of it. Unenlightened self-interest continues to prevail.

At the time of writing it is impossible to predict the extent to which the new Prices and Incomes Act will be able to safeguard the consumer from exploitation through excessive increases of wages and prices. Judging by past experience it is likely to be more effective in checking price increases than in checking wage increases.

Wage increases may be socially justified in the following situations:

(1) If the workers have contributed directly, through increased exertions or through a more efficient application of their exertions, towards the increase of productivity.

(2) If the social utility of their contribution towards the productive process has increased.

(3) If their part in the process of production becomes more difficult, more dangerous, more unpleasant or more risky, or if it has come to require more training, more skill and experience.

There is, in addition, economic justification for wage increases in the following situations:

(4) If during a deflationary period an increase in the output calls for a deliberate increase in the volume of consumer purchasing power in order to ensure the absorption of the surplus by additional consumer demand.

(5) If an expanding industry is short of the manpower it needs and there is no unemployed labour available, so that the only way in which it can attract additional hands is by offering higher wages.

(6) If the cost of living has increased through no fault of the workers.

Wage increases granted as a result of the increase of the workers' direct contribution towards increasing productivity, or wage increases resulting from the increased difficulty of their effort, or from a rise in their cost of living in circumstances indicated under (1), (3) and (6), are earned wage increases. In the circumstances indicated under (2), (4) and (5) the workers contribute nothing towards the changes leading to the increase of their wages, so that such increases must be regarded

as unearned even if they may have social or economic justification from some other point of view.

Wage increases preceded by an increase in the cost of living
are only justified if the increase in the cost of living is not the
consequence of previous wage increases obtained by those who
now claim another wage increase in order to contract out of the
inevitable consequences of their previous wage increase.

Most wage increases during recent years were largely if not
entirely unearned wage increases without any economic or
social justification. They were obtained as a result of the
monopolistic position of trade unions resulting from the
scarcity of labour, and as a result of the ability of employers to
pass on the increased costs to the consumer.

The history of the motor industry during the 'fifties and
'sixties provides the most flagrant instances of unearned wage
increases. Since the War a motoring craze has developed in
Britain, and buyers of cars are prepared to pay higher and
higher prices so long as they obtain early delivery. Their
capacity to pay the ever-increasing prices has been made much
easier by the expansion of the hire-purchase system. Motor
manufacturers are naturally anxious to satisfy this urgent
demand and are anxious to increase their output at all costs.
They endeavour to outbid each other for the limited supply of
skilled labour available. They can afford to pay higher and
higher wages, for the public is prepared to pay higher and
higher prices, so long as their costs do not increase substantially
above those of rival firms. Wage increases to skilled labour
set the pace for wage increases to unskilled labour. The latter,
too, are well in a position to hold up production unless their
demand for unearned increases of wages is satisfied.

The high wages obtainable in the motor industry have no
social justification. To the extent to which they are above the
normal level of wages paid for comparable work in other
industries the surplus decidedly represents unearned income.
The economic effects of such unearned income received by
workers employed in the British motor industry have been
little short of disastrous. For other industries, in order to avoid

losing their manpower attracted by the grossly excessive wages paid in the motor industry, have to join in the competitive bidding for labour. In Oxford, van drivers of a newspaper the profit margin of which was narrow had to be given substantial wage increases, otherwise they would have left to join the motor works in Cowley.

Wage increases in the motor industry set the pace for un-earned wage increases in other industries. Static and even declining industries had to follow their lead. Millions of workers obtained increase after increase, even though they had done absolutely nothing towards earning it or deserving it. The irresponsible behaviour of a high proportion of workers in the motor industry has become proverbial. Knowing as they do that their employers have their order books full, they exploit their situation to the utmost.

Nobody has ever attempted to calculate or estimate the cost of the British motor industry in terms of its effect on the British balance of payments. We hear a great deal about the high proportion of its output that is exported, even though it is an admitted fact that during the pre-Budget spending spree in 1968 American importers of British cars were kept on short supply. But materials have to be imported for motor vehicles produced for the home market as well as for those produced for export. Nor is this the whole of the debit side of the industry's balance sheet by a long way. The ruthless competition of the motor industry for the limited manpower set the pace of the wage inflation which greatly increased imports at the same time as reducing the volume of manufactures available for export. This inflated domestic demand, together with the higher wages, increased British prices in general, so that many manufacturers had ceased to be competitive in foreign markets and some even in the domestic market. The sum total of the net cost of the motor industry's boom in terms of increased imports and reduced exports must run into hundreds of millions of pounds a year.

But for the inflationary effect of the motor industry's boom, it might not have been necessary at all to resort to squeezes, or at any rate to not nearly the same extent. So the cost of the motor boom in terms of lost production and slowed down expansion must also run into hundreds of millions.

One Chancellor of the Exchequer after another — with the notable exception of Mr. Jenkins to whom credit is due in this respect — aimed deliberately at stimulating the motor industry as the simplest way towards ensuring prosperity. The result was considerable additions to the amount of unearned wage increases paid in that industry and, under its influence, in other industries. The admittedly creditable export performance of the motor industry did not cover more than a fraction of the cost of the inflation which that industry had generated, either from the point of view of increased total imports or from the point of view of reduced output as a result of the squeeze it has made inevitable.

Although the unsatisfactory labour relations in the motor industry during the 'sixties were largely due to ill-advised attitudes on both sides, the frequency of official and unofficial strikes at a time when wages were fantastically high shows the ruthless determination of the unions to squeeze every ounce of advantage out of the scarcity value of labour. There is often systematic slowing down for the sake of earning more overtime. The high level of earnings must have been responsible for absenteeism on a large scale and for the frequency of strikes. Workers in the motor industry could afford the luxury of leisure, for on the basis of their high pay they could lead a tolerable existence even if they only worked every other day. There was therefore a strong temptation for them to help themselves to more leisure in some form instead of enjoying additional luxuries.

There would be everything to be said in favour of a rise in the standard of living of industrial workers if it were genuinely earned and deserved. The Japanese workers who identify their interests with those of their firms and who work accordingly deserve every bit of the spectacular increase in their wages and in their standard of living during the 'fifties and 'sixties. Unfortunately the same cannot be said truthfully

about a good many British workers. They have brought to a
fine art their efforts to keep down to a minimum what they
give their firms and the community. Their attitude towards
their firm is one of malevolent hostility — they are practically
the enemy within the gates — and their attitude towards the
community is one of utter indifference. Many of them are
not even intelligent enough to realise that an increase in their
firm's profits is to their advantage. If the firm happens to be
doing well — not thanks to them but in spite of them — they
naturally claim the surplus in order to increase their unearned
incomes. But they refuse to move their little finger to help the
firm in bringing about an increase in its prosperity. Many of
them are even short-sighted enough to feel *Schadenfreude* —
thank goodness there is no English word for it — when their
firm is not doing well so long as it is not doing so badly as to
affect their own position.

Spokesmen of the Labour movement and their supporters are
in the habit of speaking in a tone of utmost contempt about
those whose incomes are derived from 'unearned' profits, dividends, interest or rents. But is there any real difference
between them and those who enjoy equally unearned incomes
out of wage increases obtained without any increase in their
own effort towards achieving an increase in productivity? If
the former are denounced as spongers and parasites the same
epithets should apply equally well to recipients of unearned
wages. Can anybody argue seriously that workers in the motor
industry really deserve higher wages than workers in other
industries, merely because their employers can afford to pay
more owing to the motoring craze? Or that workers in other
industries have really earned the wage increases granted by
their firms solely in order to avoid losing their essential manpower through the attraction of high wages which the motor
industry can afford to pay? There is no difference between
such increased incomes and increased rents charged by landlords to their tenants because the neighbourhood has improved
and because no more building sites are available in the district.

To a very large degree wage increases have been achieved as

a result of trade union restrictive practices which keep the supply of labour artificially scarce by limiting the number of new entrants, or by forcing employers to employ more workers than are really needed for doing the job, or by limiting the output per man.   Such additional incomes obtained by such anti-social means differ in no way from the additional profits made by business firms through cornering essential commodities and withholding them from the market in order to raise their prices.   Nor from additional profits made by producers or merchants by forming price rings and keeping prices artificially high.   It is bad enough if the trade unions hold the community to ransom.   But if at the same time they adopt a high moral tone and denounce others whose actions are in no way more anti-social than their own then the time has come to remind them of the immortal words of Robert Burns:

> O wad some Pow'r the giftie gie us
> To see oursels as others see us!

Many attempts have been made to ensure that wage increases should not be unearned, by adopting piecework payments or by linking wages to productivity agreement. Some of these arrangements — which covered some 40 per cent of the workers in manufacturing industries in 1961 — have been successful, because wage increases were granted on the basis of accomplished productivity increases instead of on promised productivity increases.   Outstanding among the successful productivity agreement is the Esso refinery agreement at Fawley which has often been quoted as the model, but the example of which has not been followed by many other firms.

The trouble about such agreements is that, even if they are successful, they are liable to lead to unearned wage increases in the same district through pressure on all other firms in the same district to increase the wages of their employees even if there is no inclination or opportunity to enter into productivity agreements.   Otherwise the successful firm is liable to attract the manpower of the other firms and the latter have to try to prevent that even at the cost of granting unearned pay increases. Moreover, according to a report of the Prices and Incomes Board, since techniques advance even during periods of unemployment, the resulting automatic increases of wages granted under productivity agreements make it even more difficult to control inflation in spite of the existence of unemployment which would in the ordinary way tend to deflate prices through its effect on the total spending power of consumers.

A well-known method of securing unearned wage increases is to obtain from the employers a consolidation of overtime pay into higher basic wages on the understanding that the same amount of work would be done without working overtime in return for the increase of the basic wages. But as soon as the agreement begins to operate the workers resort to their old tactics of going slow, and employers, in order to meet the delivery dates under their contracts, feel impelled to have them work overtime once more at higher rates, in addition to the recently increased basic pay.

The system of wage awards by arbitration or by conciliation has greatly increased the possibilities for bigger unearned wage increases. In theory the task of arbitrators or conciliators is to work out the wages justified amidst conditions prevailing in the industry, having regard to national requirements. In practice they fix the figures with an eye on the possibility of the acceptance of their award by the workers and, to a very much less extent, by the employers. Considerations of genuine fairness play a very subordinate part in their decision. The difference between the amounts demanded by the unions and those offered by the employers is usually split, so that all the unions have to do is to double the amount of their demand in order to be certain of an award that grants them in full what they really expect to get.

Moreover, since it is always easier to persuade employers to accept awards, arbitrators or conciliators are often inclined to meet the workers' demands considerably more than halfway. Although they may sincerely believe they aim at achieving justice and equity and safeguarding national interests, they

G

are subconsciously influenced in the sense of elaborating terms that happen to stand a chance of being acceptable to the workers without being absolutely unacceptable to employers.

Unearned wage increases generate both cost inflation and demand inflation. An increase in wages without an increase in output means an increase in the cost per unit. It also means an increase in the demand for goods and services without a corresponding increase in their supply to meet the additional demand. The rise in prices tends to be moderated by the resulting decline in real purchasing power, but the vicious spiral continues so long as wage increases exceed the rise in the cost of living as well as the increase in output.

CHAPTER SEVENTEEN

SOME MEN ARE MORE EQUAL THAN OTHERS

EGALITARIANISM, like full employment and the Welfare State, is a noble end towards which society should strive. But it is an ideal that is unattainable in real life. Even if in an ideal world an egalitarian society, having levelled up or down the worldly possessions of all its members, were to provide them with an equal start and equal opportunities for betterment, it would not mean that they would remain equal. Many of them would become 'more equal than others', in spite of starting the race from scratch and in spite of all the efforts to provide them with equal opportunities. This is inevitable, because of differences in their physical qualities, their mental capacities, their abilities and willingness to work, their abilities and willingness to assume responsibilities, their character, their personality, etc.

But ours is very far from being an ideal world from the point of view of egalitarianism as indeed from any other point of view. We are neither born equal nor are our opportunities equal, nor indeed are our physical and mental qualities or our characters anything like equal. There has been, nevertheless, a strong trend since the War towards creating more equal opportunities and towards levelling down inequalities irrespective of whether they are the result of inequality of inherited circumstances or inequality of ability or of willingness to work.

To the extent to which post-war developments have reduced the inequality of opportunities there is indeed a great deal to be said for it. The change is for better to the extent to which it has mitigated class distinctions. Reference was made earlier to a prevalent form of snobbery before the War to look down on those engaged in physical labour as being socially inferior to those engaged in office work or brainwork of any kind, and very much inferior to those gentlemen of independent means who did not need to work at all for their living. Thank goodness, all this is to a very large extent now past history.

There is now a much wider genuine realisation of the truth that anyone who is engaged in socially useful work is entitled to the respect of his fellow human beings. Indeed the need for justifying one's existence by working has come to be realised, if not in the working classes so called, at least among classes which could still afford to lead a life of leisure on their investment incomes. While before the War most girls of the upper classes and upper middle classes had led the pleasant but useless life of society debutantes, today most of them have some useful job or profession or are engaged in preparing themselves for being able to earn their living even if there is no financial need for them to do so. Every right-thinking person thinks more highly of them for this change. This is progress in the right direction. If only the working classes acted likewise!

This does not mean, however, that there is now, on balance, less snobbery than before the War. For class distinctions amongst industrial employees themselves have increased. Physical labourers look down upon those who have no direct share in the process of production. As has been pointed out in Chapter 5, the Selective Employment Tax reinforced this type of snobbery by drawing distinctions between workers employed in manufacturing industries and those in service industries. The former would be hardly human if they did not look upon the latter as inferior beings in consequence of the official distinction against them. There is also a new type of snobbery, according to which many of those engaged in the public sector look down upon those engaged in the private sector. The author had first-hand evidence of this on one occasion some years ago when his taxi-driver got into an argument with a bus-driver. 'Remove your cigarette when you are addressing the driver of a public vehicle,' shouted the latter at the former.

Possibly all this is a temporary state of affairs. The change in the balance of power has been too recent and in the course of time workers might grow used to it sufficiently not to feel the necessity of reassuring themselves of their own superiority at frequent intervals by being rude to others. But so long as the period of transition continues the new snobbery is highly detrimental to industrial discipline and therefore to productivity. Too many factory workers are too much concerned with throwing their newly-acquired weight about and too little with aiming at friendly co-existence for the sake of increasing the prosperity of their firm, their industry and the community.

Egalitarianism has made considerable progress in the economic sphere as a result of the high level of employment. Labour is no longer the weaker partner in industry. Indeed more often than not it is the stronger partner. And broadly speaking it is true that it has been exploiting its stronger position more ruthlessly than most employers did before the War. So while from a social point of view the change has been an immense improvement, from an economic point of view it has given rise to grave economic disadvantages, although it goes without saying that it is infinitely preferable to the pre-war state of affairs even from a purely economic point of view.

The egalitarian trend has made very considerable progress also in respect of reducing differentials between taxed incomes. It is true that there is much more tax avoidance and tax evasion than before the War. But, as we pointed out earlier, this is not confined to the higher income groups. Tax avoidance or evasion by the 'rich' receives disproportionate publicity, partly because the Inland Revenue has not sufficient staff to go after the large number of small evaders and partly because the bigger amounts involved make news headlines. Yet it seems probable that the extent of evasion by members of lower income groups is high and that the total amount involved is much larger even if it consists of a very large number of small amounts.

Nor indeed are well-to-do Socialists and exponents of working class point of view noted for their eagerness to contribute their share to the cost of the Welfare State. In a Press interview in 1968 one of the former 'angry young men', John Osborne, confessed that, though he loved living in Britain, considerations of taxation might force him to live abroad. And Vanessa Redgrave was reported to be planning to dispose of her future earnings against a substantial lump sum payment, presumably for considerations of taxation.

That all Left-wingers are not necessarily egalitarian was illustrated by an exceptionally long letter that appeared in *The Times* during the 'thirties by Bernard Shaw, suggesting that the rate of Income Tax should be *lower* and not higher on large incomes (such as his had been) because, after all, shopkeepers quote lower prices for customers who purchase in large quantities. But for once Shaw did not succeed in being original at the same time as being perverse. For the very same idea was suggested some eighty years earlier in all seriousness by that most reactionary 19th-century French statesman, M. Thiers, who supported this Right-wing proposal with exactly the same Right-wing argument.

It is true that there were some cuts under the Tory Governments which, taking their courage in both hands, even reduced Surtax by raising the exempted limit. But, taking the long view, this was much more than offset in the long run by the adoption of a Capital Gains Tax without any *quid pro quo* in the form of a reduction of the rate of tax on current incomes. As the Tories had conceded the principle of taxing capital gains, it was only natural that the Labour Government should take the first opportunity to increase the severity of its application. But the Capital Gains Tax came too late to prevent large increases of a great many fortunes as a result of the all-round inflationary increase of money values, and of the opportunities inflation has created for making big profits. While most stately homes had to be sold for hotels or for public institutions, and those which are still in private hands now have to admit visitors at half a crown a head to be kept going, a new set of wealthy people has come into being.

Egalitarian endeavours within wage incomes are handicapped by wide differences between the bargaining powers of various unions. Pressure in favour of wage increases for lower-paid workers is on the increase, regardless of whether they are justified by higher productivity. Their interests are well safeguarded by some of the most powerful and militant trade unions. But the craftsmen and other kinds of skilled labourers, too, have militant trade unions which are quite capable of looking after the special interests of their members. Any concession to lower-paid workers demanded for social considerations is followed by a fierce drive by craftsmen's unions to restore the former differentials. This again is followed by new demands to bring lower wages more in harmony with the rise in higher wages. Such leap-frogging wage increases continue indefinitely.

But for a long time upper-middle incomes failed in a great many instances to keep pace with the general trend. Professors, scientists, engineers, doctors and other professional people, have been treated less generously here than in many other countries. The egalitarian trend that has been progressing at their expense is mainly responsible for the brain-drain from Britain. To the extent to which this happens, and also to the extent to which the egalitarian trend acts as a disincentive in industry and commerce, it is highly detrimental to Britain's economic growth and to her progress towards a higher standard of living. It seems reasonable to assume that this disincentive effect of egalitarianism has been partly responsible for the inferiority of the progress made by the British economy compared with the economies of other leading countries in which egalitarianism has not reached the same advanced stage as in Britain.

Progress is obviously sacrificed in Britain for the sake of emotional egalitarianism. In economic terms high taxation of upper and upper-middle incomes has no justification, as the extent to which the yield of such taxation can actually benefit recipients of lower incomes is quite negligible. Some time in the middle 'fifties the Chancellor of the Exchequer, replying to a Parliamentary question, stated that if all taxed incomes above £2,000 were distributed among those whose taxed incomes were under £2,000 the latter would receive 1s. 2d. a week — that is exactly twopence a day. Although in the meantime money incomes have increased the answer today would not be materially different in real terms. So it is for the sake of the supreme ideal of securing the price of two cups of tea per week to the lower income groups that incentive and initiative is paralysed by overtaxing higher incomes. It is not really for economic considerations that spokesmen of lower income groups insist on maintaining and stepping up their policy of 'soaking the rich', but for the sake of pandering to the unattractive human failings of envy and spite.

Is it really worth while to discourage initiative for the sake of gaining 'spite-money' of 2d. per day? Even that pittance is not a net gain — if it is a gain at all. For if we allow for the effect of high taxation on productivity we must conclude without hesitation that the economic benefit derived from egalitarianism is a negative quantity. Lower income groups would have been able to increase their real incomes to a much larger degree if the egalitarian trend had not levelled down the higher incomes to the extent it has done since the War. This may sound paradoxical, and there is no means for convincing emotional egalitarians that the high degree of success of their policy is actually to the detriment of the classes which they want to help.

According to a favourite argument of egalitarians, it is the moral duty of members of higher income groups to do their best for their firms and for the community by working harder and by assuming more responsibility and taking more risk, even in the absence of any financial incentive, for the sake of being able to serve their firms and the community. This argument would carry more conviction if their lower-paid fellow-citizens, too, showed a little more zeal in helping the community in addition to helping themselves and fellow-members of their trade unions. As things actually are, the implication of the argument exhorting recipients of higher incomes to act unselfishly is that the workers alone have a monopoly in selfishness, a privilege which they refuse to share with other classes. It would of course be very convenient for them if everybody else served the community selflessly while they themselves continued to benefit by their exclusive right to selfishness.

Egalitarians are not satisfied with equal initial opportunity for all. They refuse to admit that superior skill, brain, initiative, imagination, experience, education, and the willingness and ability to take risks or to assume higher responsibility deserve higher rewards. While they are right in their egalitarianism to the extent to which it serves the purpose of doing away with abject poverty, once that stage is reached — as indeed, very broadly speaking, it has been reached in Britain thanks to the Welfare State and the high level of employment — some scope must surely be allowed for inequality for the sake of its incentive effect without which there would be a much higher degree of all-round poverty.

Of course many Socialists would object to the contention that abject poverty has been virtually abolished in Britain. They are in a position to quote many instances to prove that the poor are still with us. But then, the poor are even with the Americans and to a much larger extent in spite of their much higher average standard of living. What matters is that the proportion of the genuinely poor to the total population is now incomparably smaller than it was before the War. There is undoubtedly scope for further improvement, as there are some categories which are treated less than generously by the Welfare State. But the problem is no longer of a magnitude that would justify even from a purely social point of view the pursuit of egalitarianism beyond the point at which it becomes a dis-incentive highly detrimental to progress and therefore to the chances of raising the standard of living.

Many egalitarians are ill-informed enough to favour Com-munism on the assumption that it aims at doing away with inequality of incomes. Nothing could be further from the truth. Egalitarianism forms no part of the Communist creed. In Soviet Russia 'bourgeois egalitarianism' is a term of contempt; it is used in that sense in the official textbook on economics, passed for publication by Stalin himself shortly before his death. Differences between various grades of earnings are indeed very wide there, and there is no attempt at levelling them down by means of progressive taxation. Income Tax and Surtax are virtually non-existent, and revenue is raised by indirect taxation included in the retail price of all goods and services. Evidently Communists, after fifty years of practical experience in Socialism, believe in the need for incentive provided by income differentials.

How far is egalitarianism likely to proceed in Britain? It will not satisfy many of its supporters until all incomes are equated to each other and until conditions providing for equal social and economic opportunities are established. Carried to its logical conclusion, egalitarianism would culminate in the adoption of legislation to disfigure attractive girls, because it is unfair to plain girls that the pretty ones stand a better chance to find rich husbands or good jobs through no merits of their own, merely because of the accident of their birth — an accident that is also liable to secure inherited wealth and other 'unfair' advantages under the existing much-abused system. Fortunately such legislation is not likely ever to be passed so long as male M.P.s retain anything like their present numerical superiority in the House. Yet it is distinctly illogical to tolerate inherited inequality in the form of superior inherited pulchritude while condemning inherited inequality in the form of superior inherited financial resources.

Levelling down is demanded in the sacred name of social justice. But under a reasonable interpretation of the principle of social justice only those who are doing their best for the community within the limits of their abilities should be entitled to expect the best from the community. If this principle is accepted it is impossible to avoid the conclusion that the benefits gained from the community by British industrial workers in general since the War have been utterly undeserved, and have been therefore contrary to the principles of social justice.

Egalitarianism aims not only at egalitarian distribution of incomes but also at egalitarian consumption. During and immediately after the War when necessities were in short supply this meant rationing, a device that had in the prevailing circumstances full economic as well as social justification. Now that there are adequate supplies in necessities and lower income groups can also afford luxuries the demand for egalitarian consumption is directed largely against the rights of upper income groups to spend their incomes in the way they want to spend them — for instance on better school facilities and on special hospital facilities in private wards, etc. The abolition of public schools is advocated on the ground that they create unequal opportunities. But if it is justified to devote resources for the breeding of bloodstock, pedigree herds, etc., surely a case can be made for the social usefulness of breeding a limited set of persons eminently capable of assuming responsibility in business and in the public administration. If members of upper income groups are prepared to pay for such education, why not let them, especially if the system of education which they finance provides similar opportunities nowadays for quite a number of members of the working classes?

Egalitarianism for its own sake is open to criticism also when it aims at abolishing private wards in hospitals. If members of the upper income groups are prepared to pay heavily for their privacy in private wards of hospitals instead of being a burden on the National Health Service why not let them? The favourite argument against it is that those who can afford to pay for treatment in private wards jump the queue of National Health patients awaiting their turn for hospital beds. But a number of instances could be quoted in which Socialist Ministers and trade union leaders were 'guilty' of precisely such queue-jumping. In their case the offence is all the graver as, unlike members of upper income groups, they jump the queue presumably with a guilty conscience, knowing, if they are honest egalitarians, that it is the wrong thing to do. They may of course be able to reassure themselves that, in view of their importance from the point of view of the community, they are entitled to special considerations. But there is room for two opinions about the validity of that claim.

The most contemptible aspect of egalitarianism is when it tends to become a creed of envy. 'If I can't have this or that, let nobody else have it.' The pleasure derived by millions of working-class women from window shopping shows that this form of egalitarianism is, thank goodness, far from being universal among working people. If they can derive pleasure from merely seeing things which are beyond their means to purchase they must surely feel that it is a good thing some people can afford such things even if they themselves can't have them.

There are many people preaching egalitarianism who, like the pigs in Orwell's *Animal Farm*, are distinctly more equal than others. They are often encountered in luxury restaurants of the West End where the cost of a single meal would be enough to keep an old-age pensioner for at least a week. The author had himself repeatedly seen one of the leading exponents of the egalitarian creed during the War, partaking of sumptuous meals in one of London's most expensive restaurants, in the company of three or four Leftish politicians. And this occurred at a time when those who were less equal than this prominent egalitarian had to manage on their meagre war-time rations.

If by any chance the politician in question should read these remarks and if he should realise that they are aimed at him, it would not be advisable for him to retort that, on the author's own admission, the author himself was having war-time meals in that self-same luxury restaurant. For the answer is that the author has never pretended to be an egalitarian. Had he been an egalitarian he is sure that such a meal amidst war-time austerity would have stuck in his gullet. But presumably the prominent egalitarian politician suffered no such discomfort, either physically or metaphorically speaking. He must have felt fully justified in doing so well for himself on the ground that, in view of his great services to the cause of egalitarianism, he was surely entitled to enjoy the advantages of unequal distribution while they lasted.

CHAPTER EIGHTEEN

HAS THERE BEEN A 'BRITISH MIRACLE'?

IN the course of earlier chapters reference has repeatedly been made to the deplorable absence of a British miracle comparable with the German, Italian, Russian, Japanese, etc., miracles. On second thoughts, however, it now seems that after all it is arguable that there have been British miracles of a sort, though whether they are comparable with the above-mentioned miracles is quite another question.

If we content ourselves with small mercies we may claim that there is indeed a British miracle every single day. For is it not a miracle that, in spite of the indolence and malevolence of a high proportion of industrial workers and in spite of the unhelpful attitude of their unions and of the Government, British managements somehow succeed in getting goods produced and sold at all? Heaven only knows how they can do it in the circumstances.

When one reads the daily Press reports about all the labour troubles and other difficulties managements have to contend with — hardly a day passes without reading about at least half a dozen labour disputes — one is inclined to believe that executives must be supermen to succeed somehow in delivering the goods at all, in qualities and at prices at which they can be sold. It is true, in many instances the quality has deteriorated or at any rate its improvement has failed to keep pace with the changing requirements of an increasingly affluent society. In many more instances it takes too long to produce the goods, or their cost is too high. Above all, the increase in the national output falls considerably short of the progress shown in other countries. Nevertheless, we must take our hats off to managements for their success in ensuring that Britain is not doing even a great deal worse than she has actually been doing.

Whenever one feels impelled to criticise British management — and only too often this is inevitable — one cannot help reminding oneself that in spite of their many shortcomings they deserve the nation's gratitude, having regard to the difficulties they have to cope with owing to the behaviour of the British industrial worker. If they had been only half as unsatisfactory as their workers, Britain's decline would have culminated in her fall long before now. The nation — which includes the workers themselves — is greatly indebted to managements for keeping things going in the circumstances and in spite of the extent of the discouragement they encounter on the part of the employees, on the part of the trade unions and especially since 1964, on the part of an unfriendly Government.

It has become fashionable to put at least 75 per cent of the blame for all that is wrong in this country on the 'inefficiency' and 'incompetence' of managements, their unwillingness to depart from old-fashioned practices, their lack of dynamism. This hostile attitude towards executives is not confined to their professional opponents, Socialists and trade unionists. A high proportion of those who, because of their political allegiance or their social status or their familiarity with economics in general and with industrial matters in particular, could reasonably be expected to realise the existence of a case for British management and to have the intellectual courage to state it, are either 'neutral' or quite distinctly hostile to managements. This may be due in many instances to typical British inclination to lean backwards — to derive satisfaction from appearing to be fairminded by overstating the argument opposed to the one corresponding to their personal interests. In many other instances, however, it is due to sheer intellectual snobbery at its worst. Or it is due to sheer cowardice — to abstain from defending an unpopular point of view.

To state that Britain's decline has been due to the unwillingness of the British worker to put in a fair day's work for his pay,
and for his impatient greed to achieve a maximum of undeserved increase of his standard of living with the minimum
of delay, may be a thousand times true. But it is admittedly
not very original and its re-discovery or re-statement does not
call for any impressive intellectual qualities. To put it plainly,
any fool could stumble on that glaringly obvious answer. It
is clearly beneath the dignity of a number of the intelligent
élite to come out with such a simple answer to a complex
problem.

But to put the blame on managements is quite another
matter. It provides ample opportunity for clever, sophisticated
and original analysis of the situation. There is scope for highly
ingenious argument, both of the macro-economic and of the
micro-economic kinds. It is bound to impress not only the man
in the street who does not understand most of it but also
fellow-members of the intellectual or pseudo-intellectual élite.
The chorus of approval with which the tortuous and often
self-contradictory findings of the Report of the Brookings Institution against British management has been received illustrates
this point. It is ever so easy, and ever so cheap, to find fault
with a set of people who have been trying hard to cope with
the almost insurmountable difficulties inflicted on them by the
anti-social behaviour of the British workers and their unions,
and by the incompetence and malevolence of a Government
which has been rightly denounced as the worst Britain has had
since Lord North.

But there is ample genuine ground on which managements
are indeed open to criticism in many respects and to censure
in some respects. The last thing one should do is to attempt to
convey the impression that all faults are on one side. If the
space devoted in this book to criticising managements is brief
compared with the space devoted to criticising the workers, it is
because British managements, unlike workers and their unions,
do get their fair share of criticism by the Press, by politicians,
by trade union leaders and, last but not least, by self-castigators

and by the pseudo-intellectuals referred to above. Their relative share in the amount of criticism is incomparably higher than that of trade unions and workers. While criticism of trade unions and their members is widely regarded as amounting to *lèse-majesté*, sacrilege and blasphemy combined, no such inhibitions exist about criticising managements. The relative extent to which the Donovan Report seeks to find excuses for trade unions and blame managements and their associations, in spite of the fact that the latter were also represented on the Royal Commission, speaks for itself.

But even in everyday life, managements often come in for strong adverse comment. Executives are often accused, for instance, of being almost as slack as their workers. Many proprietors of some smaller factories and some managers of medium-sized factories are indeed inclined to arrive late and to leave early, to take off too much time for that business lunch, to help themselves to far too long week-ends and to grant themselves too generous holidays. In many instances the absence of the men responsible for giving instructions does hold up workers in addition to the effects of their own go-slow tactics and their various excuses for taking it easy. It provides them with an additional excuse for hanging about in the mornings — and a legitimate one for a change — if floor managers or foremen have no specific instructions for the day's work. But censure of the managerial class on that ground generalises from a relatively small proportion of actual instances. Most firms are sufficiently well-organised to ensure continuity of work in spite of the late arrival or temporary absence of a boss.

As a result of the increase in the egalitarian trend, many workers feel they have a genuine grievance because they have to work longer hours than their bosses. Their discontent is often expressed by slowing down once the boss is gone. Before the War, when the 48-hour week was the rule, it would not have occurred to them to think it unfair to them that the general manager should arrive at 10 a.m. or after and leave at 5 p.m., having spent two hours at his lunch. But in the prevailing atmosphere they feel it is wrong to expect them to work longer hours than their chiefs.

What does not occur to them is that work for the general manager does not begin when he enters his office and does not cease when he leaves his desk, but is almost continuous. He takes files with him to study them at home, and goes through them in his car or in the train on his way home. He is exasperatingly absent-minded in his family circle and can't concentrate on the performance in theatres or concerts, because he is trying to find an answer to some business problem. He is liable to spend sleepless nights over such problems and is never entirely free from business worries during week-ends or holidays. That is what responsibility means and should mean.

By comparison his employees may consider themselves fortunate, because they are able to forget all about their work as soon as they leave the factory or the office and need not give it another thought until they return to work next day. Allowing for this difference it is reasonable to assume that the effective working day of conscientious executives is considerably longer than that of workers — anything up to eighteen hours a day, seven days a week. Even that much-criticised and much-envied business lunch of executives with clients or suppliers or rivals or that working lunch of directors and executives in the office dining room means concentrated brainwork during meals, much to the detriment of their digestion. If they drink and eat more at such meals than is good for them, not because they really want to, but just for the sake of keeping company with their hosts or guests, it is apt to ruin their health and to shorten their lives.

Managers who set a bad example to their employees by arriving late and leaving early without due cause deserve censure, but in a very large number of instances criticism because of their shorter working days at their desks is unjustified. Even so, executives would be wise to heed such criticism. They should try to do more work on the premises instead of taking files home with them. By staying at their desks after most of their staff have gone home they would set an example that would disarm much gratuitous criticism. They should not only work hard but should be seen by their employees to work hard.

A much more serious ground for criticism than mere egalitarian envy and spite is that executives are apt to be old-fashioned and conservative (with a small 'c') and they fail to keep up with progress. No doubt in a great many instances there is much justification for such criticism. The law of inertia is a powerful influence. Owners and managers of firms which are doing tolerably well may be reluctant to go out of their way to make changes involving extra trouble and extra risk and the investment of extra capital, for the sake of trying to do even better. They may be slow in deciding to replace their old-fashioned equipment which has been earning for the shareholder a steady dividend of six per cent, even if it seems probably that more up-to-date equipment would yield a higher profit. The great deterrent is the feeling that most of the increased earnings would have to be paid out in higher wages and in higher taxes.

Instead of condemning such managements out of hand it is necessary to consider the question whether the disincentive effect of unearned wage increases, frequent strikes, go-slows, etc., and of penalising taxation, is not largely responsible for their lack of initiative. It is true, in an ideal world executives and shareholders would serve the community selflessly and would be willing to take any amount of extra trouble and risk without adequate reward. But, as we already pointed out in the last chapter, in our world the levelling down of incomes resulting from the egalitarian trend does tend to discourage progress through discouraging initiative. While there may be room for two opinions whether such an economic cost of egalitarianism is not apt to exceed the social benefits derived from the progress of egalitarianism, it is essential for egalitarians to realise the facts of the existence of such a cost instead of ignoring them or dismissing them on the ground that there ought not to be such effects.

There exist, in fact, any number of dynamic executives who

are anxious to proceed with modernisation even if the resulting
profit did not necessarily compensate their firm for the time,
the trouble, the investment of additional capital and the risk
it involved. It is usually firms with such dynamic executives
that seek to take over firms with less dynamic managements.
If critics of the executive class were logical they would enthusiastically welcome take-over bids, for in a high proportion of
instances their result is an increase in efficiency, not only
through a modernisation of backward firms but also through a
rationalisation of the combined resources of the two firms. Yet
take-over bids encounter almost indiscriminately hostile criticism on the part of trade unionists and Socialists.

The reasons for this inconsistency in their attitude are two-
fold. Take-over bids usually result in capital profits for shareholders, and such profits are a dirty word to trade unionists and
Socialists who feel that the workers should be the sole beneficiaries of the modernisation resulting from amalgamations.
While welcoming the unearned income of workers resulting
from wage increases made possible by the adoption of more
efficient production methods, they strongly deprecate the
achievement of capital gains by those whose capital is risked
when making some basic change. They disregard the fact that
shareholders suffer a capital loss if the transaction should mis-
fire, and executives risk a loss of reputation, possibly even a loss
of job, in which case they might find it much more difficult than
displaced workers to find alternative employment.

The main reason why workers and their spokesmen dislike
amalgamations lies in their fear that it might mean redundancy.
Such fears are very often well-founded. Indeed firms cannot
be made more efficient unless the elimination of duplications
in the combined enterprise and the adoption of more efficient
methods does result in the release of labour. Very often it is
possible to find jobs for those affected by the amalgamation in
some other department, or an increase in the output enables
the firms to retain them. In any case the dismissed workers are
now entitled to redundancy pay. But the risk of redundancy
is admittedly always there.

In many recent instances redundancies resulting from amalgamations gave rise to violent protests. While the attitude of those directly concerned is understandable, it is difficult to understand the support they receive from politicians who ought to realise that very often there can be no progress towards more efficient management without greater flexibility in respect of redeployment of labour. As the large majority of the workers of the firm concerned stand to benefit by the improved efficiency of the firm that emerges from the take-over transaction, and the community as a whole stands to benefit, it is difficult to reconcile the criticisms of managements for inefficiency with the resistance to the increase of their efficiency through take-overs. It is even more difficult to reconcile the demand for more efficient management with the resistance of trade unions to the adoption of modernised equipment of most kinds, or of more efficient working methods.

Managements are also often accused of callous indifference to the welfare of their workers. Beyond doubt the degree of paternalism that had prevailed in many firms has greatly declined, largely because amidst conditions that have existed since the War the workers are quite capable of looking after themselves, or, even more, they are looked after most effectively by their trade unions and by the Welfare State. The decline of paternalism is also a natural corollary to the decline of loyalty to the firm and to the 'we are the masters now' attitude. Workers are no longer underdogs and managements feel they need not be treated with the consideration due to the underdog. In many instances, as a result of prolonged bad labour relations, workers have come to be regarded by their employers as the enemy within their walls. Nevertheless, the large majority of firms still take an interest in the welfare of their workers, not necessarily for humanitarian reasons but because it is easier to acquire and retain the manpower they require if satisfactory fringe benefits are provided. But it would be idle to deny that to a very large extent the attitude of 'letting the Welfare State look after its own' has come to prevail.

Although many managements leave much to be desired,

there is absolutely no justification for the oft-repeated argument that the main reason, if not the only reason, for Britain's decline is the inadequacy of British management. It is of course very convenient for workers and their apologists to expect managements to make all the efforts for checking Britain's decline, thereby obviating the necessity for the workers themselves to work harder or to moderate their annual demands for additional unearned wages.

Exhortations addressed to managements by spokesmen of workers who abstain from contributing anything whatsoever towards raising productivity in the national interest recall a story from the first World War according to which, when a certain military unit was ordered to attack the enemy, the officers went over the top to lead the attack while the other ranks burst into frantic applause but remained safely and comfortably in their trenches.

The difference between this fictitious story and what is actually happening in British industry today is that, while the 'other ranks' in industry systematically exhort their 'officers' to carry out the attacks single-handed, they do their best to frustrate their 'officers'' zeal and to prevent the attack from succeeding. And when the 'officers' launch an attack not only unsupported by the 'other ranks' but deliberately handicapped by them, the latter, so far from bursting into applause as in the war-time story, shower the usual torrents of abuse at their 'officers', denouncing them for inefficiency, lack of initiative, etc. And if in spite of all this the 'officers'' attack achieves its objective, the 'other ranks' who have not moved a finger to assist them claim full credit for the result of the victorious operation and demand the greater part of the booty captured by their 'officers'.

It is well to remember that the standard of living has increased since the War in spite of the undeniable fact that the workers' own contribution towards productive effort has declined considerably. This can only mean that the increase in the efficiency of management has more than offset the decline in the workers' contribution to production. Exhortations by

workers' spokesmen — whether members of the Labour Government, Socialist politicians or trade union leaders — addressed
to managements calling on them to become more efficient only
means that they expect the management to contribute even
more of the shareholders' capital and to take even heavier risks
solely for the sake of enabling workers to work even less in
return for even more unearned pay. This attitude is far from
being world-wide. Trade unions in the United States and in
some European countries adopt a 'live and let live' attitude.

The task of executives is indeed unenviable. They have to
steer a middle course between the Scylla of too easy compliance
with obviously unwarranted wage demands and the Charybdis
of too rigid resistance to reasonable demands at the risk of
strikes which usually cost a great deal more than the direct
effect of meeting the demands during the next twelve months.
It is always tempting to take the line of least resistance and pay
the Danegeld, but long experience has taught them that in the
long run this policy does not pay because, in Kipling's words:

> . . . once you have paid him the Dane-geld
> You never get rid of the Dane.

Giving way too easily encourages even more frequent and
even more excessive demands for unearned wage increases.
The maximum of wage demands is determined by the risk of
a prolonged strike run by the workers, as it might cost more
in terms of lost wages than the hoped-for benefit of higher
wages. Determined resistance to wage demands at the risk of
strikes as distinct from mere token resistance tends to mitigate
such demands at least to some extent.

The choice for managements is between two evils. During
recent years they have been inclined too much to choose the
evil of giving way too easily in the hope — amounting to near-
certainty in the prevailing inflationary conditions — that they
would be able to pass on to the consumer the additional costs
of wage increases. They were right as far as domestic consumers were concerned because their domestic rivals took
usually the same line of non-resistance, but very often they

were wrong as far as overseas consumers were concerned because resistance to unwarranted wage demands by their rivals
abroad was apt to be stiffer. This also explains to a large extent
the increase of imports of manufactured goods in recent years.

It may be said without hesitation that this inclination of
managements to yield to trade union demands, however unreasonable those demands may be, justifies more criticism than
anything else they have done or have omitted to do. In private
conversation Socialists, and even the more sensible trade union
leaders, often blame managements for the ease with which they
give way even to deliberately exaggerated demands which are
only put forward to serve as a basis for bargaining. But the
behaviour of the workers and their unions has gone a long way
towards demoralising managements. It is so easy for the latter
to save themselves trouble and, instead of putting up a fight,
simply add the wage increases to their prices. Amidst the
rising trend of consumer demand executives are reasonably safe
in assuming that the rival firms act likewise, so that there is
little risk of pricing their goods out of the market — at any
rate as far as the domestic market is concerned. It has become
a habit that on each occasion of wage increases more than the
actual increase in costs is added to the prices.

The almost unbelievable folly of doing away with resale price
maintenance in the middle of a period of non-stop creeping
inflation has greatly contributed towards such demoralisation
of managements. So long as uniform retail prices of goods were
determined by their manufacturers, they were most reluctant
to raise those nationally-advertised prices. Each price increase
amounted to an admission of defeat. To avoid raising their
prices at too frequent intervals managements were inclined to
resist wage demands and other increases of costs. They
endeavoured to absorb unavoidable increases of costs through
the adoption of more efficient methods. Indeed they were
often even prepared to prevent increases of costs from affecting
their prices by reducing their profit margins.

But now that they have been deprived of the responsibility
for the retail prices of their goods they could hardly care less if

those prices were raised several times a week. They have no incentive whatsoever to make an effort to prevent such increases by keeping down their costs, knowing well that their rivals are liable to adopt the same attitude as a result of the abolition of resale price maintenance. So they willingly consent to wage increases in nationally negotiated wage agreements, even if they continue to try to resist local wage drift which would place them at a disadvantage against their rivals whose plants are situated in other districts. Instead of trying to keep down their prices to a minimum that secures them a reasonable profit, they now charge as much as the market can stand. And they raise their prices whenever they feel that the market would now stand higher prices.

Because supermarkets and other retailers cut many retail prices as soon as resale price maintenance is removed, those who are incapable of seeing beyond their noses welcome the change triumphantly as a great success for the policy of *laisser-faire*. What the public — and even their betters, economists, politicians and administrators — unpardonably overlook is the simple fact that, once the retailers have sold their existing supplies, they will have to replenish their stocks at prices which are no longer kept down by manufacturers for the sake of avoiding too frequent changes.

The prohibition of resale price maintenance in many spheres has accentuated the demoralisation of business firms brought about by the relentless pressure for more and more unearned wages and by the inflationary trend that obviates the necessity for them to abstain from resisting such pressure in an effort to safeguard the interests of their customers. In the absence of resale price maintenance they unhesitatingly add the extra cost resulting from the wage increases to their wholesale prices, leaving it to the wholesalers and retailers to act likewise. Indeed many manufacturers want to play for safety by allowing for future wage increases. Demoralisation of employers has stepped up in this way the demoralisation of their workers. Mutual demoralisation of the two sides of industry has become a vicious circle. Some managements actually disapprove of attempts at wage restraint because each wage increase provides them with an excuse for an extra price increase in addition to the legitimate increase due to higher actual wage costs.

The abolition of resale price maintenance provides an instance to show how Governments and their technical advisers are doing their best to win the last peace, in the same way as in 1939 many people in responsible positions were doing their best to adopt measures ensuring that Britain won the War of 1914. The abolition of resale price maintenance amidst inter-war deflation might have hastened the downward adjustment of retail prices. The same measure amidst non-stop creeping inflation has inevitably hastened the progress of inflation. Most managements had been against the change, but once it was made in spite of their resistance to it they hastened to take advantage of it for widening their profit margin.

Whatever criticism is made against employers they certainly cannot be accused of non-co-operation with the Government of the day in the execution of its policies, no matter how strongly they disapproved of those policies. If only the Labour Government received one tenth as much co-operation from the workers who had voted it into office as from the employers who have no love lost for it, it would have been able to give an incomparably better account of itself.

CHAPTER NINETEEN

GIMMICKS OR REMEDIES?

'To get back my youth I would do anything in the world, except take exercises, get up early, or be respectable.' These words of Oscar Wilde's Mephistophelian character, Lord Henry Wootton, in *The Picture of Dorian Gray*, could and should be adopted as the signature tune for introducing practically all pronouncements advocating any of the wide range of gimmicks that are put forward as remedies for Britain's present troubles and for halting her decline. To restore the balance of the British economy and to recover Britain's former greatness, the advocates of these various more or less ingenious solutions would like the British people to do anything in the world except work hard, live within its means or become public-spirited.

Of course most people are not even aware that drastic remedies are needed at all, because they are, or profess to be, oblivious of the disease itself. But among those who are aware that something is seriously wrong, all the best brains and many of the second-best and third-best brains have been working overtime in an effort to invent some quack remedy that would not involve the necessity for doing an honest day's work, or for mitigating the workers' insatiable appetite for more and more unearned wages, or for self-restraint needed in order to live within our means individually and nationally. The list of gimmicks by which they would like the British people to circumvent such straightforward, simple and obvious common-sense remedies is very long. None of the proposals which are put forward in great profusion is likely to inspire confidence abroad. Indeed the 'gnomes', not being fools, recognise them for what they are — excuses for deferring the inevitable evil day on which Britain would no longer be able to avoid facing realities.

The following are summaries of the most plausible among the suggested attempts to divert attention from the unpleasant but effective remedies of hard work and self-restraint called for by the situation:

(1) The most recent among the proposed gimmicks is contained in the recommendations of the Donovan Commission to solve Britain's problem by a reform of the system of wage bargaining, aiming at an increase in the relative importance of bargaining at factory or shop floor levels instead of depending too much on national bargaining as between trade unions and employers' associations, covering entire industries. Nobody would think of suggesting that there is no scope for improvement of the system of bargaining on factory and shop floor levels. But it would require an almost unbelievable degree of optimism to expect a solution through such a reform. It might possibly reduce the number of unofficial strikes, but only at the cost of satisfying local demands without undue resistance. If workers are enabled to get what they want without having to risk strikes they would step up their demands, and the result would be increase in the volume of unearned wage increases rather than their reduction.

We must remember that, judging by the large number of unofficial strikes — they outnumber official strikes at the rate of twenty to one — local leaders of workers are obviously more militant than the national trade union leaders. To implement the recommendation of the Donovan Report by further reducing the power of the latter and further increasing the power of the former would be a grave mistake. How can the proposal deliberately to reduce the importance of wage negotiations at a national level be justified in the light of the experience in Holland and in the Scandinavian countries which secured long periods of stable labour relations and relative industrial peace by strengthening the national character of wage negotiations?

This proposal, like so many other proposed solutions, has undoubtedly certain advantages. But it would only solve the major problem if its adoption were accompanied by a change in the spirit prevailing amidst industrial workers. No formula can work miracles. It is the spirit in which it is applied that matters. And if there should be a favourable change in the spirit affecting labour relations there would be no need for this gimmick or indeed for any other gimmick. The only way in which the proposal of the Donovan Report could be justified would be by proving that a shifting of wage negotiations even more to factory level would improve the prevailing spirit. There is no factual evidence or argument in the Report that would indicate that workers would be inspired by the change to become more public-spirited and would be more ready to renounce some immediate advantages for the sake of assisting in the solution of Britain's grave problem.

Those who, like Lord Henry Wootton, would seize on any patent medicine to avoid having to resort to the three effective but unpleasant devices which would bring about recovery must feel truly grateful to the Donovan Commission for providing them with another excuse for deferring the day when they would have to face stark reality. The semi-futile talking points so generously supplied in the Donovan Report will keep politicians, economists and journalists occupied for years, during which time they will have a good excuse for not getting down to the basic facts of the situation. Mr. Wilson has been placed in a position to be able to go through the gestures that will convey the impression that he is really doing something towards solving Britain's crisis by adopting the measures proposed in the Report, measures which are at best irrelevant and at worst downright damaging.

(2) The same is true, only perhaps to an even higher degree, of another widely-welcome set of gimmicks supplied by

the Fulton Report. Incredible as it may seem, there must be people who seriously believe that Britain's output could be increased and her costs and prices could be kept down, if not reduced, by a sweeping reorganisation of the system of the Civil Service. Whether the administrative improvements suggested by the Report are good or bad may be a matter of opinion. The British Civil Service, as it is today, is second to none, so that any drastic changes would involve the risk of making things worse rather than better. But in any case most proposals are utterly and delightfully irrelevant from the point of view of getting Britain out of her acute difficulties. There is one notable exception — the proposed removal of Treasury control over the Civil Service. That proposal is not just irrelevant. Its adoption by the Government will be extremely damaging. It is certain to aggravate Britain's crisis by stepping up the existing inflation resulting from overspending by the Government and will increase further the almost insurmountable difficulties to emerge from our crisis.

The Treasury's limited but by no means negligible power to check overspending is Britain's last line of defence against accelerated inflation through ever increasing waste of public money. Parliament has lost interest in the control of public expenditure. And since the experience of Mr. Thorneycroft who sacrificed his political future by resigning in 1957 in protest against overspending no Chancellor of the Exchequer, Tory or Socialist, has had the courage to take action on a political level to check the spending spree. So the Treasury is now the taxpayer's only watchdog. It is of course powerless against expenditure arising from policy decisions taken at Cabinet level. But it is still able to veto or scale down many thousands of items which are not important enough to come before the Cabinet.

One of the reasons why the Treasury had some influence over the spending Departments was its control over the Civil Service. Although clashes over Estimates were bound to occur in the course of the Treasury scrutiny of Estimates, permanent officials of the spending Departments were aware that their prospects of promotion were largely in the Treasury's hands. For this reason, when they found that the Treasury felt very strongly that a proposed expenditure item was excessive they were more inclined to meet its point of view, at least to some extent, than they would have been if they were totally independent of the Treasury.

Now that the recommendation of the Fulton Report is implemented by removing Treasury control over the Civil Service the Treasury's control over expenditure will be further weakened. It must have been weak enough during last year, judging by the record increases in expenditure in the middle of a chronic crisis.

Can anybody think seriously that an increase of inflation through overspending by the public sector will help Mr. Wilson in getting Britain out of her ghastly mess? Apparently yes. This proposal of the Fulton Report met with almost unanimous approval. And Mr. Max Nicholson, in his book *The System*, which appeared in 1967, made the self-same suggestion, only he made it even clearer that he would like to reduce the Treasury's role to that of a rubber stamp in matters of public expenditure.

(3) In addition to this, Mr. Nicholson proposed a series of other gimmicks. Outstanding in its futility amongst them was the idea that the country could be saved by combining various Departments into groups of Departments subject to the overlordship of Super-Ministers. That proposal reminds one of the frequent proposals put forward during the 'phoney war' to change the structure of the Government. On even days some M.P. proposed that several Departments should be amalgamated under the control of an Overlord. On odd days some other M.P. proposed that existing Departments should be

split into two or more Departments with a Minister in
charge of each.   Valuable Parliamentary time was
wasted on discussing such superb exercises in futility
instead of debating the gross inadequacy of the economic
war effort that had brought Britain to within an inch
of being defeated a few months later.

(4) A more serious proposal that has been made from
various directions — among others by the Brookings
Institution's Report — is to seek to increase output by
increasing the capital equipment per head of worker.
This proposal is much more than a gimmick but much
less than a remedy.   Needless to say, the idea meets
with the enthusiastic approval of trade unions — at any
rate in theory.   It would enable the worker to increase
the output per head and therefore to claim further unearned wage increases on the basis of increased productivity, without increasing — indeed by positively reducing — his own contribution to the productive effort.

But we saw in earlier chapters that when it came to
the practical application of the idea of introducing
labour-saving equipment, it encountered strong resistance on the part of the men and their unions.   In Britain
resistance to benefiting by technological progress dates
back to the fifteenth century when an Act was passed
under Edward IV banning the use of 'fulling mills' —
a primitive mechanical contraption with which to produce hats, bonnets and caps — on the ground that they
cause 'the Destruction of the Labours and Sustenance
of many Men', that is, it causes unemployment among
artisans who produce such objects 'by hand and foot'.
Although there was no effective resistance to the Industrial Revolution in the eighteenth century, in the
early nineteenth century mechanical production methods
came to be opposed by means of violent Luddite riots.

The spirit of that resistance, if not its actual methods,
came to be revived in our own days when trade unions
effectively resist and delay the adoption of labour-saving

equipment. The difference between the attitude of British and American unions towards automation largely accounts for the difference between the extent to which the two countries benefit by this latest stage in technological progress. While British trade unions strongly urge managements to increase the value of capital equipment per man they prevent the implementation of their own advice.

The fiscal system, too, operates against the adoption of the suggested remedy of solving our crisis by increasing capital investment. The high level of taxation on profits and on capital gains is a strong disincentive to investment. Why take risks? If the innovation fails the capital loss has to be borne by the owners; it is not even allowed to offset previous capital gains or current profits. If the attempt is successful most of the resulting profit is taken away in increased unearned wages and in increased taxes. Profits, even if earned by risking one's life's savings invested in unproven innovation, have become a term of abuse in Britain. In the United States trade unionists of the stature of George Meany or Walter Reuther realised that it was in the interests of workers to encourage increases of profits. Some of the more intelligent British trade unionists agree with this view in private, but hardly any of them ever dares to admit it in public. (However, when the author told an American banker how he envied his country for its statesmanlike trade union leaders, he replied with some feeling: 'You can have them!') In so far as inadequate capital equipment is responsible for Britain's decline, the fault is not so much with investors and managements as with the trade unions and with the Government. Which means that the remedy rests with them. Let the trade unions change their attitude, and let the Government change its anti-business taxation system. Capital investment would then be certain to proceed much faster.

H

But even so, it would be a necessarily slow process — much too slow to be depended upon for solving Britain's immediate problem of restoring her economic equilibrium. Unless an increase in the production of capital equipment is accompanied by a corresponding decline in consumer demand the result would be a further accentuation of the inflationary pressure and a further deterioration of the balance of payments. While it is beyond doubt true that Britain's decline cannot be checked and reversed without an increase in productivity, to a very large degree the much-needed immediate increase must result, not from additional capital equipment, but from a better use of the existing equipment by the workers, through putting in a fair day's work for their pay. Amidst the prevailing crisis the time element is of the utmost importance. The investment of additional capital necessarily takes time and, long before it can produce its beneficial effects, it would tend to aggravate the situation. On the other hand, the better results that could and should be achieved through harder and more efficient work with the aid of the existing equipment would produce immediate disinflationary results. It would enable the Government to relax the squeeze, and this in turn would encourage fresh capital equipment. The inflationary effects of its installation costs would be offset by the better use made of the existing equipment.

(5) It is a popular belief that joining the Common Market would go a long way towards solving all our problems. This idea occurred to Mr. Wilson some time between March and October 1966. During the election of March 1966 the Labour Party's declared policy was opposed to joining the Common Market — except on terms which had been quite obviously unacceptable to the Common Market. Mr. Wilson's sudden conversion, announcing in October of the same year that his Government had decided to apply for membership, seems to

indicate that something must have happened during the brief interval of seven months to induce him to change his views. No Government spokesman ever tried to give a valid explanation of the *volte-face*. We can only surmise that during the interval Mr. Wilson came to realise that Britain could not depend forever on American financial support, so that it appeared to him a piece of statesmanlike foresight to try to take out a reinsurance policy so as to obtain support out of the growing resources of the E.E.C. once American support came to an end.

Needless to say, the mere act of joining the Common Market, even if it were possible on acceptable terms, would not by itself check Britain's decline. In order to benefit by access to the Western European market it would be necessary for the British worker to work harder and to restrain his appetite for higher unearned wages. But then, if the British worker could be persuaded to do so Britain would become prosperous in or out of the Common Market — though perhaps marginally more so in the Common Market. On the other hand if the British worker could not be persuaded to do so Britain would decline, in or out of the Common Market, though considerably faster in the Common Market, because of the competitive advantages of her partners in the British market which is at present protected for the benefit of the British worker.

To those who argue that increased competition resulting from joining the Common Market would force British industries to become more efficient the answer is simple: Although the British shipbuilding and ship-repairing industries have always been exposed to international competition — to a far greater degree than any British industry would be through joining the E.E.C. — they are amongst the least efficient British industries. So much for the Common Market gimmick.

(6) Another popular gimmick through which the British

Government hopes to be able to obtain temporary respite is the creation of additional opportunity to live on borrowed money through the adoption of the Special Drawing Rights scheme, to be operated by the International Monetary Fund. Its adoption would reduce the urgency of the need for Britain to work out her own salvation. It would create more temptation and more opportunity for continuing to live beyond our means and to abstain from exerting ourselves to make ends meet, especially if the new resources were to become automatically available for use without having to obtain anybody's consent, and if they were to be made in part at least irredeemable.

If our bank managers were compelled by law to permit us to help ourselves to his bank's resources with no questions asked, and if part of our resulting overdraft were to be permitted to remain permanent, it might solve our immediate financial problems and would enable us to continue to live beyond our means. But nobody within his senses could possibly argue that this solution would induce us to work harder or to lead a less extravagant life. It stands to reason that the adoption of the S.D.R. system will accelerate Britain's decline instead of halting it and will contribute towards a further debasement of the British character.

In any case the proposed solution is bound to be purely temporary. Sooner or later Britain's limit to use her Special Drawing Rights would be reached — and owing to the demoralising effect of this solution it is likely to be sooner rather than later — and possibly even before it is reached, surplus countries might refuse to accept more book entries in payment for their exports. It is even conceivable that the artificial system might collapse because some of the participants might decide to withdraw from it by unilateral decision, like France withdrew from the Gold Pool in 1967.

(7) Yet another popular gimmick, which has actually been

put into operation after having been advocated for years, is granting to Britain a medium-term credit for the consolidation of part of her external short-term liabilities. In the form in which the scheme came to be finalised in September 1968, it enables Britain to repay part of the sterling balances held by the authorities of Sterling Area countries. But since no provision whatsoever is made for guaranteeing sterling held outside the Sterling Area, the arrangement does not safeguard sterling against panicky withdrawals by such holders. Nor is sterling safeguarded against pressure due to other causes — investment-hedging, leads and lags and pure speculation. Even in the complete absence of withdrawals by Sterling Area monetary authorities — which itself is not fully ensured by the scheme — sweeping pressure on sterling is still liable to develop through major adverse influences.

Moreover, to the limited extent to which the $2,000 million credit protects sterling against such pressure, it is bound to be detrimental to sterling in the long run, because it would make trade unions even less inclined to listen to the voice of reason than they had been prior to the conclusion of the arrangement. The Government is largely to blame for this. It presented the conclusion of the credit as a major victory which removes the cause for anxiety about sterling's prospects. Immediately after the announcement of the arrangement the Government came under strong pressure, even from usually conservative quarters, in favour of reducing the Bank rate and reflating the economy. This at a moment when trade unions were stepping up pressure for wage increases. Their reactions to this consolidation of our liabilities give a foretaste to indicate what would happen if the Government were to succeed in persuading foreign Governments to assist in achieving their consolidation on a much larger scale.

What is basically wrong is not the idea of consolidation

but that it is applied in a position of weakness and not in a position of strength. In Chapter 11 the author strongly criticised the Conservative Governments of 1951–64 for having omitted to take advantage of the confidence felt towards sterling abroad during part of their terms of office and reduce the abnormally large pursuing policies that would yield large export surpluses. The inadequate consolidation measure adopted in 1968 was the result, not of confidence in sterling but of fears generated by distrust in sterling. The Government had no cause to be proud of having brought it off, and the circumstances in which it was conceded by the participating Governments were such as to lower rather than restore the dignity and self-respect of the British nation. The transaction has further reduced the chances of a moral regeneration rather than increase them.

(8) There is yet another tempting way by which Britain could avoid for a while facing unpleasant realities — by selling out her substantial foreign investments. This was done with every justification during the two World Wars. Foreign investments are emergency reserves; they are there in order to enable the nation to meet vital external requirements when its very existence is at stake. They are not there in order to enable the nation to build more swimming pools and palatial Town Halls in the middle of a crisis, or to enable the workers to secure more unearned wage increases with impunity. Yet Left-wing Socialists are pressing the Government to commandeer privately-owned foreign investments, having spent its own holdings on the defence of sterling during 1965–67.

But Britain's foreign investments, substantial as they are, are far from being inexhaustible. Nor is all of it easily realisable, except at ruinous prices. As and when they are realised the current invisible exports represented by their yield would decline and the current balance of payments gap would widen further. Last but by no means least, the valuable reserve would cease to be available for major emergencies, and their disappearance would further aggravate distrust in sterling.

Commandeering and realising private investments abroad would mitigate the incentive for working out our salvation. It would encourage irresponsible extravagance. The Government, in adopting this gimmick, would follow the example of one of Aldous Huxley's gullible characters who gaily allowed herself to be persuaded by her villainous lover to increase her current spendings by selling out her investments. Each time she realised another amount she cheerfully compared the immediate increase of her spending power with the comparatively negligible extent of the decline of her immediate income from the investment that had been realised. By resorting to the self-same irresponsible device, the Government would of course be able to prolong the pursuit of its policy of perpetual pampering and pimping. But once the realisable investments are exhausted the British would have to face hard realities under such less favourable conditions, having lost her substantial emergency reserve as well as her invisible exports represented by the yield on those investments. However, the proceeds of such realisations, together with the utilisation of Britain's remaining borrowing power abroad, might conceivably defer the moment of truth until the election year of 1971. After that — *Après moi le déluge!*

(9) Until recently devaluation was widely regarded as the ideal gimmick for solving Britain's problems with a stroke of the pen. Politicians and even some economists who could have reasonably been expected to know better, criticised Mr. Wilson's Government for sacrificing Britain's prosperity during its first three years in office for the sake of defending sterling. Now they know better. Sterling's devaluation in November 1967 has failed to produce the miracle expected of it by its advocates. Of course they could always argue that the

devaluation was 'too late and too little' and that another and yet another dose of the same medicine might solve Britain's problem. In given circumstances the repetition of the devaluation would probably provide some temporary respite on each occasion. But we must remember that the respite provided by the deliberately excessive devaluation of 1949 lasted only a little over twelve months, while pressure on sterling which abated after the devaluation of 1967 revived after three months.

Unless a devaluation is accompanied by a change of heart on the part of the nation it cannot be expected to make any real difference to its economic situation and prospects. And the more often it is repeated the less effective it is likely to become even as a temporary remedy. The reason why the depreciation of sterling in 1931 had been beneficial was because it was accompanied by a national regeneration. The devaluation of 1967 utterly failed to produce such an effect on the Government or on the governed. The Government delayed by 6 to 12 months the measures it ought to have taken immediately to make it clear that it really intended to defend sterling at its lower parity. The so-called cuts in expenditure that followed devaluation after an unwarranted delay merely amounted to a moderate reduction of its increase which constituted nevertheless a record increase in any one year in time of peace. And Mr. Jenkins, by delaying his taxation measures and broadcasting his intention to make drastic increases deliberately stimulated consumer demand 'to beat the Budget'. Evidence of the effect of this in the monthly trade figures discredited sterling at home and abroad.

As for the effect of devaluation on the trade unions, as soon as they came to realise that the Government did not intend to adopt measures that would really hurt, they stepped up their wage demands which were conceded again and again, thereby undermining confidence in the Government's declared incomes policy. In the circumstances it was no wonder that in spite of its recent devaluation as a result of which sterling ceased to be overvalued it remained the subject of frequently recurrent scares.

(10) It is argued that Britain's problems could be solved once and for all, not by devaluing sterling again and again but by letting its exchange rate take care of itself by the adoption of the much-advocated system of floating exchange rates. This solution is urged upon the Government from a great many different quarters. The gimmick appeals not only to inflationists but also to economists of the *laisser-faire* school, who seriously believe that if only sterling were allowed to take care of itself it would find its 'natural' level at which it could ensure that trade is balanced.

As this system would do away with the incentive for defending sterling at any particular rate at the cost of keeping down public spending and private wage increases to some extent, it naturally appeals to the 'good-time boys' who are not interested in monetary stability and would prefer the orgy of overspending to continue on an increasing scale. The fact that formerly puritan opponents of irresponsible spending have become converted in favour of such an irresponsible policy is yet another indication of the extent to which the British character has deteriorated.

(11) Another tempting gimmick is the adoption of controls in the form of exchange restrictions, trade quotas or embargoes, customs tariffs, bilateralism, discrimination against import credits, compulsory deposits by importers, etc. Under the protective shield of such measures the need for working out our salvation could be deferred for some time. But the situation would become increasingly artificial, partly because import restrictions in any form would increase inflationary demand on home products — the consumer demand formerly met by imports would be

diverted to domestic goods, causing increased costs and prices — and partly because there would be no obvious inducement for resisting the resulting inflationary pressure. The restrictions would protect the reserve and would keep exchange rates stable, and this artificial state of affairs would generate a false feeling of security which would encourage demand for unearned wage increases and also public spending. British goods would become increasingly outpriced in foreign markets, and in any case exportable surpluses would be diverted to the home market as during the pre-1968 Budget increase in consumer demand. The resulting decline in exports would compel the authorities to administer additional doses of restriction in order to keep down imports to an even higher degree.

A stage would be reached sooner or later at which sterling would have to be adjusted to the decline of its domestic purchasing power. What is worse, the British example of import restrictions might be followed by an increasing number of countries, causing an all-round contraction of trade which might initiate a deflationary spiral comparable to that of the 'thirties.

Many other gimmicks have been canvassed, but the above selection provides ample examples of the ways in which it is possible to divert attention from things that really matter by putting forward suggestions of futile reforms. If some such change is wanted just for the sake of change and if the Government should be tempted to try out one of them the various proposals for Government reforms might as well be put into a hat and when the winner is drawn a coin should be tossed up to decide whether to adopt it. That is the extent of the importance of such proposals compared with the all-important need for national regeneration which alone would solve Britain's problems.

If 'national regeneration' is too vague a formula, it is possible to define it in practical though necessarily oversimplified terms. Until Britain can break even and until she can achieve a surplus to enable her to repay her most urgent external debts, everybody must work more without expecting extra pay for the additional effort. This was the simple formula adopted by the five Surbiton typists when they tried to start their 'I'm backing Britain' movement. Of course it ought to have been initiated from the top, with Mr. Wilson himself making a gesture by announcing that he and his colleagues had decided to forgo their pay increases of 1965, or at any rate part of them, for the duration of the crisis.

Instead of official encouragement we saw in Chapter 13 how the movement was strangled by the despotism of the trade union concerned. All the formidable sophisticated weapons in their armoury were mobilised to kill a mosquito with a sledge-hammer. Yet the action of the five typists rested on sound economic arguments even if they were not sufficiently articulate to formulate it or express it. As it was explained earlier in this chapter, what is called for is a more productive use of existing capital equipment, in order to reduce the inflationary pressure and thereby make it possible to increase investment in modern equipment without aggravating the pressure on sterling.

The trade union spokesmen, obviously frightened by the danger that their members might become patriotic, argued that the working of longer hours without extra pay would not help the country. Surely they are aware that there is a shortage of typists and if typists work harder it would be bound to help. What they really are against is not the working of longer hours but to work longer hours without extra pay. They do not object to longer hours — provided that they are worked against overtime pay at higher rates. They are only against increasing employees' contribution towards higher output without getting extra pay which would cancel out the resulting surplus by an increase in consumer demand to be derived from the higher overtime pay.

However false the arguments of the trade union spokesmen were, they certainly succeeded in scoring a victory over their weak opponents, not with the aid of arguments but — like La Fontaine's wolf in *Le loup et l'agneau*, who, having got the worst of the argument with the lamb, simply devoured it — by threats against those who dared to believe that amidst the existing desperate situation workers ought to place service to the community above their selfish purposes. So after a few weeks during which various other groups were hesitating whether to 'back Britain' the movement to that end was effectively strangled.

No formula, however ingenious, can possibly stand the remotest chance of solving Britain's problems if applied in the wrong spirit. No conceivable change would be nearly as effective as a return of the 'spirit of Dunkirk'. And that spirit could only be aroused if the nation could be made to realise how desperate Britain's situation is. What is more, this spirit must be upheld for some time. On this occasion it would take longer than the Dunkirk evacuation, and even longer than the Battle of Britain, to retrieve the situation.

The Government itself should be willing to practise what it has been preaching half-heartedly, by making ruthless cuts in public expenditure. Nothing it has done or is likely to do in the sphere of the private sector could possibly produce the desired result unless it set an example within the public sector which is under its direct control.

It would be in the interests of the workers to follow such a lead by moderating their own demands, because if the crisis should become prolonged and aggravated it would greatly reinforce the school of thought which sees in a return to large-scale unemployment the only way for restraining the workers' claims for unearned wage increases. But apart altogether from the risk of a return to mass unemployment as a matter of deliberate policy — admittedly a remote risk under the Labour Government — it might easily arise as a result of running short of resources to finance imports of raw materials. Even assuming that the Government should decide to sell out all the realisable private investments abroad and that the S.D.R. scheme should be activated on a large scale, the resulting additional resources might be exhausted even before a general election in 1971 could remove the present Government from office.

The extent to which additional resources could be mobilised by selling out our industries to American and other foreign investors would be limited by the discouraging effects of the Government's anti-business attitude which is liable to grow worse with the approach of the general election. A stage would be reached at which current earnings from exports would constitute the absolute limit to Britain's capacity for importing raw materials. Overconsumption and high costs, resulting from the increasing degree of pampering of unionised labour as the date of the election approaches, would keep our capacity to export at a low level. It would become difficult if not impossible to satisfy requirements of raw material imports increased by inflated domestic demand. There might not be enough to keep our factories going. So instead of the much-promised 'export-led boom' Britain would experience an 'import-led slump'.

Possibly at some stage of Britain's decline the imperative need for facing realities might come to be realised. But by that time the restoration of a balanced economy might come to necessitate such a large dose of deflation that it could easily let loose a major self-aggravating slump. In any case, such slump might easily result from measures to restrict British imports, measures which lead to retaliations by a large number of countries, leading to a slump in world trade and world-wide unemployment.

It is not wicked bankers or speculators, nor ultra-conservative Treasury officials, nor even the sinister power of gold, that are liable to bring back mass unemployment in Britain. It is the British industrial worker, urged on by his union, who by his short-sighted selfishness is likely to drive the country on to such a suicidal course.

CHAPTER TWENTY

IS LABOUR UNFIT TO RULE?

WE saw in Chapter 14 how Mr. Wilson's Government was vacillating year after year between serving the interests of the country at the expense of deferring Socialist policies and serving the interests of his political supporters at the expense of causing an aggravation of the crisis, or at any rate abstaining from dealing with the crisis effectively. The dilemma with which Mr. Wilson has been confronted ever since his victory in 1964 is admittedly far from enviable. To the extent to which he gave the public interest priority over party interests he and his Government were bound to become unpopular among the rank and file of his supporters.

Beyond doubt, Mr. Wilson has richly deserved the slump in his popularity — as indicated by public opinion surveys, by-election results and local election results in 1967–68 — owing to the gross mismanagement of Britain's affairs by his Government. Unfortunately the right thing has happened entirely for the wrong reason. His popularity declined not because he sacrificed, to a very high degree, Britain's chances of recovery for the sake of party political considerations, but because his Labour supporters feel that he did not sacrifice national interests sufficiently to make Socialist policies prevail irrespective of their effect on the country.

If only Mr. Wilson had become unpopular for the right reason, his growing unpopularity should have been welcomed by all right-thinking people, regardless of their political allegiance, as an indication of a growing realisation of the need for national regeneration. But since he has become unpopular because he was not prepared to sacrifice his party interests sufficiently for the sake of the national interest, the decline of his popularity must be regarded as yet another symptom indicating the debasement of the British character.

Even amidst the recurrent economic crises, millions of those who had voted Labour in 1964 and in 1966 expected him as a matter of course to pursue policies which would secure immediate financial benefits to them at the cost of aggravating the crisis. Instead of being prepared to accept their fair share in the sacrifices that had become necessary in order to restore a balanced economy and to create a basis for further progress, they expected the Government of their choice to pursue policies that would have suited their immediate personal financial interests, without giving a moment's thought to the obvious fact that doing so would aggravate the crisis. Indeed, Mr. Wilson received infinitely more support and co-operation for policies serving the public interest from employers and their organisations whose interests were affected adversely by his policies than from his political supporters, the workers and their trade unions, whose interests he sought to serve, even though not to a sufficient extent to satisfy them.

This deplorable experience raises the basic political question whether the British Labour Party, depending as it does for its existence as a governing party on the support of classes which appear to have become utterly devoid of public spirit, can possibly be deemed to be qualified to govern the country.

In fairness to Labour politicians, many of whom the author has known, liked and respected for many years, once they have assumed the burden of office they became willing and eager to shoulder their responsibilities. They have been largely prevented, however, from doing so to an adequate extent by relentless pressure to which they have remained subject, on the part of the millions who had elected them and on whose support their re-election will depend. It must have become obvious to them that to do the right thing would be political suicide for them. Up to a point they were prepared to risk unpopularity during the early years of Parliament's life, in the hope that long before the next general election they might be able to revoke and live down the unpopular measures they had felt impelled to adopt in the public interest, and that they might have enough time to adopt eventually truly Socialist measures without ruining thereby the national economy.

But even during the early years the Socialist Government evidently felt it could ill afford to disregard the attitude of the rank and file of its active supporters to a sufficient extent to ensure economic equilibrium.   The fact that immediately after the removal of the 1966 wage restraint on July 1, 1967, when it became obvious that there would be a very large number of wage demands, the Government felt justified in relaxing hire-purchase restrictions at the end of August in an effort to recover its lost popularity, speaks for itself.

The result of the conflict between the desire to serve the public interest or pursue Socialist policy was a compromise which, while far from satisfying the rank and file of Socialists who feel that their Government should pursue a 100 per cent Socialist programme regardless of its effect on the country, failed to restore equilibrium, made devaluation inevitable and was unable to inspire confidence in Britain after devaluation.

This is the explanation of the difference between the handling of crises by Conservative Governments and by Socialist Governments.   On the occasions during the 'fifties and early 'sixties when balance of payments crises developed the Tory Chancellors — with the notable exception of Mr. Maudling — handled the situation with a firm hand and equilibrium came to be restored, more or less, in a matter of months.   Drastic doses of the necessary bitter medicine were administered without regard for the resulting unpopularity.   In any case the bulk of Conservatives were prepared to accept sacrifices.   On the other hand, the Labour Government elected in 1964 was unable to restore equilibrium in four years, because it lacked the courage or determination to be sufficiently tough, for fear of splitting the Labour Party.   Precisely because trade unions and their members were aware of their Government's reluctance to be sufficiently tough, they did not respond adequately to the Government's exhortations or to its half-hearted deflationary measures.

To give credit where credit is due, Mr. Wilson did resist pressure to embark on full Socialist policies. His promise of 'a hundred dynamic days' became a standing joke because, owing to the crisis, he was able to meet only a fraction of the promised immediate Socialist measures on assuming office. It is true, he did increase some social service benefits at the cost of aggravating the crisis that followed his advent to office. But in order to satisfy his supporters he would have had to increase such benefits to a much higher degree and would have had to expand credit instead of adopting measures of squeeze and freeze. He would have had to pursue policies which would have produced immediate disastrous economic consequences.

The inevitable outcome of the implementation of the promise of 'a hundred dynamic days', to an extent that would have satisfied those who had elected him, would have been as follows:

(1) Wages and costs would have risen even faster than they did during 1964–68.

(2) The domestic purchasing power of sterling would have declined even more, and those classes which are not in a position to enforce an increase of their incomes would have become victimised to an even higher degree.

(3) Sterling would have become grossly overvalued in relation to the currencies of other countries where the rise in prices was more moderate.

(4) The balance of payments would have deteriorated even more, because inflated domestic demand would have reduced the exportable surplus, and would have increased demand for imported goods.

(5) At the same time, British goods would have become too expensive to compete with rival goods in foreign markets and even in the home market.

(6) Delivery dates would have become even longer and more uncertain so that Britain would have lost orders even for goods in which her prices remained competitive.

(7) Increased scarcity of labour would have produced 'bottlenecks' and would have caused a decline in

production, or at any rate the rate of increase in output would have been even less satisfactory.

(8) The budgetary deficit covered by Exchequer borrowing would have increased further, as there would have been even less resistance to the official spending spree.

(9) The public debt would have risen even more and the Government would have had to borrow on even less favourable terms.

(10) Excessive egalitarian trends and other Socialist policies would have acted as disincentives and would have discouraged initiative even more. They would have accentuated the brain drain.

(11) Foreign investments of U.K. residents would have been commandeered and used up to pay for current overconsumption. This would have reduced invisible exports represented by the yield of such investment.

(12) All these developments would have inspired distrust in sterling, accentuating withdrawals of foreign balances, including the holdings by Sterling Area countries.

(13) This, together with the adverse balance of payments, would have depleted the gold and dollar reserves and exhausted all credit facilities obtainable. In any case, in face of such policies it would have been more difficult to obtain new credit facilities.

(14) Sterling would have had to be devalued repeatedly and substantially, or it would have been allowed to depreciate in face of the pressure due to above causes.

(15) The depreciation of sterling would have caused an increase in the prices of all imported goods and would have accelerated the pace of the increase in domestic prices.

(16) Exchange controls would have been applied to foreign holdings, which would have discredited sterling and Britain even more.

(17) Inflation would have proceeded faster and faster and its demoralising effect, which is usually relatively moderate during the early phases of inflation, would have become greatly aggravated.

(18) It would have become more and more difficult to find means for financing imports of food and raw materials. Inadequate supplies of raw materials would have caused unemployment.

This is what would have happened if Mr. Wilson had yielded to the temptation of taking the line of least resistance by devaluing sterling as soon as he assumed office for the sake of avoiding adopting unpopular measures in its defence. He would have blamed the Tories for the mess they had left behind and would have pursued policies which, in the early stages at any rate, would have ensured his popularity and that of his Government and his Party.

It would be mean and unfair not to give Mr. Wilson the credit that is due to him for having refused to devalue in the first twenty-four hours on assuming office. He could have devalued and could have adopted advanced exchange control, so as to pursue full Socialist policies behind its protecting shield. Whenever the subject of his unpopularity arises he claims — up to a point rightly — that he could have avoided becoming unpopular if he had not placed the public interest above party interests.

But the role of martyrdom which Mr. Wilson likes to try to assume is quite unconvincing. Had he disregarded party interests to an extent of 100 per cent instead of disregarding them merely to an extent of 50 per cent he would go down in history as one of the greatest Prime Ministers Britain has ever had. But he tried to get the best of both worlds and, as a result, got the worst of both worlds. Although resorting to squeezes when pressure on sterling was becoming too menacing, he was sufficiently a party politician to relax them at the wrong time. He resorted to various party political measures which were damaging to sterling when he ought to have devoted all his efforts to restoring a balanced economy. And he devalued when he came to realise that the continued defence of sterling would become too costly in terms of loss of popularity. After each loss of a by-election, he was seen posing before the TV camera complete with an expression of martyrdom. But his pose fools no one who has followed his policies during 1964–68.

After the experience of 1964–68 it is unlikely that either Mr. Wilson or anyone who might succeed him as Leader of the Labour Party will have the strength of character to incur unpopularity by serving the public interest even to the limited extent to which he served it from 1964 to 1967. The temptation to take the line of least resistance, even at the cost of the consequences listed above, might be irresistible. Presumably if the clock could be put back to 1964 Mr. Wilson would now opt for devaluation for the sake of being able to pursue full Socialist policies regardless of their economic consequences.

Economic policy is not the only sphere in which Socialists adopt a Party-above-country attitude. The masonry of public schools and Oxbridge is nothing compared with the masonry of 'jobs for the boys' that exists among Socialists. There are many known instances in that respect which bear comparison with the shielding of Philby by the Foreign Office.

To give one instance, when Maurice Webb was appointed Minister of Food he told the author that his first decision was to discontinue the disastrous East African groundnut scheme which had already cost the country some £36 million. But he encountered the utmost resistance in high Socialist circles. As Sir Leslie Plummer, the head of the Overseas Food Corporation, was one of the 'boys' he had to be kept in the 'job' even at the cost of losing further millions of the taxpayer's money. So he felt impelled to tell Mr. Attlee that he would refuse to be placed in a position in which in twelve months' time he would have to defend the indefensible. It was only under his threat of resignation within weeks after his appointment that the Prime Minister decided to overrule the resistance to the liquidation of the groundnuts scheme.

In the sphere of foreign policy, too, there is always strong pressure on a Labour Government to pursue a Socialist foreign policy instead of a British foreign policy. This pressure was resisted on the whole to a commendable degree by both Labour Governments in office since the War. But there is always a temptation to give way for the sake of appeasing Socialists and disarming their active resistance to unpopular measures in the economic sphere. Some individual Socialist politicians are inclined to take the line that in the face of a conflict of loyalties their Socialism must prevail over their duties as British citizens.

During the War Dr. Dalton, in his capacity of Minister of Economic Warfare, was one of the three members of the Committee on Political Warfare, the other members being the Foreign Secretary Mr. Eden, and the Minister of Information Mr. Bracken. Dr. Dalton was the acting head and had considerable influence on the adoption and execution of political warfare measures. His idea of contributing towards victory was to try to embroil Britain in a war with Franco's Spain. As a good Socialist he thought it would be a pity not to take the opportunity of disposing of all Fascist dictatorships while we were about it. This was at a time when the outlook for victory was still very doubtful and Franco's neutrality was extremely useful from the point of view of securing Gibraltar from a German attack. When Dalton's colleagues on the Committee on Political Warfare discovered what he was up to there was a blazing row between him and Bracken and the Prime Minister was persuaded to promote him to the more senior post of President of the Board of Trade.

The author can quote an even more striking instance of the pursuit of Socialist-inspired foreign policy to the detriment of national interests. In 1924, soon after the recognition of the Soviet Union by the first Labour Government, the Board of Trade issued export licences for large quantities of arms to Soviet Russia. This at a time when the Soviet Government was openly preparing another attack on Poland. It was against British interests that Soviet Russia should become contiguous with Germany as a result of a conquest of Poland. But the President of the Board of Trade, Lord Passfield, was a great admirer of the Soviet Union and his political sympathies prevailed over national interests. Yielding to pressure in the House of Commons, the Government agreed that no further licences would be issued. The author happened to discover, however, that the existing licences, covering a sufficiently large quantity of arms exports to Soviet Russia to keep the British arms industry busy for several years, had been intended to remain valid. It took a considerable amount of further pressure behind the scenes to induce Mr. Ramsay MacDonald to implement the promises he made to diplomatic representatives of the Border States to take steps to cancel the licences already issued.

It would perhaps be too much to expect Socialists to forswear all their political sympathies and principles that conflict with the national interest the moment they assume responsible office. But surely when it comes to vital matters they must resolve their conflict of loyalties in favour of serving basic British interests. The trouble is, they have convinced themselves that whatever is to the interest of Socialists is to the interest of the nation. While in a great many instances in the sphere of foreign policy they have proved themselves British in the first place and Socialists in the second place only, in the sphere of economic policy their Socialism is given only too often priority over their duty to safeguard vital national interests.

So long as such considerations are allowed to prevail to the extent they were allowed to prevail in 1964–68 Labour will remain unfit to rule.

It is of the utmost importance from the point of view of both national interests and Socialist interests to educate supporters of the Labour Party into realisation that amidst existing circumstances pure Socialism is impracticable and that a Socialist Government, like any other Government, has to aim at pursuing a national policy instead of aiming at securing the maximum of immediate benefits for its Labour supporters. If the two considerations clash, national interests must be allowed to prevail.

That this is not impossible can be proved by the example of Scandinavian countries where the prolonged existence of Labour Governments has not prevented progress towards prosperity, simply because the Socialist regimes have pursued the aim of co-existence with much give-and-take between the various classes. Only if British workers and British Socialists come to be inspired by a similar spirit will a Labour Government be able to rule without leading the country into disaster. It is to the national interest that they should become fit to rule as an alternative to the Conservatives. After all, it would be contrary to basic democratic principles if Britain became a one-party state ruled permanently by the Conservative Party. Unfortunately the prospects of a change in the Labour attitude that would make it fit to rule are none too favourable.

Owing to the peculiar character of the British political system under which a Prime Minister with a working majority is virtually a constitutional dictator until the next general election, the country seems to be doomed to Socialist misgovernment until 1971. With the approach of the time limit for the next general election Mr. Wilson is likely to subordinate national interests to party interests to an increasing degree, so as to save the Labour Party from a repetition of the experience of 1931 when it was practically wiped out of existence.

It would be comforting if we could believe that Socialist misgovernment will at any rate make even Tory misgovernment appear almost bearable. Unfortunately for the country, there seems to be very little to be said in favour of the probable alternative to the present Government. It is true, the same considerations that effectively prevent a Labour Government from serving national interests at the expense of party interests don't exist in the case of Conservative Governments. For, very generally speaking, the Conservative middle classes on whom Tory governments mainly depend are incomparably more public-spirited than the Socialist voters on whom a Labour Government depends. When during the War the Tory-controlled Coalition Government raised the taxes on higher incomes to virtually 100 per cent the 'victims' submitted to it without a murmur. It is impossible to conceive of a Labour Government which would care or dare to impose on its supporters sacrifices of a comparable magnitude even in a war, let alone in a mere crisis. They would be certain to be stabbed in the back by the rank and file of their supporters.

It is for this reason that the British electorate instinctively feels in times of crises that it is safer to leave the fate of the country in the hands of a Conservative Government. But the difference between Socialist irresponsibility and Tory irresponsibility is merely one of degree. Whenever the author feels tempted to conclude that a change of Government might save Britain he cannot help remembering a Tory Chancellor's policies that deliberately allowed the balance of payments deficit to widen to a record level in the election year of 1964. What is even worse is the unpardonable policy adopted by the Tories while in opposition, in opposing Mr. Wilson's efforts to enforce wage restraint. They evidently could not resist the temptation to exploit for party political purposes the inevitable unpopularity of that public-spirited policy. An attempt was made by Conservatives to produce 'respectable' theoretical foundations for their policy by reverting to the 19th-century liberal dogma of *laisser-faire*, and by arguing that wage increases don't matter so long as public expenditure is kept down.

The author would be the last man to contest that excessive public spending is inflationary. But so are unearned wage increases. By encouraging the latter while condemning the former Conservatives have proved that they are no better than Mr. Wilson who is trying to discourage unearned wage increases while allowing the spending of the public sector to continue to increase. This is the reason why he feels both parties are equally, or almost equally, unfit to rule, just as the Czartoryski and Potocki factions were in 18th-century Poland. More and more people have come to the conclusion that the choice is between two evils. If the author feels that Tories are marginally less unfit to rule it is solely because the rank and file of their supporters are more public-spirited.

There would be nothing to hope for if a miracle should occur that would bring the Liberal Party to power. For the Liberal Party has long abandoned its traditional role of voicing the conscience of the nation. It is simply trying to compete with the two major parties for popularity.

What then is the answer? A coalition Government consisting of men of goodwill from all Parties. It would be able to adopt the unpleasant but vitally necessary measures without which

Britain's decline is doomed to continue and to culminate in her fall. Although the Labour Party is in a position to prolong its disastrous rule right to March 1971, most of its Members of Parliament must be aware that the electorate will then reject them. Never has a defeat been more richly deserved than their defeat will be. Unfortunately, never has a victory been less deserved than a Tory victory would be in 1971. If responsible Socialist leaders want to save their Party from extermination it would be wise for them to share with responsible elements among Conservatives the duty of adopting measures that are needed in order to enable at least a high proportion of them to survive a landslide at the next general election. To continue under the present Labour Government until 1971 would mean a continued decline of Britain at an accelerating pace. The longer the change is deferred the more difficult it would be to salvage some of the country's remaining greatness.

The other conclusion is addressed to politicians of all parties: Stop deceiving yourselves and the public by suggesting that this gimmick or that would solve Britain's problems. So long as you believe in such solutions, or pretend to believe in them, there is not the slightest hope of persuading the unions that the solution lies in their hands and in their hands alone. It is so much more comfortable to expect miracles from the adoption of the various ingenious reforms suggested than to settle down to hard and honest work. Unless and until the workers realise that no miracle can be expected through the adoption of gimmicks, they will never accept the inevitability of finding the solution in the hard way.

The final main conclusion is that workers could improve their standard of living to an incomparably higher degree, if only they were to throw themselves whole-heartedly into a national effort to increase production than they would if they persisted in their present attitude of keeping their contribution to the national productive effort to a minimum for the sake of securing immediate advantages for themselves. Would it be a hopeless task for those whose voices command respect among the workers to use their influence to persuade them to give this method a chance? If only they were to try it for a limited period it might make all the difference. The restoration of Britain's stability and of her greatness depends on their willingness to do it.

INDEX